W9-BIR-628

Children and Childhood in Classical Athens

Ancient Society and History

Children and

MARK GOLDEN

Childhood in Classical Athens

The Johns Hopkins University Press
Baltimore and London

© 1990 The Johns Hopkins University Press
All rights reserved. Published 1990
Printed in the United States of America on acid-free paper

Johns Hopkins Paperbacks edition, 1993

The Johns Hopkins University Press
2715 North Charles Street
Baltimore, Maryland 21218-4319
The Johns Hopkins Press Ltd., London

Library of Congress Cataloging-in-Publication Data

Golden, Mark, 1948–
   Children and childhood in classical Athens / Mark Golden.
      p.   cm. — (Ancient society and history)
   Includes bibliographical references.
   ISBN 0-8018-3980-7   ISBN 0-8018-4600-5 (pbk.)
   1. Children—Greece—Athens—History.   2. Family—Greece—Ath-
ens—History.   3. Athens (Greece)—Social conditions.   4. Greece—
Social conditions—To 146 B.C.   I. Title.   II. Series.
HQ792.G73G65   1990
305.23′0938′5—dc20   89-24748
                                                                      CIP

A catalog record for this book is available from the British Library

To Monica Becker, whose gift it is that my understanding of ties between human beings is not drawn solely from books

Contents

Contents

List of Figures

Preface

"Nobody cares about your birth or upbringing or education," Socrates tells Alcibiades, "or about any other Athenian's—except maybe some lover" (Pl. *Alcib. I* 122B). And about these subjects at least Athenian lovers did not kiss and tell: the evidence is scattered and scant. As a result, modern scholarship too has had little to say about children and childhood in classical Athens. Although the bibliography on ancient childhood by Karras and Wiesehöfer (1981) lists about thirteen hundred items, strikingly few concern Athens, and many of those that do date from before the Second World War. There is no book-length discussion in English.

This book investigates the place children and childhood held in Athenian public and private life from roughly 500 to 300 B.C. (I have occasionally supplemented our evidence on classical Athens, or filled gaps in it, with material from other periods and places.) The focus is on *paides*—boys before majority and girls before marriage. But after outlining the nature of interpersonal relations between children and others, I follow them into later life in an effort to explore patterns of continuity and conflict between the worlds of the household and the community. The man who acts as a citizen is still his parents' son; the head of a household and his wife retain ties with the siblings whose home they once shared; boys are first slaves' charges and then their masters. Old ties, new identities—these both clash and coexist.

Rather than seek to establish one central thesis, I have chosen to explore the interactions of children with adults and with each other in a number of contexts. This program amounts to a series of essays on socialization. That no clear-cut conclusion results is in keeping with the nature of this many-faceted process: complex, conflict ridden, discontinuous, dysfunctional. Socialization—"the process by which we learn the ways of a given society or social group so that we can function within it" (Elkin and Handel [1984] 4)—occurs in all human communities (and in some others too). Adults endeavor to shape their children, formally and informally, to take their places (or the places of their more fortunate contemporaries) in the world they know. But while men and women make societies in this way, they do not make them just as they choose: the intentions and outcomes of socialization often diverge, and the products of the process are often surprising, undesired, even undesirable.

One reason—rapid technological and social change—was less relevant in ancient Greek society than it is today. Other factors identified by students of contemporary cultures affected Athens too. For example, some psychologists now caution against imagining development to be an unbroken continuum; the events of infancy need not always determine the moods and behaviors of adolescents, still less those of adults (Kagan [1984] 73–111). Consequently, desired qualities must be reinforced throughout childhood. Yet as children grow, their social worlds expand, they enter different subgroups within society, and these may place on them incompatible demands, or at least inspire conflicting loyalties (cf. Harré [1974]). It should also be recognized that the socialization of men and women, of masters and slaves, in societies ridden (as Athens was) with sexism and class distinctions must involve the pervasive limiting of human potential, and in some cases may even contribute to widespread pathology. Finally, children cannot be regarded as purely passive objects of socialization: the process is interactive, and one in which both resistance and creativity play a part.

Thus, while the experiences, associations, and emotional ties of early childhood are not to be neglected, the child's later years are a formative force too, and the maintenance of early patterns is subject to structural conditions, especially those determining the control and transmission of property and power. This is the understanding which underlies much of this book, coming into particular prominence in its second half.

The first chapter sets out the attitudinal environment, the characteristic attributes of childhood and of its stages in Athenian eyes. These eyes, unavoidably, are adults'. In the next two chapters, however, I move a little closer to the "meaning of life as seen from the floor, or from the crib" (Thomas Wolfe's words in *Look Homeward, Angel*) by focusing on what children actually did. Chapter 2 demonstrates that they played significant and significantly varied roles within the household and the community from an early age. Chapter 3 shows that boys (especially) and girls enjoyed an extensive social life with their peers outside the household. To a surprising degree, children were part of the *polis* at the same time that they were prepared for it. In Chapters 4 through 6 I return to the household—more specifically, to its emotional environment, comparatively neglected in most studies of the Athenian family. I discuss affective relations involving children and their parents (Chapter 4), their siblings and grandparents (Chapter 5), and the slaves and other outsiders who shared the household with them (Chapter 6). I identify a number of points of tension, setting broad community expectations against personal experiences and beliefs, or ideals of family solidarity against individual and civic interests. The book concludes with a brief coda (Chapter 7) on a dimension of childhood and the household that is deemphasized throughout, change over time.

This study is based primarily on literary texts, broadly defined. Since I hope that it will be of use to those without a specialist's familiarity with classical Athens—I have translated all the Greek—a word about this evidence is in order. (For a fuller treatment, with which I am generally in agreement, see Dover [1974] xi–xii and 1–45.) Unfortunately, almost all our sources are male members of the Athenian elite, though this is not always true of their subjects or of those to whom their work is directed.

Much of my discussion relies on speeches written for delivery in Athenian law courts (or, in some cases, as rhetorical exercises in that genre). These speeches are not always reliable on points of fact. However, the speakers' ascriptions of motives and references to norms must have seemed plausible or appealing to a large panel of jurors, who were meant to represent the Athenian community as a whole. Similarly, gravestones are valuable because the sentiments they record are conventional; they too are to be given pride of place. The characters and institutions of Attic comedy—both the Old Comedy of Aristophanes (and others) in the fifth and early fourth centuries and the New Comedy of Menander (and others) in the later fourth and early third centuries—are taken from public and private life; the situations they face, despite parody and exaggeration, are recognizably those of real life (though the outcomes often are not). However, the Latin adaptations of Greek New Comedy by Plautus and Terence put us at a further remove from classical Athens. Of their plays, I make use primarily of those which are known or thought to be based on Menander or his contemporaries and set at Athens; exceptions are noted.

In tragedy, in contrast to comedy, neither characters nor institutions belong to everyday life; most plays are not set at Athens at all, and many of the kings and queens who are their heroes and heroines speak and behave in a way that is quite out of place in the world of the audience, a contrast of which Euripides in particular makes much use. Yet the playwrights and players were Athenians, and the plays were presented under public auspices at great community festivals. The issues they raise must have been not only of some interest to their audiences but also clear enough in their broad lines to be recognized on first hearing by the number and kind of citizens who might today attend a hockey game; of course, this does not guarantee that contemporary scholars will always agree on what these are. I have therefore felt free to refer to them to establish a starting point for further research in other sources, to buttress conclusions reached on other grounds (as in Chapter 6), or simply because they often express commonplaces in an unusual or powerful way. As for myth in general, I have assumed that almost all Greek myths were known to Athenians of the classical period, but not all tellings of those myths. I have naturally placed more emphasis on versions that are known to have been current at Athens or most likely were. Here again my use of this material is predominantly rhetorical, to illustrate or color.

Some other important sources—Xenophon, Plato, and Aristotle—present different problems. All three stand somewhat apart from the Athenian city-state: Plato as the fiercest critic of its institutions, Aristotle as an immigrant and noncitizen, and Xenophon, quite literally, as a long-time exile. Plato and Aristotle are besides men of extraordinary ability, and thus hardly typical of their times; Xenophon is less outstanding intellectually, but not always more conventional. Yet when their conclusions and recommendations coincide with contemporary reality, they generally provide the most articulate and thorough accounts available; when they do not, they are often guides to points of tension and contention. If only it were easier to know when these sources speak for others and when they speak just for themselves!

Finally, there is the case of spurious or doubtful works like [Pl.] *Axiochus* and [Arist.] *Problems,* in which the words are unlikely to be Plato's or Aristotle's and the ideas may not be. I include them here on the assumption that the attitudes they express do usually represent some sector of opinion from the classical period, but they (and others like them) are of course to be treated with still more caution than incontestably genuine texts.

I have invoked iconographic evidence as well, but to say that my use of it is selective is to imply a much greater knowledge of the whole body of such material than I possess. Most of the vase paintings and grave reliefs to which (mainly) I refer have been drawn from secondary sources, in particular the two recent volumes by Hilde Rühfel (1984a, 1984b). Nor is my treatment sophisticated. I have usually been content to describe images depicted on vases and gravestones without considering whether they represent scenes of everyday life or expressions of an ideal. Fortunately, for the determination of attitudes this distinction is seldom essential, but the reader should be as aware as I am of my shortcomings in this area.

My adult interest in childhood dates back some twenty years, to the occupation of the University of Toronto's main administration building in support of a demand for on-campus day care. It found a more conventional academic expression in my Ph.D. dissertation, "Aspects of childhood in classical Athens" (University of Toronto 1981). Much of that earlier work has appeared in journals; other portions have enjoyed an underground existence in friends' footnotes. All of the rest that I consider still worth saying is included in this book.

No one completes any scholarly undertaking without help, myself least of all. Virginia Hunter and Mac Wallace kindly and critically read the typescript of this book in its entirety. Others read portions in draft or replied to my requests for information or advice: Alan Booth, Per Brask, Tom Burch, Anne Carson, Cheryl Cox, Nigel Crowther, Rory Egan, Mark Kilfoyle, Don Kyle, John Oates, Dan Stone, Hector Williams. My department head at the University of Winnipeg, Iain McDougall, graciously deferred his own sabbatical so that I could take up a fellowship at the National Humanities Center in 1987–88. The fellows and staff of the Center provided an ideal environment for writing this or any book. Maggie Blades, Karen Carroll, and Linda Morgan turned manuscript into diskette, a process only a little less demanding than transforming lead into gold, and incidentally taught me how to spell like an American (though I still talk funny). Christine Bray and Marilyn Loat patiently prepared the final version. I derived less immediate but equally crucial assistance, ideas, and inspiration from the work of those responsible for the recent Roman revolution in the study of the family. However, Wiedemann (1989) came into my hands too late to be used here.

The abbreviations used in citing ancient authors and works are generally those found in *The Oxford Classical Dictionary* or in H. G. Liddell, R. Scott, and H. Stuart Jones, eds., *A Greek-English Lexicon* (hereafter cited as LSJ).

All ancient dates in this book are B.C. unless otherwise indi-

cated. Athenians dated years by the name of the eponymous ar-
chon, one of nine annual magistrates. Since the Athenian year began in the equivalent of our June or July, dates are sometimes
given in compound form (e.g., 451/0).

One

Characteristics of Childhood
and Children

The Attributes of Children

The child is father of the man, wrote Wordsworth. Some Greeks agreed. Childhood prodigies, signs of future superiority, were a staple of myth and biography. Achilles killed a boar when he was only six, Cyrus was chosen to play king by his contemporaries at the age of ten and able to give shrewd advice at fifteen or sixteen, the always arrogant Alcibiades threw himself in front of a wagon and stopped it when playing in the street "while still small."[1] The newborn Cypselus charmed his would-be murderers and signaled his future ascendancy in Corinth by smiling by divine chance; ordinary infants were thought not to smile before the age of forty days.[2] In conformity with this view, theorists of education like Plato and Aristotle stress the importance of proper training and environment from the moment of birth and even before for the development of good citizens.[3] "The lessons of childhood marvelously grip the mind," Critias remarks, apparently quoting current wisdom.[4] Aristophanes, as befits a comic poet, portrays those who have spent their childhood learning well how to act badly: the Sausage-Seller distracted the cooks when he was

1

a boy (*paidos ontos*) and stole their meat; he employs the same ruse to trick Paphlagon as an adult (Ar. *Eq.* 417–420, 1195–1200). Socrates speaks of wanting a certain something from childhood (*ek paidos*), just like everyone else; in Agesilaus's case, this was glory.[5]

Yet there was another tendency, too, to stress the discontinuities between one time of life and another. In *The Symposium,* Plato has Diotima mention the idea that a man is the same from childhood (*ek paidariou*) to old age. But, she continues, though he is called the same, he does not retain the same characteristics. He is always becoming a new person (or a young man: *neos*), physically and intellectually, in his opinions and in his temperament (Pl. *Symp.* 207D–208A). Aristotle, dealing with the various senses in which one thing is said to be formed from another, groups together the sayings "From day comes night" and "From the boy comes the man" (*Gen. An.* 1.724a23). This perspective informs the reflection, frequent in the orators, that there is no way to tell how a child will turn out (a motive for the adoption of adults).[6] It takes its most developed form in the various schemes dividing human life into two, three, four, five, six, seven, and even ten stages, based on numerology or astrology, the number of seasons or of fingers on each hand, with more or less discrete traits.[7] To cite just one example that was meant to be of practical value for life in the *polis,* Aristotle's advice on how to win friends and influence people through public speaking places a good deal of emphasis on understanding the emotions and actions appropriate to each of three periods: youth, the prime of life, and old age (Arist. *Rh.* 2.1389a1–1390b12). But his analysis, which goes on to take into account other determinants of character such as birth, wealth, and power, is not simple-minded. In other writers, too, periodization is informed by nuanced common sense. That some characteristics change more than others is one of the bases of Electra's skepticism when asked if she ever made Orestes some garment that might identify him. He'd have outgrown it, she replies.[8] So, too, change was recognized to be more likely at some times than at others, easier for a man of twenty than for one of fifty.[9]

It is within this context that we should situate Athenian ascriptions of characteristics to childhood and to children: a range of opinions on the relative importance of continuity and change within the course of human life.[10] In general, our sources stress continuity, describing children with reference to the same criteria they apply to adults—physical fitness, moral development, intelligence—and finding them wanting. Predictably, children are thought to approach adult norms more closely as they grow older; this process is marked by stages, which differ according to author and context. But children may also be regarded as so lacking in some adult qualities that they seem more closely to resemble another species altogether, or so free from others that they transcend the usual human limitations and enter into a privileged relationship with the gods.

We may group children's characteristics into neutral, positive, and negative attributes. Neutral attributes are those which children share with the dominant group through which Athenians usually defined their community, male citizen adults in the prime of life; positive attributes are those which mark children especially or much more than the dominant group; and negative attributes are those which represent a lack or shortfall of some quality adult citizens possess. In practice, of course, the use of these categories involves considerable difficulty. Designation of a quality as positive or negative must, in those frequent cases where no guidance is given by our sources, be a matter of subjective judgment. Furthermore, even an impression of the mix of these different categories of characteristics in the makeup of the Athenian idea of childhood is hard to come by. Though Athenians clearly recognized that children could see and hear and possessed other senses from infancy (e.g., Pl. *Phd.* 75B), our sources usually pass over those qualities which are shared with adult males like themselves (and so seem unremarkable), in favor of those which differentiate children.

This interest in the *differentia* of children in contrast to adults unfortunately pushes distinctions between boys and girls into the background. Such divergences were certainly noted, from a boy baby's tendency to move more in the womb to the higher pitch of a girl's voice; we can even find a trace of the modern schoolboy taunt, "You throw like a girl."[11] But we learn less of them from explicit statements in our sources than we would like. (How exactly, for example, was the characteristic virtue of a girl unlike a boy's? Plato's Meno does not say: Pl. *Meno* 71E.) These sources, all male, are slanted in another way as well: the material presented here stems all too often from the opinions of two exceptional residents of Athens, Plato and Aristotle. This is a weakness no account can avoid, a reflection both of the volume of their work and of the special interest they seem to have taken in childhood as a mirror for human nature and in children as the raw material of the citizen community.[12] As much as one can tell, however, their attitudes toward children's moral and intellectual qualities are not atypical, though their views on the physiology of childhood sometimes represent only strands in a complex debate in the ancient scholarly literature.

The first section of this chapter, then, presents a *catalogue raisonné* of Athenian conceptions of children and childhood. By *children* I mean those the Athenians called *paides:* boys before their admission to their deme at the age of seventeen or eighteen, girls before their marriage.[13] Most of the texts drawn upon do indeed include some form of the word *pais;* but other terms and expressions are found as well. It is thus possible at times that very young children only, or youths just of age, are meant, but such instances are too few to affect my general conclusions. This collection of qualities primarily provides information on the ideas and attitudes of adults. But such ideas, and especially such attitudes, do find expression, even if it is only muted. If—when—they do, they must contribute to some degree to children's definitions of themselves. My catalog, therefore, is also a blueprint, however faint. Full discussion of the terminology of childhood at Athens and the relationship between this vocabulary and popular and philosophical notions of childhood's stages I leave to the chapter's second section.

What I have called negative attributes predominate in this catalog. Though characters in tragedy occasionally envy children their freedom from the burdens of adult life, especially those they must bear themselves, the Greeks of the classical period were generally not nostalgic for childhood.[14] It was a privilege of the gods, or of those they especially loved, to pass through childhood quickly, to be born with many of the powers they would display when grown. So, in their first days of life, Apollo slays Python and founds his oracle at Delphi, Hermes steals his brother's cattle, Heracles kills the snakes Hera sends against him in his cradle.[15] They are not just miniature versions of their adult selves—Hermes, for instance, when seized by the angry Apollo, wins his release by dirtying his diapers. But they are certainly free from the usual limitations of their age group. In contrast, when Zeus is temporarily overcome by Typhon (or Typhoeus), he finds himself in the Corycian cave, much like the one where he was born, with the sinews of his hands and feet severed so that he cannot walk. In defeat, he is a helpless baby (Apollod. 1.6.3). And the Boeotian poet Hesiod expresses the degeneracy of his Silver Race by saying that children then stayed with their mothers for one hundred years.[16]

Children were regarded as physically weak, morally incompetent, mentally incapable. (It is to indicate the Cypriot king Evagoras's extraordinary nature that Isocrates' eulogy recalls his "beauty and strength and good sense" as a child: Isoc. 9.22.) Aside from scientific writings, our sources seem much the least concerned with physical infirmity, perhaps because it was too obvious to occasion specific comment.[17] At any rate, one of the few literary passages to make mention of children's lack of strength is in fact concerned with underlining the impotence of a group of old men; members of the chorus of *Agamemnon,* "no better than a child," refer to their "child-like strength" (Aesch. *Ag.* 75, 81). Elsewhere, bodily weakness is often linked with other limitations, as in Cyrus's explanation of why men have the advantage of boys in learning to ride. (Men are cleverer than boys, and also abler at putting into practice what they have learned because of superior strength: Xen. *Cyr.* 4.3.10–11.)

Moral incompetence, as we might expect, is primarily a philosopher's problem. Plato's outlook seems to be summarized in a scene in which Socrates praises the Spartans for their temperance (*sōphrosynē*), orderliness, easy-going temperament, greatness of spirit, discipline, bravery, endurance, willingness to work, will to win, and love of honor. In all these respects, he tells Alcibiades, the Athenian is like a child by comparison (*Alcib.I* 122C); in all, a child would be wanting. Aristotle thinks that children have free will but not *prohairesis,* "resolve, purpose," and cannot therefore be really happy or moral.[18] But morality is also the subject of a comment by the orator Aeschines, who regards the ability to distinguish right from wrong as the mark of the adult male citizen.[19] It was courage that children were felt to lack in particular;[20] children might seem brave, but this was dismissed as mere ignorance and thoughtlessness.[21] Readily frightened as they were, children were easy prey for stories about female bogies like Empousa, Gello, Gorgo, Lamia, Mormo (or Mormolyke).[22] Vase painters portray Athena doffing her helmet, or wearing the aegis, the emblem with the fearsome face of the Gorgon, back to front to avoid alarming the baby Erichthonius.[23] Such fears may have inspired Aeschylus to invent the bloodsucking Erinyes of the *Oresteia* in order "to reawaken them in an adult audience."[24]

Intellectual incapacity is touched on far more often, and in sources of many different kinds. One of the most popular Greek proverbs, "Old men are children again," always refers, as far as we can tell from ancient commentators and extant examples, to mental incompetence.[25] Aeschylus's Prometheus says that Hermes is "a child and even more mindless" if he expects to learn his secrets.[26] In Sophocles, Oedipus hesitates to give his children advice because they do not yet possess *phrenes,* "wits" (*OT* 1511–1512). Old Comedy makes much ado about humor so crude only children laugh—thick, red-tipped codpieces, "Megarian jokes."[27] Pericles, so the story goes, compared the Samians to children who cry while accepting scraps, because the Samians didn't appreciate Athenian rule (Arist. *Rh.* 3.1407a2).[28] Xenophon's idealized Cyrus knows Astyages is drunk when he does things he would not allow even children to do; his Agesilaus shows Tissaphernes to be a mere child at intrigue.[29] Hyperides recalls that the dead he is commemorating were once *paides . . . aphrones,* "mindless children," though now born anew, as it were, as valiant men (*Epit.* 29). The fullest compendium of children's intellectual shortcomings comes from Plato, concerned as he is with knowledge as a key to ethical development as well. Plato (or his speakers) claims that children know little, are gullible and easily persuaded, can understand only

6

the simplest things, talk nonsense, make unreliable judges.[30] Some adults, we are told, tease children (and amuse themselves) by talking to them in a high-flown and mock-serious manner (Pl. *Resp.* 8.545E); it is of course the incongruity which makes the joke. Superiority is expressed by saying a man makes others appear like children or less than children; inferiority is denoted by the taunt, "Even a child could refute you"; an argument is made conclusive by the clincher, "Not even a child would deny this."[31]

Plato often groups children with women, slaves, and animals.[32] These are also associated in Aristotle, for whom boys bear a physical resemblance to women (because they do not yet concoct semen), animals stand in the same relation to humans as children to adults, and both animals and children are as inferior to adults as bad and foolish men are to good and wise ones; as one consequence, the opinions of animals and children are regarded with equal contempt.[33] Children are also linked with the sick, the drunk, the insane, and the wicked.[34] No sensible person would choose to live with their powers of reasoning, or to return to childhood once he left it.[35] One specific weakness that Aristotle adds to Plato's list is a short memory.[36] Children, it seems, are simply in too troubled and unstable a state to acquire knowledge and exercise sound judgment (Arist. *Phys.* 7.247b19).

Of course, the child has the potential to outgrow all these limitations; as Aristotle says, he is not yet complete and whole.[37] It is interesting, however, that the child is seldom a symbol of what is to come, and that when, as rarely, he is, the future hopes he represents are often unrealized. Hector's son Scamandrius is called by the people of Troy Astyanax, "defender of the city"; he is to be Hector's successor in this role, but first father is killed and then son, and the city that looks to them for help is destroyed. More often, children figure in images that ignore their future capabilities in favor of their futility in the present. The child builds castles in the sand, and then whirls them away.[38] The child chases a winged bird, which flees from his grasp.[39] Most moving of all is the beautiful picture first presented in Sophocles' satyr play *Lovers of Achilles* and later proverbial:

> Lovesickness is a joy mixed with pain. I can make a good comparison, I think. When the frost has come in bright weather, and children seize a solid lump of ice in their hands, at first they find a new delight; but finally their desire won't let it go, yet what they have will not stay in their hands. So the same passion often lets lovers love and not love at the same time.[40]

Even in this inelegant translation the metaphor is apt and full of resonance. We are attracted (or so some thought) to our lovers by their sparkle and charm; yet love itself is fleeting; childhood too does not linger; and the youth, *pais* in the terminology of Greek homoerotic poetry, whose love is sought by the lovers of Achilles will himself be as short-lived and as brilliant as a piece of gleaming ice. Here we have a vision of childhood rich with loss and longing. But there is beauty and grace in the image as well, for children have qualities adults lack, and some of these are thought to be attractive.

Most prominent among the positive physical characteristics of children are the sweet smell of their breath and skin and their softness. Mentioned in contexts full of pathos by parents in tragedy, these are also discussed and explained by the philosophers.[41] According to the *Problems* ascribed to Aristotle, a child's smell stays sweet until puberty, at which point the sweat becomes saltier and stronger-smelling.[42] Plato explains the softness of children's bodies in an interesting account of the aging process. When they are young, creatures are formed of firmly interlocked triangles of matter. These are soft, as they are newly produced from marrow and nourished on milk. As older and weaker triangles that make up food and drink come into contact with them, they overcome these invaders and so grow. In time, however, the body's triangles begin to weaken after so many battles, and can no longer assimilate new ones to themselves. They are divided by newcomers and decay, the process that is called old age (Pl. *Tim.* 81CD). The plasticity and malleability of the child, physical and intellectual, is a fundamental starting point for Plato's regimen in both of his major utopian treatises.[43] Crying, too, was a childhood trait, sometimes an unwelcome symptom—Plato seems to disapprove—and sometimes viewed as an exercise contributing to the child's growth (Aristotle's opinion).[44] Children's wailing is described by distinctive words, *blēkhanō* (otherwise used of sheep and goats) and *brykhaomai* (usually applied to the bellowing of beasts and the raging of storms).[45] Their mode of speech also was their own. As among other species (except cattle), children have higher voices than adults.[46] Plato's Callicles takes pleasure in listening to small children lisp.[47] Baby talk is quoted on the comic stage and in Theophrastus's character sketches.[48] In addition, we are told that children have dense bodies (and so suffer from leprosy less than men), are snub-nosed, get thinner in the summer, are particularly prone to head lice, and are especially likely to get dizzy if they look at things a long way off.[49] And, sweet though their skins may be, their body products are not, a perception exploited for comic purposes.[50]

One physical characteristic has implications for children's temperament. In a number of places in the Aristotelian *Problems,* we read that children are moister and hotter than adults.[51] As a result, they are more hot-tempered as well, greedier and angrier than men.[52] Aristotle elsewhere notes their passion, and regards childhood as the time when the appetite for pleasure is strongest.[53] All this is in agreement with Plato, who says the young are "fiery," and ranges children with slaves, women, and the lower classes as those who have the most desires, pleasures, and pains.[54] Specific pleasures include sweets—a honeycomb stuffed in a newborn's mouth might stop its crying—and music.[55] Passionate as they are, children are energetic, unable to keep still in body and voice, susceptible to crying out or leaping about in a disorderly fashion.[56] Because their reason is as yet uncurbed, they are treacherous, fierce, hubristic; in short, the most difficult to manage of all wild creatures.[57] Lack of discipline renders them changeable; Plato regards children's tendency to alter their games from day to day as dangerous (Pl. *Leg.* 7.797B). Yet variability and unpredictability may also be termed playfulness and are sometimes viewed more favorably by those with less concern for controlling all aspects of community life. In a play by Sophocles, the satyr Silenus (unsuited by temperament for service as one of Plato's rulers) presents a pleasant vignette of the charm of a child's random responses. "Whenever I bring [the baby Dionysus] food, he straightway touches my nose and reaches for my bald head, smiling sweetly all the while" (Soph. fr. 171R.).

As the rhetorical use of children to denigrate opponents indicates, to behave in a manner appropriate to an earlier stage of life was generally regarded as a regression. Aristoxenus, an associate of Aristotle who lived at Athens in the later fourth century and is best known as a writer on music, is perhaps most explicit: children should not behave like infants (*nēpiazoien*), youths like children (*paidarieuointo*), adults like young men (*neanieuointo*), and old men should not become crazy.[58] So Bdelycleon taunts his father for proposing to tell a children's story in adult company, Socrates puns on the root of *paizein* when he hesitates to appear to be playing, though he is an old man.[59] What about precocity? We have already alluded to the motif of early achievement as a sign of great things to come. Of course, attitudes must to some degree depend on just what is achieved. Both Alcibiades and his son of the same name were rebuked for sexual activities inappropriate to their status as minors.[60] Less controversial activities elicited two rather different reactions, respect and affection.

Immature and lacking in experience, children were also believed to be innocent, and so were easily associated with phenomena outside the usual areas of citizen interaction: nature and the gods.[61] As a proverb put it, "Wine and children tell the truth";[62] children's chance comments might be credited with oracular force, their advice be valued for its special insight.[63] Herodotus, who knew a good story when he heard one, passes on an excellent illustration (5.49–51). When the Greeks of Asia Minor were planning to revolt from Persian rule, Aristagoras, the tyrant of Miletus, came to Sparta to enlist the aid of king Cleomenes. At first, Cleomenes was inclined to help his fellow Greeks. But when Aristagoras unwisely revealed that the distance from the coast to the heart of the Persian empire was some three months' journey, he changed his mind. Aristagoras then turned from persuasion to bribery, and had upped the ante to fifty talents when Cleomenes' daughter Gorgo, a girl of eight or nine, cried out, "Father, the stranger will corrupt you if you don't go away." Cleomenes, pleased by his daughter's advice, left, and Aristagoras went away empty-handed; in the event, the revolt ended in disaster. For another illustration, we may turn to Athenian drama. One of the techniques of Greek tragedy is to express its themes in verbal and visual imagery alike. In Sophocles' *Antigone,* Creon insists on the proper deference due to certain set hierarchies: man over woman, father over son, king over subjects. Others, Antigone and his own son Haemon among them, invoke different considerations, and Creon's rigidity has a tragic result, not least for himself. Tiresias is the one who brings home to Creon that he is in error. A boy leads the blind seer on stage, the same boy who had earlier reported to him the rejected sacrifices that mark the displeasure of the gods. The boy (he says) is his guide, as he is a guide to others (Soph. *Ant.* 1012–1014). The boy's role, and Tiresias's respect for his contribution, underline one of the play's themes, that true wisdom may come from unlikely sources; children, young women, and an old, blind man may understand the gods' wishes as well as their social superiors do.

A second response involves a combination that is characteristic of the Athenian attitude toward children: their limitations are recognized, they themselves are loved and enjoyed. From this point of view, clever comments and wisdom beyond their years are neither regarded as special delivery from the gods nor dismissed with contempt. Either reaction would constitute taking the children too seriously; the comic Strepsiades' proud recital of his son's attainments as a boy—making toy houses, boats, wagons, and frogs from pomegranate peel—is treated with gentle mockery (Ar. *Nub.* 877–881). They are simply cute. Our most developed portrait of what we would today call a cute kid comes in the account of the young Cyrus's stay with his grandfather Astyages, king of the Medes, in Xenophon's *Cyropaedia.* Of course, Xenophon would hardly trouble to compose his romance on Cyrus's early years if the boy had not become a great king and conqueror, his methods a model for the Athenian's own day. For the author, there is always a subtext in these stories; they are early signs of Cyrus's exceptional success. But the other characters involved in them, the adults who witness Cyrus's precocious perspicacity, cannot know his destiny. Their response is often simply appreciative laughter. When Cyrus imitates the cupbearer Sacas, and puts on his serious and decorous countenance, both his mother and her father laugh heartily (Xen. *Cyr.* 1.3.8–9). They find him entertaining (1.3.12). Xenophon himself seems sympathetic to this view, for he sums up Cyrus's long disquisition on justice and the law with the words, "So Cyrus often used to chatter" (*elalei:* 1.4.1, cf. 12), and he says that his hero's loquacity and relentless curiosity did not seem unpleasant because he was so fresh and naive (1.4.3) The young Cyrus, in fact, was like a pet puppy (*skylakōdes:* 1.4.4). Later in this work, we are introduced retrospectively to another cute kid. Cyaxares offers Cyrus his daughter with these words: "This is the girl you often used to pet when you stayed with us as a boy. Whenever anyone asked her whom she would marry, she used to answer, 'Cyrus'" (8.5.19–20). We might be tempted to take this as simply another example of truth out of the mouths of babes. But it is clear in the telling that Cyaxares does not mean to imply that the marriage has been made in heaven, fated in any way. His intention is rather to reawaken in the adult Cyrus the same feelings of warmth he had for the girl when they were both children and she said such cute things.

The Vocabulary of Childhood and Its Stages

Broadly speaking, the words for *children* we find in our texts were chosen according to three criteria: their denotation, their resonance of connotation and tone, their suitability to the genre to which the text belongs.[64] For example, of the common words for those in transition from child to adult, *neaniskos* and *meirakion*, absent from tragic drama, are found in the verse of comedy, which employs a more prosaic vocabulary than other genres of poetry. On the question of connotation and tone it is less easy to be so categorical, as a brief examination of the two most common words for *child* in the sense "offspring," *pais* and *teknon*, may indicate.[65] They are distinguishable in many ways. *Pais,* formed from an Indo-European root meaning "small" or "insignificant," means both "child" and "young person"; it has a very broad range, it and its derivatives being applied to others of subordinate status, slaves and the junior partners in homosexual couples, from an early period; it is rarely found in emotional appeals from parent to child or from old to young, at least in early Greek verse; and at times it is so lacking in affective overtones that *pai* is later used as an ejaculation, much like our "Oh, boy!"[66] *Teknon*, related to *tiktō*, "I give birth," never means "young person" but always means "child" (literally or metaphorically); in early Greek poetry, it is frequently used by parents to address their children in contexts of consolation, exhortation, and reproof. Given these facts, it is natural for standard reference works to seek to establish thoroughgoing and more or less strict differences of usage between these words, such as the dictum that *pais* has special reference to the father, *teknon* (the more emotive term) to the mother, in tragedy above all.[67]

But such formulations cannot be pressed. In Aeschylus, Xerxes is often termed the *pais* of his mother, Atossa, Clytemnestra calls her son Orestes *pais* as well as *teknon,* and Danaus addresses his daughters as both *paides* and *tekna.*[68] In Euripides, Hecuba addresses her daughter Polyxena as *teknon* and *pais* in the same line, and the phrases *ateknos paidōn* and *apaidas teknōn* seem synonymous.[69] Certainly *teknon* may sometimes increase the emotional intensity of a passage, as it does when Oedipus uses it to address his suppliant subjects in the opening words of *OT.* The word indicates his paternal concern for the citizens of Thebes;[70] it also initiates the ironic undercurrent running through the play, in which the regal father figure will be humbled, revealed as sinner and son. But in many other instances the choice may depend more on aesthetic effects (such as alliteration) or on wordplay than on recognizable patterns of connotation.[71] And of course poets in particular may choose to stretch or even subvert a word's usual usage for effect.[72]

Any discussion of the ages denoted by various words for *children* must consider an important question: How much does vocabulary reveal about social history? In the opening chapter of his path-breaking book on the history of childhood, Philippe Ariès notes the wide range covered by the word *enfant* and the absence of words for *baby* and *adolescent* in early modern France. He argues that these are significant indicators that the notions of infancy and adolescence as separate stages with their own positive attributes were correspondingly late to develop.[73] Michel Manson's work on Roman childhood has pursued this theme. According to Manson, *infans* and *infantia* begin to refer to early childhood only in the late first century B.C.; this represents "a reflection of the discovery of the small child" at that time.[74] But contrary opinions are persuasive. Other recent studies in Roman social history exhibit close attention to legal and philological niceties while at the same time insisting on the inadequacy of such evidence to express the realities of institutions and those who live within them, and indeed on its potential to mislead. For example, examination of the epigraphic record reveals that the mother-father-child(ren) triad was at the core of Roman kinship relations despite the fact that neither of the common Latin words for household, *familia* and *domus*, regularly refers to the nuclear family.[75] I suggest here that the Athenian vocabulary for *children* neither mirrors nor seriously misleads. Though classical Attic had several nouns designating infants, children in their earliest years, most were not in common use and several were elastic; and no other stages of childhood were delineated by a single word. Yet artists and writers certainly show an awareness of and interest in this and other stages of the child's development.

Ancient authors occasionally present neat and plausible schemes in which words are presented in order of the age group to which they refer or even with what look like exact definitions attached. The most extensive list is that of the Hellenistic scholar Aristophanes of Byzantium. Designations for males include *brephos*, the newborn; *paidion*, the nursling; *paidarion*, the child who can walk and speak; *paidiskos*; *pais*, roughly, the child who can be educated; *pallēks* or *boupais* or *antipais* or *mellephēbos*; *ephēbos* (and its local equivalents); *meirakion*; *meiraks*; *neaniskos*; *neanias*; and so on until old age.[76] An account derived from Hippocrates includes seven stages of life, each identified with a set age span; the first four are *paidion* (until age 7), *pais* (7–14), *meirakion* (14–21), *neaniskos* (21–28).[77] These two systems are loosely compatible—at least, each places the terms *paidion, pais, meirakion,* and *neaniskos* in the same order. But other evidence is less easy to assimilate to them. For example, in a passage of Menander the order runs *ephēbos, meirakion, anēr, gerōn (Men.* fr. 867aE.); in other Athenian authors *neaniskos* rarely refers to a youth who has not yet reached the age of majority, sometimes to an ephebe, sometimes to a young man who is old enough to participate more fully in civic life;[78] and *meirakion* and *neaniskos* are often interchangeable; *pais* and *paidion, paidion* and *paidarion,* on occasion.[79] Usage is thoroughly inconsistent.[80]

Some words do indeed have a well-demarcated chronological reference. *Pais* itself is quite clearly defined both as a technical term and in common usage. When it does not mean "child of," it refers to a male child before his enrollment in a deme and his consequent entry into civic life, and (less strictly) to a female child before her corresponding change in status, her marriage.[81] A number of words refer to very young children in particular. Most, however, belong to the language of poetry, and some may be applied to older children as well. *Nēpios,* common in epic and later poetry, seems always to mean "baby," but the noun is quite rare in Attic prose.[82] *Brephos* is still more unusual outside poetry; it occurs only in two passages of Xenophon. In one of these, newborn children are referred to both as *ta neogna brephē* and as *tōn neognōn teknōn,* which implies that *brephos* on its own was not felt to express extreme youth more clearly than *teknon.*[83] (In later Greek prose, it may describe a child as old as six.)[84] The noun *mikros,* "the little one," is rarer still, attested only in a comedy by Menander; *mikkos,* found twice in a satyr play by Aeschylus, is Doric dialect and thus probably not current in Athenian speech and prose (though it is found as a personal name).[85] Among more common words in prose diction, *paidion* and other diminutive forms such as *paidarion* and *teknidion* are, as we would expect, often applied to very young children. But not invariably. All three of Socrates' sons, two small (*smikroi*) and one large (*megas*), are referred to as *paidia.*[86] This is a characteristic of other diminutives as well; *meirakion* and *meirakiskos, neanias* and *neaniskos* are sometimes synonyms.[87] Further elaboration is required to give even *paidion* and *paidarion* the meaning "small child" unequivocally, an adjective or a descriptive phrase.[88] It seems that classical Attic had no terms to refer to any stage of childhood except the first, and even for this its vocabulary was far from precise. But this should not be taken as evidence that the Athenians themselves did not trouble to distinguish this and other age levels within childhood.

Newborns attract special notice, not always for any distinctive qualities of their own but because they exhibit the characteristics of children in general to a very high degree. For example, the skin of children (*tōn paidōn*) is said to be closely packed, as if their pores were closed—and the skin of young children (*tōn paidiōn*) most of all (Theophr. fr. 9.18 Wimmer). Newborns have the smoothest body of all; even the bones in their head are soft.[89] They exemplify less attractive attributes too, lack of intelligence and of strength. When Cassandra suddenly speaks words it is willing to hear, the chorus comments, "Even a newborn child would understand that" (Aesch. *Ag.* 1162–1163). Similarly, according to a picturesque passage in a lost tragedy, "Not only a woman but a newborn child may tickle the bristly boar with a tender hand and throw him easier than any wrestler" (*Trag. Adesp.* fr. 383K.-S.). Orestes' nurse, summing up her charge's early days, indicates that the philosophers were not alone in perceiving children, especially small ones, as akin to animals:

> I got him from his mother and reared him, enduring shrill summonses which kept me walking about all night and which were troublesome and unprofitable for me. You have to rear something which doesn't speak like an animal. . . . The child *en sparganois* doesn't say anything if it's hungry or thirsty or needs to urinate; the young guts of children are a law unto themselves. I had to be a prophet, and often I got it wrong, and had to clean his clothes.[90]

More neutrally, Aristotle indicates that newborns have white hair, eyelids, and eyebrows, and eyes a shade of blue;[91] they sleep a lot in the first stage of life;[92] though they laugh and cry in their sleep, they do not dream until they are four or five;[93] they are bigger on top than their elders, smaller where their weight is supported—it is for this reason that they can't walk.[94]

Unable to speak, eat, move, or control their bowels even as well as older children, infants and toddlers were catered to through special equipment: feeding bottles, potty-stools, cradles, perhaps walkers.[95] They also wore *spargana,* usually translated (as by the lexicographers) as "swaddling clothes."[96] Plato recommends that children be swaddled until the age of two; Soranus, a medical writer of the second century A.D., regards tight wrapping as of great importance for modeling the infant's body, stipulating that the bonds be drawn most tightly at the knees and ankles (to produce finer joints), less so in the region of the thighs and calves.[97] Late reliefs show infants swaddled according to this prescription, with only their hands and feet free of their bonds, and Plutarch approvingly says that Spartan children were unique in Greece in not being swaddled.[98] Yet (aside from Plato) there is no archaic or classical evidence that children were in fact bound in this way; and babies depicted on *choes,* the drinking vessels associated with the Athenian festival of the Anthesteria, and on other vases, are usually shown unclothed. Though children are sometimes to be observed wrapped more or less tightly on archaic and classical grave reliefs, they may simply be wrapped in blankets rather than swaddled.[99] The story that Cronus ingested a rock enveloped in *spargana* under the delusion that it was his son Zeus is itself a little easier to swallow if we imagine the rock as completely covered with cloth, but hardly plausible nonetheless, since no real baby could survive such a thorough wrapping (Hes. *Th.* 485–491). It is possible that our late sources, Plutarch and the lexicographers, merely reflect their contemporary customs and that Plato's plans, as often, do not; *spargana,* then, would be rather like our diapers, rags that could be placed on a baby's bottom as required and easily removed.[100] But it is safer to accept that children were swaddled for a very short period after birth—the forty or sixty days Soranus speaks of?—and that Plato's eccentricity lies in his recommendation of a much longer period. We may then assume that babies shown unswaddled are older than this, or that artists have chosen to depict them without swaddling bands; in modern cultures, cradle boards, swaddling bands, and similar restrictions on infants' body movements are typically applied for only part of the day.[101] Whatever their precise nature, however, *spargana* were as unique to very young children as the other apparatus mentioned here, material reminders of their special nature.

Still other stages are identified in art. Greek artists were slower in establishing conventions for the depiction of children than they were in determining those for other age groups, perhaps because there was no widespread agreement as to which of the many ways in which children differed from their elders most merited emphasis; the lack of a stereotypical image for children in turn made it difficult to develop methods of displaying variations within the category.[102] Yet some striking attempts survive. On the grave stele of Apollonia, found on the island of Ikaria in 1933, a woman sits with a naked boy (perhaps ten years old) standing before her; a baby sits on her lap, a naked child crawls on the ground, two other older boys, different in size—her brothers?—are off to the right. In this relief there are five children, apparently of five different ages.[103] The grave stele of the shoemaker Xanthippus shows this dead father flanked by two daughters, one much smaller than the other.[104] Another stele, about fifty years later, bears a relief of a seated woman and two children; these are once again of different sizes, and further distinguished by their clothes.[105] On each of these gravestones the younger daughter is the more demonstrative. In addition, *krateriskoi,* small vases of a distinctive shape, from Brauron often differentiate older and younger girls;[106] and *choes* feature crawlers, toddlers, older children, youths.[107] Though these monuments are of varied genres and not all are well realized, they do reveal an awareness of childhood's diversity.

Among literary sources, the aims of narrative often preclude close investigation of a character's age. Eurysaces, son of Ajax in Sophocles' play, is sometimes presented as very young, sometimes as old enough to help carry his father's body. Sophocles is more concerned with appealing to the pathos of the situation, and with underlining the new family responsibilities Eurysaces will now have thrust on him, than with establishing the precise stage of his development.[108] We must turn to didactic treatises for explicit expressions of opinion on the stages of childhood and their characteristics. Plato and Aristotle give the fullest and most self-

Fig. 1. The shoemaker Xanthippus and his daughters

conscious accounts in their programmatic works *Laws* and *Politics*.[109] It is Plato's Athenian spokesman in *Laws* who recommends that the baby be swaddled from birth until the age of two and then carried about by its nurses until the age of three (7.789E). The period from three to six is to be characterized by games with other children and the administration of mild forms of discipline (7.793E). Then, at seven, boys and girls begin to live separate lives and formal education begins (7.794C). Boys of ten will study literature for three years, and those of thirteen will go on to master the lyre for three years more (7.810A). *Laws* offers other characterizations of the periods of childhood which are not entirely consistent with these. During the first three years, the child is said to make a lot of noise, but not to understand language, so a nurse can judge his wants only from his crying (7.791E–792E). During his first five years, he is thought to grow more quickly in height than in the next twenty (7.788D).[110]

Ten is a benchmark in another Utopian work, *The Republic,* where all the residents of the ideal city of Magnesia who reach this age are to be sent into the fields to work (*Resp.* 7.540E–541A). In a third dialogue, influenced but not written by Plato, Socrates outlines the particular problems to which stages of childhood are prone. The newborn, beginning life in grief, weeps because of need or cold or heat or a blow, not yet able to say what he wants and able only to cry to indicate discomfort. But when he turns seven, he drains sorrow's cup to the dregs, tyrannized by *paidagōgoi* (the male slaves responsible for his conduct) and teachers, and as he grows older he takes on still other instructors as his masters ([Pl.] *Ax.* 366D–367A).

In *Politics,* the critical ages are two, five, seven, and fourteen. Up to the age of two, children are to drink plenty of milk but little wine, to exercise as much as possible, and to become accustomed to the cold (7.1336a2–24, 1336b36); from two until five, the child should continue to exercise through play, but both the forms of play and the stories told to children of this age must be supervised by officials, the *paidonomoi* (7.1336a24–40). Children are to be reared at home until the age of seven, and protected as much as possible from indecent talk and images; one consequence is that they are not to be permitted to attend comedies and similarly scurrilous dramatic fare (7.1336b1–36). At seven, children begin formal education outside the home, a period divided into two halves, before and after *hēbē,* puberty, at fourteen (7.1336b36–1337a7). Other authors confirm the significance of the age seven, when baby teeth (or "milk teeth") were thought to be replaced, a connection as ancient as Solon.[111] The importance accorded the ages five, six, and seven finds parallels in many cultures studied by anthropologists, in which this is commonly a time for the child's attributes and social roles to change; it is also reflected in some leading theories of cognitive development.[112] *Hēbē* too is an important time for other Greek writers; again, their view of its crucial characteristics—the breaking of the voice, the beginning of the growth of hair on the chin, cheeks, armpits, and genitals, and sexual maturity above all—is hardly unique.[113]

Incidental information on specific ages from other sources is less coherent. For example, one speaker in an Attic lawsuit, Lysias's client, describes himself at thirteen as ignorant of what oligarchy was, without any financial motives to wish his father ill, and quite incapable of rescuing him from harm; his intention is to free himself of any guilt for the actions of the Thirty.[114] A second litigant says he was thirteen when his brother was born and was therefore old enough for his assertion that they are both sons of the same man to be trustworthy (Isae. 12.10). As always, we must evaluate this seemingly contradictory evidence with the understanding that the orators were not primarily concerned to provide precise information to the jurors, let alone to us. But in each passage there is a trace of the common-sense conviction that children near or in their teens are very nearly able to act with adult force, if not foresight, as indeed a slave not yet twelve is said to have done in almost killing his master with a knife (Antiph. 5.69).

Broader portraits of more vaguely defined stages are not uncommon. For example, in *The Republic,* Glaucon terms *trophē,* the stage between birth (*genesis*) and formal education (*paideia*), the most difficult.[115] In respect to children's speech, we again find an appreciation for change over time within the period of childhood. Aristotle observes that children at first can't talk at all and then

21

stumble in their speech for a long time.[116] They begin by calling every man "father" and every woman "mother" until they learn to whom these special terms apply (Arist. *Phys.* 1.184b12). Cyrus, or so Xenophon supposes, grew less talkative as he matured, his voice became more subdued, he didn't interrupt as often (Xen. *Cyr.* 1.4.1–4). Tastes, too, change over the course of childhood: very small children (*ta pany smikra paidia*) prefer puppet shows, older ones (*hoi meizous paides*) comedies (Pl. *Leg.* 2.658CD). The thrust of all this evidence is that stages of childhood, though legally and politically irrelevant and only irregularly and imprecisely marked off in the Attic vocabulary, were widely recognized at Athens.

It would be easy enough to demonstrate that these ideas about children, childhood, and its stages for the most part mirror the social reality of classical Athens—at least as seen through a glass darkly. Children as a group failed to measure up to adult male standards of strength, spirit, and sense; they were therefore excluded from the political and legal privileges of citizens who had come of age. Again, just as childhood was widely believed to be divisible into stages leading to maturity (though the demarcations of these stages differed, and they themselves left little trace in the language), so also young Athenians took their place in the household and in the world beyond by degrees; some, but by no means all, of this process of integration into the adult community was signaled by formal ritual acts. Yet it is worth noting that the steps in children's admission into Athenian society do not always match up with the stages of childhood discussed above. I take this as a welcome reminder that mirrors merely reflect reality; they do not reproduce it in the round. Similarly, the imposition of patterns on the evidence, necessary though it is, may sometimes obscure a complexity that is in itself a matter of interest. This conviction underlies the next chapter, in which I will show that children's participation in household and community life was more widespread and more varied than is generally recognized.

Two

The Child in the Household
and the Community

The Child in the Household

Athenian children were social beings almost from the beginning of life. Being born, a biological event, was insufficient to make a child a member of an *oikos* or *oikia,* a household. Even those with two citizen parents had no automatic right of entry; they had to be accepted by the *kyrios,* the household's head, and his decision was based on a complex of factors, impossible to identify in any one case, but certainly including cultural constructs such as gender—girls were rejected more often—and the optimum size of the family.[1] Two ceremonies marked this acceptance.[2] The *amphidromia,* which took place on the fifth or seventh day after birth, involved a sacrifice; the father (naked, according to one late source) carried the child around the household hearth; women purified themselves; friends and relations sent traditional gifts, octopuses and cuttlefish, but did not attend unless they had been present at the birth. It was presumably at this time that the family decorated the doorway of its home, announcing the birth of a boy with a wreath of olive, that of a girl with wool "because of their spinning."[3] Girls and the children of poorer families might be named at the same rite. However, those who could or would bear the extra expense bestowed the name at a second celebration, on the tenth day after birth, the *dekatē*. This, too, involved an offering to the gods, but was rather more festive—it featured a dance by women, who were rewarded with a special cake—and open (presumably by invitation) to outsiders.

Athenians had just one personal name, most often made up of two elements with more or less transparent connotations; an example for boys is Hegesistratus, "army leader." Shorter names occurred as well, generally formed from the same elements that appear in compounds (Hegesias, Straton) or referring to personal characteristics (Pyrrhus, "fiery, red-haired") or circumstances (Didymus, "twin"). Girls' names were for the most part simply feminine forms of boys' (Hegesistrate, Pyrrha, Didyma). Such speaking names gave parents the opportunity to express opinions on public issues—Lacedaemonius, son of Sparta's ally Cimon, bore a political manifesto as much as a name—and also to mold their children's sense of themselves; they were at the same time indications of family (or broader community) values and a means of maintaining those values and transmitting them to others.[4] The use of names such as Hegesistrate for girls, who were not encouraged to grow up to lead armies, may be taken to reflect the dominance of (culturally defined) masculine attributes at Athens and the role of women as transmitters of goods and status rather than as actors in their own right. The forms of certain names, however, did send a message to and about women. Some women bore names identical with abstract nouns (Euphrosyne, "happiness"; Philia, "friendship"; and so on); others bore names in the form of diminutives, grammatically neuter in gender, such as Boidion and Lysion. These may have contributed to a tendency to depersonalize and objectify women, to present them as things—and rather insignificant things at that.[5]

Though they had no surnames or family names, the Athenians could use personal names to advertise a child's membership in the family. The Athenian system of nomenclature included the personal name; the father's name, the patronymic, in the genitive case; and the demotic, which indicated the deme to which the family belonged. Hegesistratus might more fully be referred to as Hegesistratus Hegesiou Kephalethen—Hegesistratus, son of Hegesias, of the deme Cephale.[6] Such a system of nomenclature has an obvious hereditary component, the patronymic. Deme membership, too, was passed down in the male line, being based on the area where some paternal ancestor had lived when Cleisthenes redesigned the political map of Athens in the late sixth century. Besides these formal family links, moreover, personal names themselves often ran in families.[7] In Plato's *Politicus,* Socrates says that two young strangers, Theaetetus and Socrates, are related to him after a fashion—Theaetetus because they look a little alike, Socrates because they share the same name, "which implies some sort of kinship" (Pl. *Pol.* 257D). Grandsons were regularly named for grandfathers—more precisely, a man's first son after his father. The family of Hagnias of the deme Erchia included five men named Dromeas, three named Hagnias, and four named Diocles. Other "family names" involved the sharing of one syllable (or a variation), usually the first, with the same semantic element. For example, Callicrates of Erchia named his sons Calliphanes, Callisthenes, and Callistratus. We know the names and patronymics of some twenty-six hundred Athenian males attested before 300; just under one-third bear names that are identical to or share one element with their father's, and thus mark them as members of his family. This figure, excluding as it does sons named for other family members, represents the minimum number of those identified in this way almost from birth. The number of women whose fathers are known is much smaller, but large enough to assure that daughters were linked by name with their fathers significantly less often than sons. So, too, their role in the devolution of property was more marginal, their opportunities to bring the family fame much fewer.

Children were also admitted into family-based social groups, the *genos* and the phratry, at an early age. We know of three introductions to *genē,* exclusive groups of unknown origin associated with certain cults.[8] One involves the adoption of an adult heir (Isae. 7.13, 15, 17, 26, 43); the others, exceptional circumstances. Callias introduced to his *genos,* the Ceryces, a child he had denied before his phraters several years before; Phrastor sent away his wife, and then relented and tried (unsuccessfully) to introduce her child into his *genos*.[9] How old were these boys? Phrastor's wife was pregnant when he sent her away. He grew sick and accepted the child soon after—it must have been very young indeed. Callias's son was quite grown up when he joined the Ceryces, but he was much younger when Callias rejected him before his phraters, probably newborn, and it is likely that he would have been introduced to the *genos* as well as to the phratry at that time if Callias had accepted him. This admittedly imperfect evidence suggests that children were usually introduced into their *genē* soon after birth.

Unlike the *genē,* which were restricted to a portion of the citizen body only, phratries were open to all Athenians, male and female (though this need not mean that all in fact belonged to one).[10] Our evidence for them is consequently fuller, but not more straightforward. Children were introduced at the Apaturia, a festival held each autumn.[11] But our sources do not agree on the age of those introduced. Some suggest they were newborn, under a year old, or very young; an ancient commentator on Plato sets the age at three or four years; and other passages imply a child could be still older—even seven—though a late introduction might be irregular or suspicious.[12]

A related problem is posed by evidence for a double introduction to the phraters. Two offerings, the *meion* and the *koureion,* are mentioned in the decree of the Demotionidae.[13] That decree also provides for the listing of those who will one day undergo the scrutiny of the phratry Deceleieis. Each person's name is to be registered "in the first year or in the one he sacrifices the *koureion*" (line 118). The natural reading of this decree is that there were two possible times for admission—at the first celebration of the Apaturia after birth and at the time the *koureion* was offered.[14] The text requires registration at either or both of these times; this may imply that only one of these sacrifices had to be offered. Since the *koureion* was obligatory (the date of the scrutiny was set as the year after the *koureion*), the *meion* may have been an optional ceremony for the year of birth. Perhaps here, too, only the wealthy risked extra expenditure on a newborn or very young child; others may have omitted the *meion* entirely or offered it only when a child's survival seemed more assured.[15]

The *koureion* probably takes its name from the offering of hair made on the part of those introduced to the phratry; these may have waited until this occasion to cut the topknot, which distinguishes boys on some vases.[16] Hair styles demarcate age and status elsewhere in the ancient Mediterranean, most elaborately perhaps on Crete, and a change of fashion makes a fitting accompaniment for a rite of passage.[17] In the absence of any direct evidence, Labarbe (1953) has put forward an ingenious argument that boys offered the *koureion* at the age of sixteen. His case is based on the sixth speech of Isaeus, which deals with the attempt of Euctemon to introduce the son of a woman called Alce to his phratry. After an initial setback the boy is admitted (Isae. 6.18–26). After these events (*meta tauta*) Euctemon's son Philoctemon is killed off Chios, and sometime later (*hysteron khronōi*) his son-in-law Phanostratus sets off on an expedition with Timotheus (27). Labarbe, concerned to establish the chronology, sets the expedition at the end of the summer of 366/5, on the strength of *IG* 2² 1609, which associates Timotheus and Phanostratus with a cleruchy to Samos. Philoctemon's death is put a short time before, at the end of 367/6 or the beginning of 366/5; the rejection by the phratry at the Apaturia, in the fall of 367; and the boy's acceptance at the Thargelia, the next spring (at the end of 367/6). Labarbe dates the speech before the summer of 363/2. Alce's son was then *oupō hyper eikosin etē* (14), not yet twenty-one, and was, therefore, born in 383/2. Consequently, he was sixteen at the time of the *koureion*.

Unfortunately, appealing though it may be, this is a very fragile reconstruction. The inscription *IG* 2² 1609 may refer to 370/69, not to 366/5.[18] The intervals between the acceptance of Alce's son, Philoctemon's death, and Phanostratus's departure need not be nearly so short as Labarbe imagines.[19] Moreover, there is no justification for the supposition that Alce's son was not accepted by the phraters at the regular time, the Apaturia. The failure of any one of the elements in Labarbe's scheme renders the whole invalid. And yet it is possible that the *koureion* did involve sixteen-year-olds after all.

The question is tied up with a complex of issues regarding *hēbē*, a word with a number of related but distinct connotations. In the first instance, *hēbē* refers to the onset of puberty, usually set at fourteen.[20] The word is also used of legal maturity; the Athenians provided for the sons of those killed in battle until *hēbē*, that is, until their admission to a deme in the eighteenth archon-year after their birth.[21] But the orators also express legal maturity in the context of entry into an inheritance by using a curious phrase, *epi dietes hēbēsai,* "to be two years older than *hēbē.*"[22] One lexicographer brings this term into conformity with the age of majority by setting *hēbē,* eccentrically, two years later than usual; but among most scholars of antiquity the assumption is that *hēbē* here is puberty, to be thought of as fourteen, and that the age in question is therefore sixteen.[23] How are we to explain this belief, which seems so completely at odds with Athenian practice during the classical period? I would suggest that the expression *epi dietes hēbēsai* was originally applied to boys at the time they offered the *koureion* and were registered in their phratry. While fourteen was the age generally identified as the onset of *hēbē,* it was well known in antiquity that boys did not all mature at the same rate.[24] To delay ritual recognition for two years would make it more likely that the boys involved had all, in fact, reached puberty;[25] this argument gains force if all boys born in the same year offered the *koureion* at the same festival, in the same way as they were admitted to a deme in the same archon-year. It is generally agreed that, before Cleisthenes' reforms, admission to the phratry was the equivalent of entry into the citizen body and to such citizen rights as inheritance.[26] It would be natural enough for an old phrase used to express legal maturity before Cleisthenes to become fossilized and remain in use with its former force, even though its literal meaning no longer corresponded to the age of those it described; all the more so since phratry membership was often adduced as proof of eligibility for citizenship and the two events could be regarded,

Fig. 2. A father takes his son to the shoemaker's

both causally and conceptually, as related stages in the process of coming of age.

The child, then, was a member of a family, a family's phratry, perhaps a family's *genos*. But such formal definitions could have only limited significance, especially to a small child. Children apprehend the social world more concretely, classifying persons and relations primarily by the things they do to and with them. A mother is not a kinship category, but someone who provides food and comfort and so on. An Athenian son would know his father as the man who took him to the shoemaker's or accompanied him (and perhaps his *paidagōgos*) to the theater.[27] (On each occasion, he would incidentally learn a lesson about how to be a man, competent in commercial interactions, a conduit of community culture.) Along the same lines, to approximate a child's experience of the family, we must, in Beryl Rawson's words, "also take account of what activities families undertook together."[28] Such a project may also afford incidental insight; it is suggestive both for Roman ideals of family life and for Roman conceptions of entertainment that (as Rawson points out) married men, women, and schoolboys all sat separately to watch plays, gladiatorial shows, and some other spectacles, while they watched the horse races at the Circus together.

I begin with religion. *Amphidromia, dekatē,* introductions to *genos* and phratry—all include ritual acts. Religion, of course, pervaded Athenian life, from the invocations to the gods which prefaced decrees, to the plays presented in Dionysus's theater in his honor, to the temples on the Acropolis, which dominate the city's skyline even now. That families are so often involved in cult activities of one kind or another is another index of its importance. Some of these (like those already discussed) revolved around the children themselves. And we should not imagine that children were always bystanders—Eubulides, for example, distributed the meat at his celebration of the *koureion.*[29] In others, some children had distinctive responsibilities. Athenian marriages reserved an important role for the *pais amphithalēs,* a child with both parents living; such a child served as an index of one household's good fortune and (so it was hoped) an omen for another's.[30] On the night before the marriage, the groom slept in the bride's house accompanied by a *pais amphithalēs* who was male (cf. Poll. 3.40). At the ceremony itself, a boy *amphithalēs,* crowned with a wreath of thorns and acorns, circulated among the guests, distributing bread from a basket that resembled a child's cradle.[31] *Amphithaleis* also accompanied the processions of the bride and groom and then of the wedding gifts on the day after the ceremony.[32] At other times, children took part in ritual activity simply as members of the family, as at funerals, another important occasion for the assertion of solidarity.[33]

Families sacrificed together too. A fourth-century votive relief from Brauron is framed by a young man holding a bull and a woman bearing a stool, both probably cult functionaries or family slaves. Between them we see a bearded man, two women (one a nurse?), and four children of different sizes—all about to make an offering to Artemis.[34] In general, an effort was made to include children in cult observances, at least within the city itself, though

Fig. 3. A *pais amphithalēs* rides in a wedding procession

exceptions seem to have been made in the case of rites involving abusive language (Arist. *Pol.* 7.1336b18).[35] Euxitheus's relations took him to the temple of Apollo Patroos and other sacred places (Dem. 57.54). The Superstitious Man wants his children and his wife (or a nurse) to accompany him to Orphic rites (Theophr. *Char.* 16.12). Theophrastus brought his sons to religious ceremonies all over Attica and introduced the adopted one, Astyphilus, to worshipers of Heracles, "so that he might share in their association" (*koinōnias,* Isae. 9.30).[36] As this phrase alerts us, there is more at stake here than piety alone. Such acts, solemn and significant as they must have seemed, would naturally bind together children with those who shared in them. Worshiping in concert as a manifestation of common purpose, fathers strengthen bonds with their sons, families gain the gods as witnesses (and with luck guarantors) of their unity. Astyphilus's career illuminates one explicit way

Fig. 4. A family sacrifices a sheep to Asclepius

in which families fostered a sense of identity in children. Right from childhood (*eutheōs ek paidiou*), his uncle and other relatives told him how his natural father had met his death, and he never spoke to the son of the man responsible once he reached the age of reason (Isae. 9.20). The cult activities mentioned here are clearly another means to this end.

Secular activities, too, afforded children a chance to contribute. Arethusius and his brothers sent a boy from the city, likely a family member, to Apollodorus's farm to pick some roses; they hoped that Apollodorus, taking him for a slave, would handle him roughly, and so leave himself open to a charge of *hybris* ([Dem.] 53.16). Work inside and outside the family home was a more straightforward way to lend a hand. Children make economic contributions to their families in many cultures, in ways which differ so greatly in respect to age, social status, gender roles, and organization of labor that any except the most careful use of comparative material is hazardous in the extreme.[37] One thrust of recent research does seem to be of wide relevance, however: to stress children's indirect contributions, undemanding but time-consuming work that frees adults for more highly skilled tasks. Included here are such activities as running errands, housecleaning, collecting firewood, caring for animals, and (especially) minding younger children. Nor should we slight the value of children's share in the primary production of food and other necessities; their productivity in some areas of agriculture (cutting fodder, for one) may be nearly as great as adults'.[38] There can be no doubt that Athenian children took a hand in many of the tasks children do in peasant societies today, though our scattered and largely anecdotal evidence permits few generalizations. Childcare, a major responsibility of girls (though not theirs alone) in many cultures, was probably a common enough chore for Athenian girls, such as those we see minding a smaller girl and boy in a swinging-scene on an archaic amphora.[39] Because of its relevance to male-female relations at Athens, I will defer discussion of childcare until my treatment of siblings in Chapter 5. What is worth mentioning here is that in this regard, as in others, girls help out in their family of birth while they prepare for their future role in their husband's household. Similarly, Ischomachus's wife learned little except to make a cloak from wool and to give spinning out to maids before her marriage, presumably as a result of pitching in on domestic duties when she was younger (Xen. *Oec.* 7.6); a sixth-century votive offering to Athena Ergane, the goddess associated with handicraft, displays a woman working wool while a girl sits on the ground nearby.[40] So, too, girls must have learned another aspect of women's work, food preparation, hands on—one derivation suggested for *thygatēr,* "daughter," is "preparer of the meal."[41] Boys also might learn adult roles in the course of contributing to the work of the household. A potter's sons help out in their father's workshop, observing all the while; then they begin to pot themselves.[42] The tradition that Solon released sons who had not been taught a trade from the obligation to support their fathers must be based on the prevalence of this pattern (Plut. *Sol.* 22.1).

We cannot say how early children began to participate in this

Fig. 5. Older girls mind small children while they swing

way. It was perhaps true of Athens, as of some modern small-scale societies, that children in larger families tended to work more and earlier than those who had fewer siblings, partly because of the model older brothers and sisters provide.[43] Plato furnishes our only evidence on the ages thought appropriate to certain tasks, recommending that all Magnesia's residents over ten be sent into the fields (*Resp.* 7.540E–541A). The contributions of poorer children were probably of special importance to their families. Phrynichus had to tend sheep in the fields while a wealthier boy was at school in the city.[44] According to his rival Demosthenes, Aeschines helped his impoverished father run a grammar school by

Fig. 6. A woman works wool while a girl sits nearby

grinding ink, sponging benches, and sweeping the schoolroom, "the function of a servant, not a free boy"; Demosthenes himself was spared these indignities.[45] In comedy, Cnemon's daughter accompanies him to the fields (Men. *Dysc.* 333–334). If she is to be thought of as sharing his labor (which the text does not exclude), this is perhaps a symptom of the old man's niggardly ways; he requires her to work even though he has the resources to hire or buy other help.[46] Greeks in the classical period generally regarded sons and daughters in menial occupations as substitutes for slave labor.[47] It is possible that the children of some slave-owning families did chores too, to release slaves for other tasks or as a form of discipline and training. To quote Aristotle: "Some menial duties are honorable for free men if performed when they are still young" (*tōn neōn, Pol.* 7.1333a8). But his own criticisms of the license allowed to the children of the very rich tell against such practices at the top of the social scale (*Pol.* 4.1295b15, 5.1310a24).[48]

The ancient economy was primarily based on land. The agricultural labor of children—clearing stones from fields, breaking

Fig. 7. Boys feed chickens

up clods of earth, tending animals—therefore carries an extra weight in any evaluation of their contributions to the family as an economic unit.[49] The consumption of food and drink, like their production, is also an important arena for social interaction and may provide a means to measure social status. The symposium, "the group of men which expresses its identity through the ritual drinking session," has been called the organizing principle of Greek life, responsible (among much else) for the form and content of lyric poetry and for the ascendancy of painted pottery as a form of art.[50] The right to dine in the *prytaneion* was the greatest honor the *polis* could bestow; the *prytaneis,* the representatives of the democracy, ate together in the *tholos* in their month of office.[51] An army messmate might be preferred to kin as an heir (Isae. 4.18). At Rome, patron and *clientes* ate together to manifest their solidarity; but they might eat different food, and status distinctions could be reinforced through seating arrangements.[52] Family eating patterns at Athens also are both complex and instructive. Children might be included in invitations to parties, such as the neighborhood celebration with which the audience is teased in *Lysistrata* (Ar. *Lys.* 1065–1071). But they (and their mothers) are generally out of place at evening symposia. (One of the distinctive features of Socrates' simple *polis* is a focus on family life, including dinners at which citizens will feast in the company of their children [Pl. *Resp.* 2.372B].) When children are (exceptionally) allowed to attend, they are distinguished from adult male symposiasts by sitting. Autolycus, a special guest at a symposium held in his honor after a victory in the boys' *pankration,* sits by his father's side while the others recline "as usual."[53] Reclining and drinking alcohol are regarded by Aristotle as attributes of maturity.[54] After the meal and the libations, however, it was customary for children to make an appearance in order to entertain the guests.[55]

On less elaborate occasions, too, fathers fed their male visitors apart from the rest of the family. When Euphiletus has a friend over to eat with him, they go upstairs, which is temporarily serving as his male quarters, the *andrōn* (Lys. 1.23). In what looks like an unusual case, Theophrastus's Obsequious Man bids his host's children join them at dinner (*Char.* 5.5); they are presumably male, for otherwise the guest's conceit that they are as like as figs to their father would be no compliment. Normally the children would eat with their mother, who would not be expected to attend a meal with strangers.[56] Xenophon's Utopian account of life among the Persians provides a reversal of normal Athenian practice; he relates that Persian boys up to the age of sixteen or seventeen eat not with their mothers but (when their rulers so order) with their teachers (*Cyr.* 1.2.8). Boys of this age might be called *meirakia*, like the sons of Lysimachus and Melesias. These friends of Socrates, resolved to take better care of their boys than most Athenian fathers, pride themselves on sharing their table with them rather than just letting them go their own way (Pl. *Lach.* 179AB, cf. Xen. *Mem.* 3.14.4). Less attentive fathers might find their sons carrying on like Conon and his fellow *meirakia*, who formed a gang, the Triballi, and gathered together to dine on such disgraceful delicacies as the testicles of pigs sacrificed to purify the assembly (Dem. 54.39). Exceptional at opposite extremes, each example confirms that teenage boys did not usually eat with their fathers. The children's main meal seems to have been at midday (Ar. fr. 360K.-A.). When Evergus and his gang burst into an enemy's house, they find his wife, children, and a freed slave nurse at lunch in the courtyard; one of the children is a boy ([Dem.] 47.55, 61). I see no reason why a father might not join them if he happened to be home.[57] In general, however, children ate with their mothers, not their fathers; and boys who were admitted to the men's club of the symposium were clearly set apart from their elders. Eating and drinking, then, far from offering the whole family an opportunity for communal activity, tended to express and reinforce cleavages within it. Boys, social inferiors destined to inherit the father's dominant role, were placed in an ambiguous position. They usually ate with their mothers and sisters, but might also be granted an early taste of privileges to come.

The Child in the Community

Until they reached the age of majority, boys could not vote in the assembly, serve in the armed forces, represent themselves in a court of law, make a will, or enter into contracts (at all or for more than a set amount); girls were lifelong minors.[58] In respect to interactions with adults, children's lives were generally circumscribed within the circle of the family and its connections. "From the beginning" (as Demosthenes puts it in his funeral oration) "the dead were outstanding in every aspect of their upbringing, practicing what was fitting at every age, and they pleased all they should, their parents, friends, relations. . . . But when they arrived at manhood, they made their quality known, not just to their fellow citizens, but to all" (*Epit.* 16–17). Aristotle, struggling to define citizenship, concludes that the sons of citizens aren't citizens in the same sense as adults, but are only incomplete citizens, citizens *eks hypotheseōs,* "by presumption."[59] On a more practical plane, when Hyperides wants to stress how flagrant is the corruption of his enemies, he says that even little children in the schools—who would not be expected to have any interest in politics—know about the speakers who take Macedonian money.[60] Children's lack of competence in the public realm provides the basis for a joke in a comedy by Eupolis (fr. 133K.-A.). *Mē paidi tēn makhairan,* "no knife for the boy," was a popular proverb, found also in a variant form, "No sword for the boy," and related to a number of other sayings that suit contexts in which someone harms or may harm himself.[61] So, when a phrase begins *mē paidi,* Eupolis's audience expects the usual completion, a knife, a sword, or some other dangerous weapon. Then a twist: the concluding words are *ta koina,* "the community." The humor arises not from the change alone, but also from the fact that the spectators must shift their focus in an unexpected way. Eupolis's parody depends for its effect on the fact that the proverb normally implies that the child is at risk. Suddenly, the onlookers, detached up to now, are forced to recognize that the danger this time is to themselves; they sit up and take notice. Of course, the impact of the change is all the greater because children's qualifications for managing *ta koina* were thought to be so slender.

But we should not imagine that the barrier between childhood and the adult world of the *polis* could not be crossed, or that the transformation at majority was complete. Even after they came of age, Athenian men were still too young for certain responsibilities, such as service on juries or on the Council of 500.[62] By the same token, minors were not completely excluded from civic life; though they could not share fully in the community, they were part of it nonetheless. Given the profound interpenetration of family and *polis* in classical Athens, it is only to be expected that their involvement was usually mediated through the family and its members and expressed in its terms.[63] We have already seen that fathers introduced their sons and (less often) their daughters to fellow citizens who belonged to the same phratry or *genos;* such an introduction was important proof of citizen status in contested cases. Less formally, too, fathers might make their sons, in particular, known to a wider circle; Lysimachus may first have met Socrates when he was a boy and accompanied his father to a shrine or some other gathering of their demesmen (Pl. *Lach.* 187E). On the ideological level, the land of Attica is sometimes described as mother, the political community as mother or (more frequently) father of all Athenians.[64] As such, the city is concerned with the birth of children, the support of boys (at least) whose fathers were killed in war (or in restoring the democracy at the end of the fifth century), and the dowering of the daughters of those who had earned its thanks; and it deserves the support, *tropheia,* owed to parents in return.[65] In addition, the Athenians often brought their children into public discourse, adducing them as motives for revolution or counterrevolution, invoking them to persuade jurors to convict in political trials, swearing on their heads to guarantee commitment to a political position, including them in exhortations before battle.[66] A two-way street: jurors are urged to remember that they will have to report what they have decided to their wives and children.[67] In all these ways, both boys and girls are clearly regarded as the children of the *polis,* not the family's alone.

What is more, in some ways children might be very much like adults. Despite their legal limitations, minors were apparently liable for involuntary homicide on the same basis as other Athenians. One of Antiphon's rhetorical exercises deals with the death of a boy, struck and killed when he walked into the path of a javelin tossed by a youth, a *meirakion* or *neaniskos.* The dead boy is certainly underage; the unlucky athlete probably is, as his father not only speaks on his behalf but refers to himself, too, as the accused.[68] Though the father of each boy argues that it is the other who is to blame, neither suggests that age diminishes their responsibility. Likewise, trials for the intentional murder of minors were held at the Areopagus, just like those in which the victims were adult citizens. It is also possible that children (boys anyway) were able to testify in Athenian lawsuits. Certainly they were present in courtrooms; adults could testify to what they saw or knew as children (Isae. 12.10); and the testimony of another group without full legal rights, slaves, was admissible (though only if obtained under torture).[69] As it happens, however, our only instances of boys' giving evidence or of taking an oath to support a prosecution (both hypothetical) concern cases of homicide, and it is best to assume that these, involving as they do questions of pollution, make up a special class of crime.[70]

Indeed, religion provided the main avenue for children into the life of the *polis,* just as cult observance was perhaps the most important family activity. Cult might even take them outside the city, as envoys of a kind; boys joined ephebes in the Pythais, an expedition to Delphi undertaken in response to lightning strikes.[71] Children also regularly took part, sometimes at center stage, in a number of city-wide religious festivals at Athens itself. Children may have been a focus of the Diasia, the most important Attic festival for the serpentine Zeus Meilichius, "the kindly one." It was on this occasion that Strepsiades bought his six-year-old son a toy wagon, and a famous votive relief shows a man and a young boy standing in front of an image of the god in the form of a snake.[72] The Anthesteria, held ten days before the Diasia in the spring month of Anthesterion, is certainly connected with children, especially its second day, Choes. In fact, it seems to have been an occasion for otherwise marginal groups in general to join a city celebration; slaves took part too. But details involving children are less clear than some authorities' confident accounts allow.

According to a standard English-language book on the Athenian festivals, "It was an Athenian custom on this day [Choes] to crown with flowers children who were three years old."[73] But the wreaths for children ("in the third year after birth") are mentioned only in a late work, *Heroicus,* usually ascribed to Philostratus (35.9 De Lannoy), and he does not even identify the festival by name (though it is probably what he has in mind when he refers to the month of Anthesterion). A more critical point: the time Philostratus refers to in this work is not the classical period, but the years

Fig. 8. A father and his son stand before an image of Zeus Meilichius

just after the Trojan War. Now, the Athenians may well have celebrated the Anthesteria at this time, but we cannot expect Philostratus to have been an eyewitness; nor is *Heroicus*—a fantastic
demonstration that the heroes of the Trojan War were still alive—
the most reliable of repositories of antiquarian lore. It is much
more likely that Philostratus's reference is to the Athens of his own
day (which he knew well); it is still more so because he shifts to
the present tense to bring in the wreaths, the only other evidence
for a set age of participation in the festival of Choes is roughly
contemporary with him, and crawlers on *choes,* who should be
under two years old, are occasionally wreathed.[74] The notion that
choes were used as grave gifts only for those who had died before
they reached the age of two (or three) should therefore also be
rejected.[75]

These *choes* are miniature wine jugs of peculiar shape, bearing
in many cases (though far from all) illustrations of children, boys
chiefly, undertaking a wide variety of activities. Most date from the
last half of the fifth century and the early fourth. Since some depict
elements known from literary evidence to be connected with the
Anthesteria, scholars have often concluded that the children's activities also represent events at the festival. A *chous* showing Orestes (connected in legend with the festival's founding) is thought to
illustrate "some parody of the story of Orestes, played by little chil-

dren at the festival of the Choes"; other suggestions have included crawl-offs, dogcart races, ball games, and wrestling.[76] The *choes* themselves, pint-size versions of the vessels used in the drinking contests that characterize the festival, are evidence of such mimicry of adult activities, since they were probably given to children as gifts at this time. But many of the scenes are found on vases of other shapes, and few are connected to the Anthesteria in literary sources.[77] It is therefore best to explain these depictions differently, as products of the whimsy of artists and their customers (e.g., those showing children as Silens or Erotes or racing in carts drawn by deer), as records of informal play at the festival, or as portrayals of everyday life.[78] Children's involvement in one festival activity, however, is beyond doubt. This was the Aiora, a rite in which they sat in swings tied to the branches of trees. It is not quite clear whether this is to be thought of as a fertility rite (and so took place on Choes) or as a rite of purification (on the third day of the Anthesteria, Chytroi).[79] Children's roles may tip the balance toward the first of these views.

Still another festival with special significance for children was the Oschophoria, held in the autumn just after the Apaturia and, like it, much concerned with the coming of age of Athenian boys. Those who took part in the procession and foot races from Athens to Phaleron were ephebes, not boys.[80] But fables and stories were part of the rites as well, and these were apparently directed toward children (Plut. *Thes.* 23.3). All too predictably, we know nothing about them. They were perhaps devoted to the exploits of Theseus, who rescued the Athenian boys and girls destined for the Cretan Minotaur but then inadvertently caused his father's death; a boy among boys on his departure, he replaces his father as king on his return. It is also possible, however, that they (or some of them) bore some relation to a story we do know. The old men in Aristophanes' *Lysistrata* taunt their female contemporaries with the tale of Melanion, which they heard as children (*eti pais ōn*). Melanion was a young man (*neaniskos*) who fled marriage, pursuing a life in the mountains; here he hunted hares with his dog, set snares, and loathed women so much that he never came home (Ar. *Lys.* 781–796). Pierre Vidal-Naquet has drawn attention to the cross-dressing that is a feature of the Oschophoria—the two youths leading the procession appeared as girls—as it is of other passage rites. Melanion's flight from women may seem to mark the opposite pole; but in fact it is analogous, a move beyond the norms of male culture in the *polis*. And Theseus, too, fought against women, the Amazons. Melanion's story would suit this festival.[81] Children themselves provided the text at another festival held at the same time, the Pyanopsia. Carrying the *eiresiōnē,* an olive branch wreathed with wool and decorated with model lyres and vases and with fruits of the earth, they went from house to house begging for treats and singing a song of plenty. A late Hellenistic calendar frieze shows one boy, a *pais amphithalēs,* bringing the *eiresiōnē* to the Temple of Apollo.[82]

All adult Athenians—like all other Greeks and even slaves— were eligible for the Eleusinian mysteries. A vase showing children among those walking in the procession to Eleusis confirms what the admission of slaves suggests, that they, too, could become initiates.[83] Some children played a prominent role. Each year, a boy or girl was elected by lot and initiated at public expense to serve as the *pais aph' hestias.*[84] According to the late author Porphyry, the *pais* was an intermediary between the other initiates and "the divine," placating the gods like priests who perform sacrifices for their cities (*Abst.* 4.5). Similarly, it is a child (whether a boy or a girl is uncertain) who presents (or accepts) Athena's robe, the *peplos,* on the east frieze of the Parthenon.[85] In each instance, it is presumably children's very marginality which makes their role appropriate. Not yet fully integrated into the social world of the *polis,* they are interested outsiders, a status they share with the gods with whom they intercede.

Children enjoyed theatrical presentations, puppet shows, musical contests, the spectacles Plato says delighted the young at sacrifices, going so far as to spur on those competing on stage (perhaps in recitations).[86] Casual references in Plato and comic appeals to the audience guarantee the presence of boys at the great dramatic festivals in honor of Dionysus, and (though they go unnoticed, as often, in our sources) the connection of women with the god in other contexts provides a plausible justification for the attendance of girls as well.[87] It has even been proposed (rather implausibly) that satyr plays, said to be simpler in style and moral framework than other genres, were used to teach children dramatic conventions and to reward them for sitting through the three tragedies that preceded them.[88] But did boys actually appear on stage? Boy actors won prizes even against adult competitors during the Roman period (though they may simply have recited passages from plays rather than performed them), and mosaics indicate that boys took supernumerary roles in Hellenistic productions of New Comedy.[89] The ability of boys to fill the numerous but relatively minor speaking and nonspeaking roles for infants and older children in both tragedy and comedy is therefore not in question. Nor would their appearance in choruses in such plays as Euripides' *Suppliants* and Aristophanes' *Wasps* (and perhaps, too, his *Peace* and *Frogs*) be out of place, similar as it would be to their role as choral singers in any festival.[90] It is therefore tempting to follow Sifakis (1979b) in his contention that children both appeared on stage and sang their own parts. Children in tragedy, he says, are depicted in a conventional role—helpless, in danger, seeking protection. This stereotype demands an equally conventional portrayal of children on stage. Yet the children of tragedy say much the same things, in much the same language, as adults. What, then, does their conventional portrayal involve? Sifakis asserts that children are regularly depicted as small adults in Greek art until the Hellenistic period, and that tragedy must have used a similar convention. "Children . . . must absolutely *look* their very young age. The cardinal point here is size" (73). Therefore, child actors must have represented children.

Unfortunately, however, the parallel from art is misleading (quite apart from the fact, which Sifakis admits but evades, that children are sometimes shown realistically).[91] A vase painter can distinguish children and adults only through external characteristics, unless he adds identifying inscriptions. On stage, however, the means of identification are many; direct address is only the most obvious. There is no *need* for children to be distinguished from adults by size. And Sifakis's remarks about convention, though sound enough in general, are applied rather arbitrarily. It is one thing for children to appear in a conventional role, another for that role to be further emphasized by a distinctive physical representation. We might even argue that the children's conventional role rendered any further differentiation unnecessary—it is, after all, precisely the nature of the convention that is at issue. This might indeed have been to show children as small, or (just as easily) for men to play all roles, those of children and women. Other alternatives, such as children's lines being delivered by adults offstage or even on, also could be passed off as conventions.[92]

The appeal to convention is thus less convincing than Sifakis thinks. Nevertheless, the balance of probabilities does favor his case, in comedy as much as in tragedy. Appealing, too, is the notion that child actors were members of theatrical families learning their trade.[93] If this is so, one of Athenian drama's most important themes, the conflict of *polis* and *oikos,* would be undercut in the very way some plays were produced, much as the presentation of war orphans in armor at the City Dionysia expresses an ideology made problematic in Sophocles' *Philoctetes,* featuring as it does a young man (Neoptolemus), orphaned by the Trojan War, who balks at his military role.[94]

In all these festivals, one or more children join in the city's rites as adults' equals or as their representatives. Less directly, too, cult activity brought children into community life, by preparing them for their future. This can be seen most clearly through a brief examination of some cult functions of girls, whose ritual life was on the whole richer than that of boys.[95] Four of these are listed in an often-cited speech by the women's chorus in *Lysistrata* (Ar. *Lys.* 641–647).

> As soon as I was seven I was an *arrhēphoros*. Then at ten I was an *aletris* for the foundress, and shedding my saffron robe I was an *arktos* (bear) at the Brauronia. And once I carried a sacred basket, a fine girl wearing a chain of figs.[96]

Brelich has argued that these verses outline four grades (*arrhēphoros, aletris, arktos, kanēphoros*) of what was once a system of initiation tied to the four-year cycle of the Greater Panathenaea, and which still retained some of their initiatory character in the classical period.[97] According to Brelich, the passage from *Lysistrata* shows that every Athenian girl in Aristophanes' time passed through the grades the chorus mentions. Since later evidence indicates that there were just two (or four) *arrhēphoroi,* that only girls of noble birth could be *aletrides* or even perhaps *arktoi,* and that not every girl could be a *kanēphoros,* Brelich must imagine that the rite became exclusive only after Aristophanes' time (237).[98] Now, already in archaic Athens Harmodius's sister was declared unfit to carry a basket. As the slur is more likely to have been against her chastity than against her family's status, however, a more fundamental objection is in order.[99] *Lysistrata* is, after all, a comedy. Aristophanes' women are portrayed as putting a case, arguing that their training gives them the motive and experience to manage the city. There is surely a touch of irony here: how better to undercut what must have seemed an uproarious claim, at least to the men in the audience, than have the women obtain the benefits of many more rituals than any one girl would share in, and so show just how ill-prepared they really were?[100] Understanding its tone in this way clears up one of the passage's puzzling features, the implication that service as an *aletris* was simultaneous (or nearly so) with being a bear at Brauron. One solution, to read *kaita* as "and then shedding," puts the two activities into a sequence, but still allows for little time between them; *arktoi,* too, were ten years old.[101] And *arrhēphoroi* may have served for more than one year, perhaps from one Greater Panathenaea to another, so that they might also be ten—another overlap.[102] I suspect that the impression of a jumble of activities is intentional, and is accentuated by the use of *pote,* "once," as if carrying a basket had to be fit into the chorus's hectic schedule. This could only make the women's pretensions seem still more ridiculous, sound and fury signifying nothing of practical value to the *polis.*

These four offices might still make up a series of initiation rites, but one that only a few girls of elite families went through completely or in part. Such a program would also be of great interest to other Athenian girls. (Mother Theresa and Imelda Marcos are influential examples of rather different definitions of female excellence, even though—perhaps because—so few can ever fill their shoes.) Identification would be easier if each *arrhēphoros* represented all the girls born in the same year.[103] But we know very little about the *aletrides*, nothing that shows that they were involved in any initiation rite. And there were *kanēphoroi* for so many divinities, Dionysus and Apollo among them, that the nature of the rite referred to here is impossible to specify.[104] We should regretfully reject the proposed initiation system, even as a vestige.[105] But this is not to deny the role of public rites in preparing girls for later life. On the contrary, they served two important purposes.

First, these ceremonies often set girls in duties or apparel that reflected their training in women's work.[106] Two *arrhēphoroi* went on a mysterious nighttime journey to the underground precinct of Aphrodite on the Acropolis (carrying, it may be, images of children or even live infants, and returning with a stone swaddled like a child).[107] But they (or two others) also had a more mundane task, helping to set up the weaving of Athena's *peplos*.[108] *Arktoi* worked at weaving as well.[109] The *aletrides* ground meal for a special kind of cake, the *popana*, offered to Athena.[110] *Kanēphoroi* at the Panathenaea were powdered with barley flour—baking again (Hermippus fr. 26E.). In other rites, too, girls had the trappings suited to their sex. Other girls actually wove the *peplos*, the *ergastinai*.[111] On the sixth day of the spring month of Munychion, girls walked to the Delphinion carrying boughs of olive wrapped with wool (Plut. *Thes.* 18.1). Two girls, called *loutrides* or *plyntrides*, washed the statue of Athena on the Acropolis (Ar. fr. 849K.-A.). *Deipnophoroi*, "food carriers," more likely girls than married women, took part in the Oschophoria, representing the mothers of the Athenian children sent to Crete.[112] In every instance, these girls served the gods in ways women were to serve their households; that they gained honor in doing so must have made the activities themselves more desirable.

The second contribution public cults made to the socialization of women is still more important. Marriage marked the biggest break in a girl's life; it made up, in fact, the transition from girl to woman, a transformation dramatically highlighted by the marriage rituals themselves, which bore many similarities to those of funerals.[113] But marriage did not involve a change in legal or political status, for wives were as subordinate as daughters. It signaled a change in control: the husband replaced the father (or, in his absence, the brother or another male family member) as a woman's *kyrios*.

At marriage, a young girl had to leave the family with whom she had spent almost all of her life and join another, quite separate, *oikos*. It is true that her dowry provided, in law, an important ongoing connection with her original household. But this can have had little immediate impact on the trauma of separation. "We women are the most wretched of creatures," says Medea. "A wife comes to new customs and habits, and she has to be a prophet to tell how to treat her husband. She doesn't learn at home."[114] Marriage was a responsibility that a girl raised entirely within her own household might have been unwilling, or psychologically unable, to take on. It was the public festivals, which joined girls from many *oikoi*, which did the most to allow the Athenian girl to see herself in a social context outside the women's quarters, the *gynai-kōnitis*, as a member of a larger group than her own household. They were a necessary link between a girlhood spent in a father's house and a woman's life in a husband's.

It is fitting to close this chapter with religion, for cult observance is a thread running through the child's life in both the family and the community. Or rather a coat of many colors to cover each area. For while children's innocence, especially sexual purity, is usually invoked to explain their service in cult, it is worth noting that their functions are not always the same; nor do their roles always stem from the same view of their relation to *oikos* and *polis*.[115] In some cults, children retain what may be called their secular guise, as when listening to stories at the Oschophoria. But there is nothing childlike about the dark descent of the *arrhēpho-roi*. Furthermore, some children seem to owe their role to their membership in a successful and surviving family—for instance, the *paides amphithaleis*. Others, however, such as the *paides aph' hestias* (who did not have to be *amphithaleis*), were recommended precisely by their social separation from other, adult initiates. Girls may be considered a special case. Forever marginal and yet essential for both the family and the community, their roles in public cults paradoxically stress their domestic duties. I prefer to end by stressing diversity in this way because this very complexity affords the clearest indication that children were more developed as social creatures than their legal and political liabilities might suggest. Restricted though they largely were to the sphere of religion, they displayed therein a range of roles almost as rich, an identity nearly as many-faceted, as the roles and identity of adult Athenians. Like them, too, they enjoyed a variety of social contacts with their age mates of the same sex, the subject of my next chapter.

Three

The Child and His or Her Peers

The Social Life of Boys

I turn now to boys' interactions with their contemporaries outside the household. I begin with children's play, the sphere least under adult control, move on to sex and schooling (where the *kyrios* and his agents much influenced what went on), and conclude with a discussion of boys' cultural and athletic competitions at religious festivals within the city and outside it, contexts created and controlled by representatives of the entire citizen community. As this plan signals, the link between the child's peer groupings and his life in the adult community—contrast and continuity—will be an important theme.

Very young children knew little of what went on outside the household, few people except those who shared or entered it. But as boys aged they began to move out into the community and to make friends. No doubt many friendships failed to last; Aristotle comments on the ease with which the young make and drop friends, in part because they change so quickly and develop in such different directions.[1] But some ties continued. One of the inducements Astyages offers his grandson Cyrus in persuading him to visit is to provide *sympaistores,* "playmates"; years later, some

Medes volunteer to follow Cyrus because they had known him as a child and were his friends.[2] This is fiction, but not far-fetched. Demosthenes' father chose as guardians for his wife and children two nephews and a man who was not a relative at all. This was an unusual choice, and might be thought imprudent—after all, the guardians allegedly cheated Demosthenes and his sister on a grand scale. Demosthenes, anxious to absolve his father of negligence, explains it by saying the man was a friend from boyhood (Dem. 27.4, *ek paidos*). Perhaps there were some among the jurors who felt that the elder Demosthenes had got just what he deserved, agreeing with an unnamed associate of Socrates that the friendships of children and wild beasts are usually harmful (Pl. *Clit.* 409DE).

But the belief that boyhood friends were loyal in their affections was widespread enough for Isocrates to bring as character witnesses those who knew him in youth, and for Demosthenes to deny that those who testify on his behalf do so from friendship arising between contemporaries.[3] So strong were such links that Cleocritus can appeal to opponents on the field of battle, supporters of the tyranny of the Thirty, to stop the civil war on the grounds that he and the others on his side have shared with them in the city's rites and festivals, served in choruses together—and been at the same schools.[4] More than this, there was a suspicion in some circles that children might exert a formative influence on one another. Encouraging the Athenian stranger to expound his views in the opening book of Plato's *Laws,* Megillus tells him that his family once represented Athenian interests in his native Sparta. "Your Athenians hurt us," Spartan boys would say to him from his youth, or "Your Athenians helped us." As a consequence, Megillus delights in the Athenian manner of speech (though he finds it perhaps less pleasing at the end of the stranger's interminable discourse) and regards Athens as a city of special virtue (Pl. *Leg.* 1.642BD).

Astyages' offer, the cynicism of Socrates' friend, Megillus's memoir—all testify to adult interest in children's interactions with their peers. In fact, the most important forums for such interactions were organized and controlled by the adult community, the religious festivals in which boys competed as performers and athletes. Less formally, too, community standards influenced the choice of friends and the forms of friendship, most notably in the conventions that shaped homosexual relations among boys and young men. Even playmates could be selected only from those available, and relatives and family connections must have been numerous among them. In one sphere, however, children seem to have been free to do as they liked, following recognized patterns, to be sure, and under adult eyes, but on the whole able to interact in ways that (whatever their origins) must have been experienced as very much their own. This sphere was children's play.[5]

On a linguistic level, the Greek conception of childhood is inextricably intertwined with play. *Pais,* "child," shares the root of a family of words including *paizō,* "I play," *to paigma,* "play, sport," *hē paignia,* "sport, game," *to paignion,* "plaything," *hē paidia,* "child's play, pastime." Play characterizes children in contrast to adults, who are involved in more serious and more consequential activity,[6] and it may therefore be used by comic poets and philosophers to ridicule humans and their pretensions to importance, to suggest that they are mere children *sub specie aeternitatis.* In *Birds,* Aristophanes presents two older Athenians, Pisthetaerus and Euelpides. Anxious about an avian attack, they formulate a plan of action in terms taken from *khytrinda,* a child's game combining elements of monkey-in-the-middle and tag.[7] In this moment of tension, when they are trying to pass themselves off as brave soldiers, they risibly take on the tactics of children.[8] Institutions, too, might be mocked in this way, as Plato the comic poet mocks ostracism by associating with it *ostrakinda,* a chase game involving two teams.[9] Plato the philosopher describes the earth as a child's ball and humans themselves as playthings of the divine.[10] Though children's play may be pleasurable to observe, grown men who join in invite contempt; it is the obsequious man who plays with his host's children.[11] Later in antiquity, stories played on the paradox of famous figures of the period of Greece's greatness—Agesilaus, Archytas, Socrates—wasting time in childish pursuits; in one tale,

Heraclitus prefers playing knucklebones with children to taking part in the political life of Ephesus, thus neatly turning his fellow citizens' contempt for such pastimes against them.[12]

Despite its denigration, however, children's play was of surprising interest to the Athenians, an interest reflected in the popular art of Old Comedy and in the more esoteric dialogues of Plato.[13] Plato's concern is not just casual or illustrative. Sounding rather like a modern functionalist—an anthropologist king—he identifies certain qualities and consequences of children's play and then prescribes accordingly. Children love to play and will invent games whenever they come together (*Leg.* 7.793E–794A). But it is irresponsible simply to allow them to play as they like; "lawless" games make children unruly, unlikely to mature into serious, law-abiding men, and constant chopping and changing and the love of novelty may threaten the established order.[14] The enthusiasm for play is to be diverted into productive channels: play should help identify aptitudes, toys should prepare the child for his or her role in life—future builders should construct toy houses— and skills should be taught with the aid of games, as among the Egyptians.[15] Aristotle is in agreement with the thrust of this program (*Pol.* 7.1336a29–34).

But the interpenetration of child's play and adult life is less tidy than these theorists would prefer. That some pastimes were thought appropriate to one age alone is suggested by the term *ephēbikē,* "the ephebe game," applied to a team ball game otherwise called *episkyros* or *epikoinos* (Poll. 9.104), and symbolized by the dedication of toys by girls before marriage and by boys at puberty, especially to Artemis and Hermes, all over the Greek world; these include clay animals, dolls, rattles, small cymbals and other noisemakers, tops, knucklebones, and balls.[16] It is knucklebones, *astragaloi,* which seems most strongly to characterize children in contrast to adult males. As a cynical saw attributed to a number of political leaders puts it, "You fool children with knucklebones, but men with oaths."[17] Polyclitus's statue of two boys, "considered by many the most faultless work of sculpture," showed them playing *astragalismos,* and *astragaloi* are commonly included in school scenes.[18] And it is these which Aristophanes' jurors (wrongly) assume their boys will want as a gift from the wages for their own weighty duties (Ar. *Vesp.* 295). Other pursuits, however, were carried over into manhood; Socrates says that no one can be an expert at *petteia* and *kybeia,* games making use of counters and dice, except someone who has concentrated on them from childhood.[19]

In still others, there is an oblique connection to later life. Tests of strength (like *helkystinda* and *ephelkystinda,* varieties of tug of war) or games of flight and pursuit (like *ostrakinda*) had an obvious utility in a community that went to war on foot and fought it hand to hand; blood sports, too, like cock-fighting, might prepare a boy for battle.[20] Less predictably, Xenophon finds cheating at *posinda,* a children's guessing game, to be good preparation for the deception he regards as so important in warfare.[21] Other forms of play combine mimesis of adult life with commentary on it in a tone Plato might not approve of. A cup shows three boys playing school; one, who sits and holds a rod, is the teacher.[22] They (and other boys shown on a similar *chous*) may well be playing their roles straight, but it is hard to believe that this was always so.[23] Rather, elements of satire and caricature were probably involved at times, as in another *chous,* which shows a boy with an oversize comic mask apparently aping older actors.[24] According to Otto Raum, such ironic reflections of adult values and behavior may be as significant in children's mimicry as more respectful imitation; he describes Chaga children playing "school and teacher," parodying their (white) teacher's obsession with time by placing a large sand clock in front of their make-believe school.[25]

Another complex reflection of social reality is provided by one of the names of the game usually called "bronze fly" or *myinda.* This is *drapetinda,* "runaway slave," a designation perhaps invented by the players themselves.[26] In *drapetinda,* the boy who is "it" covers his eyes and tries to catch the runaways, who must replace him if they cannot escape. Such games of alternation help instill the perception that social relationships depend on the serial adoption of roles of one kind and another. In this instance, however, the reversal of roles implicitly challenges the master-slave hierarchy fundamental to classical Greek society. Among similarly subversive games we may adduce ring-around-the-rosy, in which (ac-

Fig. 9. Boys play school

cording to one view) children model the social system by acting in concert only to destroy it by collapsing.[27] I don't think we should underrate the element of hostility expressed here; children are, after all, very much social subordinates, subject to adult authority and control in many ways, and so not necessarily enamored of the system in which they seemingly play so minor a part. But there is more to such games than that; they are positive as well as negative. Games like *drapetinda* give children a chance to manipulate and even deny social categories that structure their world and the world of adults too, an opportunity to display even when young the power they may expect (or at least wish) will come to them as they mature. It is, I suspect, very rare for play of this sort to lead to a revolution, such as the abolition of slavery; to that extent we may regard it as analogous to the reversals and transgressions of normal rules marking many festivals that end with the reestablishment of order. But we should admit the possibility that the feelings of competence and creativity aroused in such games may not be aroused merely to be appeased; instead, they may be fostered, at least for individual children, and contribute to an abiding interest in change.[28]

Men took a more active interest in boys' sex lives. At least in comedies and satyr plays, admittedly a raunchier environment than everyday Athens, boys were identified as sexual beings from an early age, addressed as *posthōn,* "penis," and referred to as *posthaliskos,* "little pecker."[29] The satyr Silenus even propositions the baby Perseus, promising a space in his bed with Danae and a share of the fun (Aesch. fr. 47a.805–814R.). Aristotle, straighter-faced, observes that boys enjoy rubbing their penises before (though only shortly before) they are able to ejaculate, just like men who are unable to reproduce.[30] Awareness of boys' interest in the subject leads Xenophon to approve of the Persian reluctance to discuss sex in front of the very young lest their lack of discipline lead to excess (Xen. *Cyr.* 1.6.34).[31] For most boys, puberty would of course precede legal majority and passage from the group of *paides* by several years. But their outlets for heterosexual activity were limited. Though Mnesilochus, pretending to be a citizen wife, claims to have had a young lover from the age of seven, Mediterranean machismo and its legal incarnation, Solon's law condoning the murder of men caught in the act of adultery, made such escapades risky in real life (though this is not to say that some did not take the risks).[32] Slave girls and prostitutes were safer as well as more available. I expect that sex with the household's female slaves was the prerogative of its master and other citizen males, including adolescents; it seems to have been something of a family joke for Euphiletus and his newlywed wife.[33] As for prostitutes, we have already seen that a boy's whoring could provide ammunition to political enemies, especially if such precocious predilections could be presented as precursors of adult license. Extravagance, squandering one's patrimony, was usually a major count in such an indictment of an *apolesioikon meirakion,* "a house-destroying youth."[34] But some fathers, in life as in New Comedy, were probably amused and even pleased by adolescent randiness. It would be interesting to know whether an introduction to female sexuality was sometimes thought to be one of a father's legacies to his sons. There is no evidence for this that I am aware of; but a curious hydria by the Harrow Painter may just possibly show a father accompanying his son (or sons) to a brothel.[35]

It was only in homosexual relations that Athenian boys could achieve sexual intimacy with other Athenians and (perhaps as important) demonstrate their success in attracting their peers.[36] At what age were such relationships acceptable? Among later writers, Strato praises the charms of a boy of twelve (*Anth. Pal.* 12.4). Xenophon, writing in our period, says that Episthenes of Amphipolis was moved by the beauty of a boy just reaching puberty, say fourteen or so (Xen. *An.* 7.4.7). There is no clear-cut evidence from Athens itself. It was certainly illegal to sell a boy's favors or force them (as prostitution and sexual assault incurred penalties when adult Athenians were involved as well).[37] But David Cohen has suggested that homosexual relations with an underage boy might be regarded as *hybris,* "outrage, abuse," even if they were entered into freely, without payment or violence, because Athenian law had "some notion equivalent to statutory rape in modern legal systems."[38]

This seems unlikely. In his speech on love in Plato's *Symposium,* Pausanias praises those who love boys only when they begin to acquire understanding, which he associates with the growth of the beard. Before that, boys are young and thoughtless, easy to take advantage of, and there ought to be a law against sex with them (Pl. *Symp.* 181DE). Pausanias's perspective is perhaps unusual— it is changing partners, promiscuity for lack of a more neutral word, which he most disapproves of. But his statement must mean that no such law existed at this time, whether we take that to be the dramatic date of the dialogue (416) or its period of composition (the early fourth century). I do not deny that others might feel unease about homoerotic relationships involving boys; I merely suggest that Cohen's grounds are misstated. Cohen's case rests heavily on a few passages in which *hybris* and its derivatives clearly refer to instances of sexual relations between consenting adults. But there is no need to conclude that these texts employ *hybris* in a technical legal sense, even the one in which words of this family occur in a forensic context. Euphiletus says Eratosthenes, his wife's seducer, committed *hybris,* but as much against him and his household as against her (Lys. 1.4, 16, 25). It is Euphiletus's status as *kyrios* which has been flouted; the sexual nature of the insult is essentially irrelevant. This distinction is directly relevant to the case of boys.

In its public manifestations, at least, Athenian male homosexuality was shaped by a number of conventions. It did not involve equals. As Dover puts it, "Homosexual relationships . . . are regarded as the product not of the reciprocated sentiment of equals but of the pursuit of those of lower status by those of higher status."[39] Both parties might be young men, but one, the *pais, erō-menos,* or *paidika,* is normally younger than the other, the *erastēs.* Common Greek views on the appropriate relations of men of different ages require that the younger partner be regarded as subordinate to the other, and he plays the passive role in sexual activity. Yet certain conventions de-emphasize or deny his subordinate status. Thus, the older partner has to court the younger man or boy, to approach a social inferior as a suppliant. In addition, on vases depicting homosexual activity, it is the older partner who bends his knees and not infrequently his head before the younger one; the latter, for his part, stands upright and shows no sign of either constraint or pleasure, neither under the authority of his partner nor in the grip of pleasure or any other emotion.

Many students of this institution have regarded these conventions as a way to distinguish the younger partners from women; I prefer to stress the importance of drawing lines between citizen *paides* and those other *paides,* the slaves they associate with and are thought to resemble in so many ways. There is little disagreement, however, on the benefits that were said to accrue to the boys themselves or on the role of male homosexuality as an institution of transition between boyhood and maturity. Broadly speaking, regular intimacy with an older member of the citizen elite provides a boy with a model of appropriate attitudes and behaviors, a source of wisdom. And the good conduct of the older partner is fostered by this role.[40] In individual instances, involvement with a particularly well-connected or gifted partner may prove socially and politically valuable, not just for the boy but for his whole family.[41] Since this was a kind of passage rite, a boy was supposed to outgrow his role as a junior partner, first by taking on the active role and acting as an adviser and model for a younger protégé, and then by assuming a new (though by no means exclusive) sexual identity as the husband of an Athenian citizen woman, *kyrios* of a household, father and master of *paides.*[42]

This is obviously a drastically schematized representation of the emotional and social complexities involved in such relationships. Its very crudity, however, serves to reveal the points of tension within these homosexual liaisons involving boys. If a boy had the wrong partner or partners, his social standing might be threatened or at least not advanced; if he continued to play the passive role as he grew older, he called into question both the Athenian conception of conduct appropriate to an adult male citizen (remaining too "womanish" or too "slavish") and his own capacity to live up to it. It is with such matters that our sources concern themselves. Boys are said to give themselves to lampsellers and the like in preference to the traditional elite (Ar. *Eq.* 736–740). Dover rightly emphasizes that the comic poets reserve their ridicule for adult males who play the passive part; they do not express contempt for active homosexuals.[43] A passage from Aristotle is instructive (*NE* 7.1148b15). Here we do find a condemnation of boys' passive homosexuality, the position espoused by Pausanias in *The Symposium*. It is not the liaisons themselves that are problematic, however, but rather their consequences for the future, since Aristotle believes that enjoyment of so unnatural a pleasure in adult males must be based on habits inculcated in boyhood.[44] In other words, passive homosexuality may potentially cause problems, but it is not necessarily wrong in itself.

Most Athenians were probably less worried about the effects of homosexuality on boys in general than about the particular partners boys chose. Laws, *paidagōgoi,* peer pressure—all operated to prevent undesirable matches. Much of a boy's time, especially among the elite, was spent in a gymnasium or a palaestra, taking formal instruction or just working out and conversing with friends.[45] The Greeks exercised in the nude, or very nearly so. These athletic facilities were therefore prime pick-up points, and the law consequently forbade slaves to exercise or anoint themselves with oil in palaestrae.[46] How about other locales where boys might gather in groups? The law restricted the hours of operation of schools and regulated visits to them (Aeschin. 1.9–12). Boys on their way to school or elsewhere outside the home were the focus of admiring eyes; *paidagōgoi* went along.[47] Of course, such measures alone could not prevent boys from taking up with their schoolfellows. But when Critobulus fell for Clinias, his father put him into Socrates' hands (Xen. *Symp.* 4.24). Sometimes, however, friends might be on the other side. In Plato, we are told that initially, at least, a boy may be turned against a suitor by schoolmates or others who say it is disgraceful to have sex with him; and that a boy's friends will call him names to dissuade involvement with someone a father disapproves of.[48] The impression this evidence gives is that a boy's sexual friendships were taken seriously, and that a father's opposition was no mean obstacle; no wonder Pisthetaerus's ideal city is one in which a father would reproach him for *not* fondling his son (Ar. *Av.* 137–142).

Yet it is important to recognize that some relationships did meet with approval. Xenophon's *Symposium* is a fictional account of a dinner party held by Callias in honor of his lover Autolycus, who has just won the boys' *pankration* at the Greater Panathenaea, and of Autolycus's father, Lycon; father, son, and lover all go to the party together (Xen. *Symp.* 1.2–3). Later in the evening, Socrates takes Lycon's presence as a sign that the friendship of Callias and Autolycus is spiritual, not carnal; the noble *erastēs* keeps nothing secret from the father of the one he loves (8.11, cf. 19). Socrates' distinction, one often made in Plato's dialogues, is even less convincing here. Like Plato, Xenophon is interested in exalting spiritual relations among men above physical sexuality, though unlike him he offers heterosexuality as an alternative. (His *Symposium* ends with boy and girl slaves, representing Dionysus and Ariadne, tenderly kissing, a scene that so inflames the guests that the unmarried resolve to end their bachelor days and those with wives ride off to enjoy them: 9.2–7.) But Lycon's role rings true. It is echoed in the episode in which Critobulus, judged by the two young slaves to be more attractive than Socrates, is urged to claim his reward, a kiss from each—but not before obtaining the consent of their *kyrios,* their Syracusan owner (5.4–6.1). Though the boy in this instance is a slave, the suggestion a joke, some such approach to a boy's father might well have preceded conventional and approved relations between citizen young men and boys. I do not think a breach of etiquette was a crime in itself. But failure to conform to this convention might certainly cause an outraged father to feel his authority had been mocked, and he could conceivably try to convince a jury made up of other household heads that this amounted to *hybris,* just as Euphiletus did.

I have already mentioned schoolfellows among a boy's friends, including those who remained friendly in later life; schoolboys made enemies as well.[49] Schools were important areas of peer interaction.[50] But this activity took place under strict supervision, not only by the teacher himself but by the slave *paidagōgos* who accompanied at least the better-off boys to school and into the schoolroom. Schooling was not compulsory, nor were schools organized or staffed by the community (though education was encouraged and schools were regulated by law);[51] attendance was essentially a private matter between a boy's father or guardian and the teacher, an independent entrepreneur.[52] The *paidagōgos,* a familiar member of the household, afforded the boy some continuity between home and the school environment. More important, however, he was the *kyrios*'s agent, an instantiation of his interest and an extension of his authority into the teacher's classroom. Certainly both fathers and mothers took an interest in their children's education. Niceratus's father had him learn Homer by heart, and fathers arranged contests in recitation during the Apaturia.[53] Some fathers could even make a nuisance of themselves, going to the schools and palaestrae and taking up teachers' time with idle chatter (Theophr. *Char.* 7.5). A mid fifth-century cup by the Sabouroff Painter depicts a boy reciting to a group of women, and, some two generations later, Xenocrateia dedicated a shrine to Cephisus and other deities at Phaleron in recognition of her son Xeniades' education (*didaskalias*).[54]

The later literary tradition and the evidence of school scenes on Attic vases combine to assure the existence of education outside the home as early as the beginning of the fifth century.[55] Boys probably attended from the age of seven or so, as suggested by Plato and Aristotle.[56] Traditionally, schooling was divided into three areas—reading and writing (*grammata*), physical training (*gymnastikē*), music and the poetry that was sung to it (*mousikē*)— and sometimes a fourth, painting and drawing.[57] Plato's *Laws* puts forward a system of stages, in which letters and the lyre are taught in turn, and an authority on ancient education has recently argued

Fig. 10. A boy recites to a group of women

that "such a pattern was traditional in the Greek world." [58] I suspect, however, that this is a pet theory of Plato's, like his call for compulsory schooling (Pl. *Leg.* 7.804D). [59] One often-overlooked indication of concurrent education in several subjects: Epicurus, a student at Athens in the late fourth century, is said to have turned to philosophy in disgust at the shortcomings of his *grammatistai* at fourteen (Diog. Laert. 10.2). This is some time after he would have come into the hands of the teacher of *mousikē*, the *kitharistēs,* if *Laws* represented Athenian reality.

More than one subject could be taught at the same spot, but physical training often required special facilities. Boys might therefore have to visit more than one locale in the course of their day's schooling. We would expect that these schools were reasonably close to a boy's home, and that boys from the same neighborhood attended together, as, according to Aristophanes, children from the same *kōmē,* "region of the city," did (Ar. *Nub.* 965). We might also expect better-off boys to go to different, perhaps more expensive, schools (as Demosthenes implies), but this may not always have been so; at any rate, some Athenians regarded equality in education for rich and poor as a mark of democracy. [60] There certainly were distinctions. Wealthy children began school at a younger age and attended for a longer period, and *mousikē* may have been regarded as an unnecessary luxury by the poor. [61] But even Aristophanes' Sausage-Seller can read and write, and, in the words of a popular saying, only dunces don't know their letters or how to swim.[62] Athenian schools, then, would be rather like contemporary neighborhood schools in bringing together boys of somewhat different social and economic status who lived in the same region of the city; the need to travel between schools, however, would bring them out into the community more.

Relatively cohesive to begin with, students might be made more so by the harsh discipline of the classroom. We should not ignore the role of schools as simply agencies of social control. Boys needed some occupation; as Aristotle puts it picturesquely, education is an older child's rattle (Arist. *Pol.* 8.1340b26). At the level of the individual school, teachers deserved respect: Plato regards the failure of pupils to heed them (and their *paidagōgoi*) as a way station on the road to tyranny; Aristotle brackets them with gods and parents as those it is wrong to contradict.[63] But respect was not always forthcoming, especially, perhaps, from the richer students, those who are described by Aristotle as unused to submitting to authority even in school (*Pol.* 4.1295b15). So teachers imposed their authority through beatings; *paideuō,* "I teach," also has the meaning "I correct, I discipline" in classical Attic.[64] Judging by the story that Heracles repaid his music teacher Linus by killing him with a stool, such treatment was expected to instill in boys some hostility toward their teachers.[65] Herondas mentions, and a later gem shows, boys helping the teacher administer a beating, and this may well have taken place in classical Athenian classrooms too; a tactic of divide and rule.[66] But the *paidagōgos* must have assisted here more often, if only because boys greatly outnumbered their teachers.[67] We hear of schools with 60 and 120 pupils, though not at Athens.[68]

The stress on discipline and punishment reflects the goal of Athenian schooling, to produce citizens with the hoplite virtues of courage and self-control rather than to teach skills. As Hyperides puts it in his funeral oration, "We educate children so that they may become good men (*andres agathoi*), and they show that they were well educated as children by being especially brave in battle."[69] According to Protagoras, parents urge teachers to pay more attention to good behavior (*eukosmia*) than to progress in letters or *mousikē* (Pl. *Prot.* 325D). Significantly, it is in this moral realm that the *polis* can be said to educate its citizens.[70] Methods of instruction, like the emphasis on order, seemed tailor-made to stifle originality and self-expression, relying as they did on mimicry and memory. Boys learned to write by following the furrows of an inscribed alphabet and tracing letters lightly sketched in wax, and concentrated on memorizing texts, from lists of words (if we may judge from papyrus finds from Hellenistic Egypt) to the works of Homer and other poets.[71] But competition, a critical feature of Athenian boyhood as of adult life, provided opportunities for the display of individual talent and for attention and acclaim. Only in later literary sources do we read of boys praying to the muses for success at school or thanking them for a victory in penmanship (and a prize of knucklebones).[72] But vase paintings indicate that contests in recitation and *mousikē* were known already in classical Athenian education.[73]

Boys also met and matched themselves with one another through musical and athletic competitions at the city's major religious festivals. Here, too, they mingled under the close supervision of adults, but their interaction was structured and superintended according to terms established by the *polis,* not their own fathers.

Choruses of boys competed at the Hephaesteia and the Prometheia (*IG* 2² 1138.11). More is known of their activities at the City Dionysia and Thargelia. At the City Dionysia there performed dithyrambic choruses of fifty boys, each under a choragus chosen from one of the ten Attic tribes.[74] Five dithyrambic choruses of the same size took part in the Thargelia, each representing two tribes.[75] Fourth-century regulations required that the choragus be more than forty years of age.[76] This was not the rule in the fifth century; the speaker of Lysias 21 was choragus for the Thargelia in the year following his majority at age seventeen or eighteen, and Alcibiades was not yet forty when he assaulted a rival choragus.[77]

Antiphon's speech *On the Chorus Member* affords welcome insight into the workings of these competitions (Antiph. 6.11–14).

65

The speech, which concerns the poisoning of Diodotus, a member of a boys' dithyrambic chorus at the Thargelia in the later fifth century, is delivered by the man accused of his murder, the choragus. The defendant outlines his preparations for the contest, indicating how seriously these competitions (and victories in them) were taken.[78] He fitted out a training room (*didaskaleion*) in his house, had the boys come to practice there, and arranged for four men (two with previous experience in this line) to see to their needs, all at his own expense. The training room was the one he had previously used for the Dionysia; we may assume, then, that day-boarding was in effect for that festival at least. He notes, as a special point in his favor, that he recruited the chorus without fining, or even antagonizing, a single parent. The implication is that the choragus could press into service any boy he wished; his office let him overrule a *kyrios*'s control of his child. Perhaps this became more controversial in the fourth century, and the requirement that a choragus be an older citizen was an attempt to enhance his authority.

It is more plausible, however, that the demand for older choragi "had something to do with changing attitudes to pederasty."[79] Public officials in charge of ephebes had to be forty years old as well (Arist. *AthPol* 42.2); in those days before the invention of the mid-life crisis, they were thought to be more sober and sexually self-controlled than younger men. But we should not imagine that the welfare of boy choristers alone was at risk. The Athenians were well aware of the disruptions the erotic attractions of the young could cause; Plato refers to "the passion for *paides,* both male and female, which has given rise to countless evils for individuals and for entire cities."[80] Why should such entanglements appear more dangerous in the fourth century than before? As will become evident in Chapter 7, I am generally skeptical about answers to questions of this type, and I do not exclude any I offer here. But it is hard to read the most articulate members of the Athenian oligarchical elite—Xenophon, Isocrates, Plato—without concluding that their society was volatile and unstable (in their eyes at least), and only too likely to erupt in civic strife. The change in the age of choragi may be regarded as an attempt to remove one potential point of tension.

These competitions, set as they were amid the city's celebrations of its gods, must have given the boy singers a powerful sense of belonging to the community and contributing to its welfare. Their preliminaries had a similar effect, smaller in scale but more immediate. We have reason to believe that boys attended schools in their own neighborhood, and other evidence, too, suggests that they had only a narrow experience of Attica. (About twenty years old and ambitious to make his mark in public affairs, Glaucon has never been to the silver mines at Laureion: Xen. *Mem.* 3.6.12.) In the choruses, however, they shared quarters with other boys of their tribe and (at the Thargelia) with boys of another tribe as well. Of course, the tribes were not geographical entities; each grouped Athenians from all over the city. Choral competition therefore brought boys face to face with their peers from elsewhere in the *polis* at the same time that it introduced them to the community as a whole. In this way, a boy's circle of acquaintances could extend beyond his family and neighbors. Moreover, he was not the only one to benefit. Since the tribe was the basic organizational unit of the Athenian armed forces, this boyhood identification with the tribe and camaraderie with its members could only improve Athens' military morale and effectiveness when boy singers became adult soldiers.

Competition and its rewards were features of all these areas of Athenian life, but nowhere more than in sports. Sports gave boys a chance not only to identify their place within the community but perhaps also to escape it.[81] In local competitions for Athenians alone, they set themselves against their fellows in individual sports, joined with their tribesmen in team events. At the Panathenaea and the great Panhellenic games, they found themselves on a wider stage, Athenians among Greeks from all over the Mediterranean world. Successful athletes at Athens and elsewhere could win glory or material rewards that might help them transcend their origins.

Boys competed at all four major Panhellenic games: the Olympics (traditionally founded in 776) from the year 632, the Isthmian Games, the Nemean Games, and the Pythian Games at Delphi from the time of their reorganization in the earlier sixth century. At both the Olympics and the Pythian Games athletes were divided into two age classes, boys (*paides*) and men (*andres*); at the Isthmian and Nemean games there was an intermediate class, "the beardless" (*ageneioi*). The boundaries of these classes are quite uncertain.[82] There was apparently a minimum age for competitors, at least in some events, for Pherias of Aegina was excluded from wrestling with the *paides* at the Olympics of 468 because he was too young; he was still a *pais* in the competition four years later, but this time he participated and won (Paus. 6.14.1). The youngest winner we know of is Damiscus of Messene, fastest in the Olympic *stadion* race in 368 at the age of twelve.[83] The upper limit of the *paides* age class at Olympia and Delphi was probably seventeen; any boy who turned eighteen in the year of the games was excluded.[84] (Nicasylus of Rhodes, eighteen, had to wrestle with the men at Olympia [Paus. 6.14.2].) It may be with this threshold in mind that Aristotle recommends that boys not begin hard training until three years after puberty—in other words, at seventeen (Arist. *Pol.* 8.1339a1).

Defining *ageneioi,* and establishing the effect of this class on the age limits of the others, is still less straightforward, and it is complicated by the likelihood of variation over time and place and the fact that almost all our evidence is post-classical.[85] So "Pythian boys" (*paides Pythikoi*), presumably named for the boys' age class at Delphi, are younger than "Isthmian boys" (*paides Isthmikoi*) in late games, while boys at the Panathenaea (which also had three classes of competitors) are said to be older in late sources.[86] This is really the realm of guesswork, but it cannot be too much of a mistake to imagine *ageneioi* as young as sixteen and as old as twenty. Precision is perhaps as undesirable as it is unattainable. The ancient Greeks had no birth certificates, many Greek states probably considered all children born within the same year to be the same age for civic purposes at least (as Sparta and Athens did), these years did not all begin and end at the same time: the allocation of athletes to the proper age class must have been left to the judgment of those in charge of the games, influenced (no less importantly) by the arguments of the competitors and their supporters. (It was owing to the intercession of King Agesilaus of Sparta that the son of Eualces of Athens, "biggest of the boys," competed with the others at Olympia.)[87] And the athletes themselves could sometimes choose to ignore age boundaries. When Pythagoras, a Samian wrestler of the early sixth century, was laughed out of the competition for boys at Olympia because of his long hair and purple robe, he promptly entered the men's event and won.[88] A later athlete is said to have won four victories on one day at Nemea, competing both as a *pais* and as an *ageneios* (Euseb. *Chron.* 1.212 Schöne).

Whereas children's games only rarely and indirectly reflected adult activity, the program for boys in these games more or less paralleled that for men, though there certainly were differences. (For example, the *pankration,* one of the most dangerous events, was first open to boys only in 346 at Delphi and in 200 at Olympia, and boys used a light-weight discus in the *pentathlon:* Paus. 1.35.5.) In one festival or another, boys competed in the *stadion,* a race of about 200 yards; the *diaulos,* 400 yards; the *hippios,* 800 yards; the *dolichos,* a long-distance run; wrestling; boxing; *pankration,* which combined elements of each of the other combat sports and forbade only biting and gouging; and *pentathlon* (the *stadion,* discus, javelin, jump, and wrestling). Little is known of the boys' place on the program, though in Plutarch's day, at least, their competitions often preceded the men's, either as a bloc (as at Olympia, where the boys ran, wrestled, and boxed a day before the men) or in each separate event (as at Delphi: Plut. *Mor.* 639A).

At Athens, athletics were a part of a number of religious festivals—the Heracleia at Marathon, the Eleusinia, the Oschophoria.[89] The Hermaea, celebrated by boys and youths in the palaestrae and gymnasia of which Hermes was an important patron, featured athletic contests in later antiquity and probably in the classical period as well.[90] A series of second-century inscriptions supplies the boys' program for the Theseia, including *stadion, diaulos, dolichos,* wrestling, boxing, *pankration,* and fighting in armor (*IG* 2² 956–965). Of particular interest is the division of *paides* into three groups, the first, second, and third ages, perhaps permitting younger boys than usual to take part; the youngest boys, the first two groups, did not run the grueling *dolichos.* The torch race, run perhaps in relays, included teams of *paides, ephēboi,* and *neaniskoi;* here younger children might be thought too irresponsible to handle fire. In neither case can we be sure that the format dates back to the classical period, and it is in later festivals that we hear the most of such a multiplication of divisions.[91] But the myth of Theseus included the rescue of Athenian boys and girls from the Crete of the Minotaur, and his festival might therefore have been thought to be especially suitable for the participation of younger children right from its inception in the early fifth century.

For the Greater Panathenaea, celebrated every four years in honor of the goddess Athena, we have a very important piece of evidence, an inscription from the early fourth century, fragmentary and incomplete but richly informative (*IG* 2² 2311).[92] This sets out both program and prizes. Athletic events included the *stadion* race, *pentathlon,* wrestling, boxing, and *pankration* for boys and *ageneioi;* the same events were apparently held for men as well, but that section of the stone has been lost. Also listed were an ambitious equestrian program, competitions for singers and musicians, and other events. Unlike the four great Panhellenic festivals, the so-called crown games, the Greater Panathenaea gave value prizes, including second-place awards in the athletic and equestrian events. In every case, they were smaller for boys than for *ageneioi,* but only somewhat so. Thus, the winner of the boys' *stadion* race received fifty Panathenaic amphorae of olive oil, the second-place finisher ten, while the *ageneios* who won this event received sixty and the next competitor twelve. The victorious boy pancratiast won forty amphorae, his leading rival eight; the *ageneioi* who finished first and second won perhaps fifty and ten (these lines are missing). In the other athletic contests boy winners received thirty amphorae and runners-up six; *ageneioi* winners were awarded forty amphorae and runners-up eight. (Our only evidence on men's prizes, an epigram for the Corinthian pentathlete Nicolaidas, unfortunately dates from a much earlier period, the late sixth or early fifth century. Nicolaidas won sixty amphorae of olive oil: Simonides, *Anth. Pal.* 13.19.) That boys' competitions were not regarded as unimportant is further indicated by the prizes for pyrrhic dancing. Winning tribes in each class—boys, *ageneioi,* and men—received the same prizes, 100 drachmas in money and an ox.[93]

The Greater Panathenaea was not unique in the attention it directed toward boy victors. Boy winners at the great Panhellenic games, like other victors, dedicated statues or had statues dedicated for them—Pausanias describes many in the sixth book of his *Description of Greece*—and were the subjects of odes by the paid praise poets, Simonides, Pindar, and Bacchylides.[94] Their triumphs were sources of pride for their communities; the Clazomenians dedicated a statue for the boy runner Herodotus because he was their first Olympic victor.[95] A city's first victor among the *paides* also was likely to gain special recognition.[96] We know of few Athenian *paides* (or *ageneioi*) who won at the great Panhellenic games during the archaic and classical periods.[97] One is Epichares, who finished first in the Olympic *stadion* race for boys in the early fourth century, winning "a wreath for the city," and was respected, we are told, as long as he lived.[98] His achievement is among his grandson's claims on the sympathy of a jury.

Winners at these games also received gifts from the community;[99] at Athens these included meals in the *prytaneion* and a grant of money, said (on dubious authority) to be one of Solon's measures, 500 drachmas for Olympic victors, 100 for Isthmian.[100] There is no reason to exclude boys from these generous benefits. At the Greater Panathenaea, of course, the prizes themselves were substantial. It is naturally difficult to calculate a modern equivalent for the value of fifty large jars of olive oil, but by any reasonable estimate these awards were very large indeed, tantamount to a year's wages or more, enough to buy a house or several slaves. They raise the question of athletics as a means of social mobility. According to a scenario sketched by David Young, a boy of natural ability but moderate means might win such a prize at the Greater Panathenaea (or at smaller local games), buy with it the leisure and training necessary to succeed at other age levels, and so establish himself and his family among the city's elite. This is speculation. The little we know of the social origins of Athens' champion athletes confirms the usual view that most were already privileged by birth or wealth before their victories, and we cannot point with confidence to any example of the curriculum vitae imagined by Young.[101] Yet it is not implausible, and something like it may lie behind the story of Melesias, who won the *pankration* for *ageneioi* at Nemea in the later sixth century, subsequently repeated as a man, and then became a famous trainer.[102] Plato says his was a great family—it included his son Thucydides, an important rival of Pericles—but Melesias is in fact its first known member (Pl. *Meno* 94D).

The Social Life of Girls

Though I will argue in Chapter 5 that girls spent a good deal of time with their brothers as children, restrictions on their movements and Athenian ideas on the sexes' separate spheres generally kept boys and girls apart outside the home. Plato sets the age for them to go their separate ways at six (Pl. *Leg.* 7.794C). This line of demarcation is roughly confirmed by the iconography of Athenian funerary monuments, on which boys and girls some years after infancy are usually depicted with different characteristic attributes: wagons for boys, ducks (and some other fowl) and dolls for girls.[103] (Pheidippides was six when his father bought him a toy wagon during the Diasia: Ar. *Nub.* 861–864.) Adolescent sexuality increased the stakes in separating the sexes. Plato's idea that youths (*koroi*) and girls (*korai*) should dance together so as to encourage better-informed choices of marriage partners must have scandalized many Athenians, even without the added fillip that they wear as few clothes as decency allowed; just as the Spartan practices that informed it did.[104] Even with the daughters of other families, Athenian girls' involvement was more limited than their brothers' with other boys. They did not compete in athletic festivals in other Greek centers or (again unlike Spartan girls) in public contests within the city itself during the archaic and classical periods.[105]

Fig. 11. A schoolgirl and her slave (?)

Nor is it likely that they attended school outside the home. It is true that at least some Athenian women were functionally literate, and vases do show girls taking instruction in dancing and in *mou-sikē,* playing flute, cithara, or lyre.[106] But lessons might well have been taken at home; this is especially plausible in the case of vases on which only one girl is shown (though not only then). One vase, which depicts an older girl carrying writing tablets by a strap, much like boys on other pots, is the best evidence for girls' schooling outside the home: she is attended by another girl of the same size, perhaps a slave playing the part of a *paidagōgos.* But even in this case only the girl's literacy can be assumed, not the locale where she learned it; and the shape of the vase, a vessel for drinking wine, may suggest that she is an educated (and expensive) hetaera, not a respectable citizen girl at all.[107] Similarly, I take a red-figure phiale on which a girl and several women dance under the eye of an instructor to be an illustration of the training of courtesans.[108] Most girls' contacts, then, were with kin or neighbors, another reflection of their smaller social world. Two younger cousins live next door to each other and are raised together in Menander (*Asp.* 122–129). A joke in comedy takes off from the possibility that a mother might invite her daughter's friend, a neighborhood *pais*, to share in a celebration for Hecate (Ar. *Lys.* 700–702).

We know little enough of other activities. Swimmers on archaic vases may represent citizen girls; they are nude among themselves, clothed in the presence of men.[109] Girls played *khelikhelōnē*, "tortoise," a tag game rather like *khytrinda*: the "tortoise"—an animal associated with the home, woolworking, and the love of children[110]—sits in the middle while other girls circle her, engaging in a series of queries and replies which ends with her attempt to catch one of them:

> Tortoise, what are you doing in the middle?
> I'm weaving wool and Milesian thread.
> What was your son doing when he died?
> From white horses into the sea he was—jumping.[111]

The game is one the poet Erinna, who lived perhaps on the island of Telos in the early Hellenistic period and gives what is as close as we can get to a first-person account of Greek girlhood, played with her friend Baucis.[112] These girls had dolls as well and played with them (so Erinna writes) on a sleepover at Baucis's house. One of the early commentators on Erinna's poem interpreted its fragmentary text as a description of the girls' imitating young mothers caring for their babies, but extant examples of dolls and their depiction on gravestones, from Athens and elsewhere, indicate that they were meant to represent girls of marriageable age.[113] If the *nymphai* of the poem does refer to brides and is not, as sometimes, simply another word for "dolls," a plausible explanation is that Erinna and Baucis dressed their dolls as

Fig. 12. A girl and a tortoise

the brides they hoped one day to be, a pastime consistent with the dedication of dolls to Artemis and other deities at the time of a girl's marriage.[114]

Marriage, of course, meant an end to or at least a change in girls' friendships, involving as it did not only a shift in role but also, in many cases, movement from one part of the community to another. A "speculative discussion" suggests that at least as many Athenian marriages were contracted between those whose families belonged to different demes as between those belonging to the same deme, and some of those involved must still have lived at or near their ancestral homes.[115] Lamented by Erinna, this transition is the background to the abduction of Persephone—she was playing and picking flowers with her friends when the ground opened before her and Hades carried her off (*Hym. Cer.* 4–19, 414–428).[116] It was mediated by the participation of young women, along with youths (*korois te kai korais*), in the wedding itself, notably as singers on the morning after.[117]

Choruses were important institutions of socialization for girls in other parts of the Greek world. At Sparta, Alcman's *Partheneion,* or "Maiden-song," was performed at a festival (for Helen?) by a choir of adolescent girls as one of their rites of initiation.[118] Less formally, Sappho's young female friends may have sung some of her poems together on archaic Lesbos; this expression of female solidarity before the group's dissolution at marriage would mirror an important theme of the wedding songs, the movement from a life spent among other young girls to the world of men. Such coteries were unknown, such passage rites less prominent, at Athens, where the individual household bore more of the burden of socializing female citizens, but choruses of girls did sing and dance there, too, on special occasions such as the Greater Panathenaea and perhaps some other festivals as well.[119] These girls must have spent some time together at practice, but we should not assume that they spent as much time away from home as boy choristers, nor did groups of girl choristers compete. An early first-century inscription that records a vote to honor the *ergastinai* who wove Athena's *peplos*—perhaps as many as one hundred—may indicate that they lived at home, though their fathers' supervisory role is mentioned only in a restored portion of the fragmentary text (*IG* 2^2 1036). Some religious rites, however, did require girls to live together outside their homes for a time; at Athens too, then, cult practices served not only to integrate girls into the larger community but also to form them into a community of their own. The *arrhēphoroi,* two or four in number, lived on the Acropolis during their tour of duty; they had the use of a field on the way to Aphrodite's shrine "in the garden," and a hydria of the later fifth century shows them there playing ball, Aphrodite in their midst.[120]

More significant in terms of the numbers involved were the Thesmophoria and the Arkteia. Since the Thesmophoria, a fall festival for Demeter and her daughter Persephone, mainly concerned

Fig. 13. *Arrhēphoroi* play ball

natural and human fertility, some have assumed that only married women took part.[121] But a participant carries a baby girl at her breast in a comedy by Aristophanes; ancient scholars refer to noble maidens and virgin priestesses; and in fact the rites, especially the curious exhumation of piglets cast into caves some time before, and the myth of Persephone attached to them, seem peculiarly relevant to girls who themselves are to be transformed from wild beings whose sexuality must be checked into chastely wedded wives.[122] Perhaps, however, some girls stayed at home to look after their fathers and brothers. For during the three days of the festival, Athenian girls and women camped out near the Pnyx (the meeting place for the Athenian male citizen assembly) and made up a city of women separate from and parallel to that of men. Like theirs, it was a city with divisions. The women celebrating the Thesmophoria were apparently arranged according to the demes their husbands and fathers belonged to, so that ties among men were privileged even in this setting (cf. Isae. 3.80, 8.19); links among girls and women would reinforce men's. Two further elements that might drive women apart, the exchange of abuse and scourging, are attested from other rites for Demeter (the Eleusinian Mysteries) and from fertility cults. We can only speculate on their effects here; much, of course, must depend on form and feeling. On the one hand, even ritualized mockery might arouse resentment, and so work against community feeling. Yet if strong emotions, even negative ones, are aroused, and then put to rest—which seems likely in this case—group solidarity is not just maintained but often enhanced.

The Arkteia, for Artemis, was quite different, held far from the center of civic activity at Brauron, on the east coast of Attica, and aimed solely at girls; something similar is attested for Munychia as well. Most of our (late) literary sources indicate that all Athenian girls spent some time in the sanctuary of Artemis Brauronia serving the goddess as *arktoi,* "bears," before their marriage.[123] Against this, we may note that a scholium on Aristophanes refers to "selected maidens" (*epilegomenai parthenai*), and that if (as the original excavator thought) a three-sided Doric stoa in the sanctuary was the residence of the *arktoi,* it appears too small for the numbers we would expect it to have housed.[124] But Athenian girls customarily carried out other ritual tasks before marriage, such as a sacrifice to Athena on the Acropolis; not all "bears" need have stayed at the sanctuary at the same time; and the identification of the stoa is in any case uncertain. The evidence clearly favors the tradition that participation in the *arkteia* was widespread, if not universal.[125] It is all the more disappointing, then (though not exactly unprecedented), that we know so little about the activities of the "bears." Indications that they took part in contests—footraces, perhaps even spinning bees—are especially tantalizing, although the evidence, almost entirely iconographic, is open to other interpretations.[126] If they did, we could conclude that the *arkteia,* like boys' athletic competitions, afforded girls more than just an opportunity to meet their peers; it also made possible the display of exceptional merit among them. A crucial (and characteristic) difference is that boys' superiority was exhibited and publicized to the whole community and even (at the Greater Panathenaea) to outsiders, while girls won recognition only within their own group. Dedications to Artemis Brauronia found on the Acropolis often fail to indicate even girls' family affiliations. And other differences among them are denied in the main public manifestation of the cult, the long procession from Athens to Brauron (about twenty-five miles) every four years.[127] This included all those who had served the goddess since the last celebration of the Brauronia, many hundreds of girls. They reestablished old acquaintances certainly, but, just as important, they asserted the unity of the group before the eyes of onlookers, including men (cf. Ar. *Pax* 872–876).

Four

Parents and Children

Personal Relations within the Household

Aristotle begins his *Politics* with a discussion of the residential household, the *oikia* or *oikos*. Consisting of the nuclear family, its relatives and dependents, its possessions, animate and inanimate, this is viewed as the basis of the *polis*. It includes both people and things; appropriately, Aristotle starts off with an analysis of the relationship of the master of the household with one of its constituents which is both person and thing, the slave. He regards the slave primarily as part of the property of the household. But things, he says, are less important in household management than people, and he promises to examine the household's human relations later in his account. In the opinion of most commentators, however, this promise is not fulfilled.[1]

Better late than never. In this chapter and the next two, I propose to carry out Aristotle's program. It may be surprising to some that such a project needs doing, since W. K. Lacey's intelligent and valuable account of the ancient Greek family has existed for more than twenty years (1968). Lacey's book, however, is at the same time too broad, too narrow, and too successful. It treats much more than the classical Athenian family, devoting chapters to Homer, archaic Greece, women, Plato, Sparta, Crete, and "the family in other states"; as a result, less is said about Athens than might be. It also focuses (as the index's subhead signals) on "legal, political and religious aspects"; interpersonal relations are slighted, touched on only in passing. And though Lacey is well aware that slaves and others shared the *oikos,* his concern with the family itself prevents him from treating them at any length. Finally, with Lacey's book so firmly established in the field (and flanked by another with similar concerns, Harrison [1968]), there has seemed little need to work on the Greek family. The spate of research that has revolutionized our understanding of the Roman family has passed by what classicists call "the Greek side," and as a result Lacey's shortcomings have not been made good.

I would not deny that the forms and directions feelings take depend to a great extent on the social structures and property relationships among which consciousness comes to be; to set these out (as Lacey and others have) is therefore the first important task for students of the family. Perhaps it is even the task of first importance; but it is not the only one. More should be said about the emotional relations among those who shared the household, on the assumption that these were important constituents of the environment in which the child's consciousness developed. In my discussion of those relations, I will begin with the members of the nuclear family, devoting this chapter to parents and children, and the next to siblings, grandparents, and grandchildren. I will then move on, in Chapter 6, to newcomers who enter the household from parts of the community outside it (stepparents, adopted children, friends) and to those outsiders who might, paradoxically, have been part of the household since its formation, slaves.

My aim is to sketch what was expected of, or at least desired in, each relationship in question. But the discussion will not be restricted to ideals: conflict, too, will play a part, especially that which developed as children grew into roles outside the household. I will endeavor to identify some sources of tension, some methods taken to alleviate it, and some of the consequences of each. Finally, I hope throughout to make necessary but often ignored distinctions between the sexes: between fathers and mothers among parents, and between sons and daughters among children. Diachronic differences, on the contrary, will play a less prominent part than might be expected in a historical essay, simply because I think changes within the classical period have for the most part been exaggerated.[2] This is not to say that I reject the possibility of change over time *in toto*. But I will reserve the subject for a separate examination of the dowries of New Comedy, in the last chapter of this book.

Parents and Children

I begin with a query: Did the Athenians care when their children died?[3] Here, as often, M. I. Finley provides a cautious and seemingly compelling response:

> Any Greek or Roman who reached the age of marriage could look forward to burying one or more children, often very small ones. . . . I do not suggest that Greeks and Romans buried their children and spouses without a sense of loss. . . . What I do suggest is that in a world in which such early deaths and burials were routine, so to speak, the intensity and duration of the emotional responses were unlike modern reactions, though I confess that I know no way to measure or even to identify the differences.[4]

Finley's remarks come from an article that begins with an outline of ancient demographics; despite his diffidence, they amount to a suggestion that demography largely governs emotional responses. Other historians have asserted this demographic determinism much more confidently. Philippe Ariès, Ivy Pinchbeck, Margaret Hewitt, Edward Shorter, Lawrence Stone—all have argued that affection and love were not expected in preindustrial populations, because high mortality made emotional commitment, especially to children, too dangerous for individuals and insupportable for their societies.[5] Stone's expression of this view has been the most influential.

Writing on early modern England, Stone (1977) argues, "The omnipresence of death coloured affective relations at all levels of society, by reducing the amount of emotional capital available for prudent investment in any single individual, especially in such ephemeral creatures as infants" (651–652). In other words, "to preserve their mental stability, parents were obliged to limit the degree of their psychological involvement with their infant children" (70). As a result, the children suffered neglect, "caused in part by the high mortality rate, since there was small reward for lavishing time and care on such ephemeral objects as small babies" (81). As Stone notes, a vicious circle. Others have identified as one aspect of parental neglect the practice of putting children into the hands of wet-nurses, usually outside the household, even far away in the countryside; out of sight, out of mind. Shorter's words on the subject (1976) are particularly striking: ". . . mothers viewed the development and happiness of infants younger than two with indifference" (168); "that is why their children vanished in the ghastly slaughter of the innocents that was traditional child-rearing" (204).

Much in Greek (and Roman) society appears consistent with this view. Infant mortality was high—how high we can only estimate, but perhaps 25–35 percent in the first year of life.[6] Infant deaths were to be expected; it is noteworthy that on extant epitaphs from all over the Greek world, children under the age of two are never (or hardly ever) said to have died *ahōros,* "untimely," on extant epitaphs from all over the Greek world, though the term is so widely used that it can be applied to a woman of seventy-three.[7] In death, as (allegedly) in life, children made little impact; they were rarely commemorated and were often allowed burial within the boundaries of cities, even within the confines of houses.[8] Some adults said straight out that they were not much of a concern. "Most men treat their private business in a careless manner," says Plato's Laches, "that concerning children and other things too."[9] Parents who lose children must be satisfied with the cold comfort that they can have new ones.[10] Finally, among the elite at least, it was customary to entrust children to the care of slave nurses and *paidagōgoi;* and children were sent out to be raised in the households of others.[11] No wonder, then, that Stone's thesis attracted even so skeptical a scholar as Finley.[12] And yet it cannot be applied to many high-mortality populations studied by modern anthropologists, and it may be misleading even for the society with which Stone himself is most concerned.

Far from being indifferent, members of cultures in which children are at risk often make sure that their infants are in almost constant contact with a care-giver, quickly see to them when they cry, and feed them whenever they suspect they are hungry—precisely because they know the danger that they will die if they are not attended to. So, among the Kalahari Desert San, infants are frequently held, looked at, smiled at, and spoken to, and their demands are generally indulged. In fact, to quote one student of this society, "the natural environment . . . resembles . . . a well-designed infant stimulation program."[13] If that sounds too idealized, we may think of this pattern of child rearing as another observer does, as a kind of "constant medical alert."[14] Either way, it is clear that children receive a good deal of attention from adults. Concern for children is at a similarly high level among a group whose cultural practices may be thought more directly relevant to the ancient Mediterranean, the Sarakatsan shepherds of central and northern Greece. "Children from the day of their birth are the centre of attention and interest in the family. The needs of the infant take priority over all others."[15] This care must itself increase the value put on children; "rearing children often proves a stronger elixir of love (*philtron*) than giving birth," in the words of a tragic fragment of uncertain date (?Biotus 205 F 1 Snell).

Of course, this care cannot guarantee health and survival. Why are such attentive parents not devastated by the death of their children? I leave aside the validity of metaphors such as "emotional capital," which imply that humans can love (or experience any other feeling) only to the limits of some imaginary budget. One important reason is that parents believe that they are following customary and well-accepted child-rearing practices, and they therefore feel relatively little insecurity or guilt about their behavior at any given stage of the process.[16] Another is that child rearing in high-mortality societies is often diffused, not the responsibility of parents alone, but shared to some extent with other adults and with older children; as a result, the burden of loss also is distributed more widely than in some cultures. A third reason is related to this (and is the most relevant to ancient Athens): many traditional cultures have more-or-less elaborate ritual practices and eschatological beliefs that help parents come to terms with their grief.[17] A real sense of loss exists;[18] but it is vented by following a set series of actions, often over an extended period of time, not by individual, self-expressive outpourings of emotion.[19] These actions are often shared by others in the family and outside it, who thus provide personal support and social validation during the grieving process. Furthermore, these individuals are perhaps more likely to provide comfort because they, too, have so often suffered similar experiences.[20] Finally, a child's death may be rationalized by appeal to beliefs such as that in "repeater children," who are destined to be born over and over again.[21] Something similar is supplied by the pessimistic reflection expressed movingly in Sophocles' *Oedipus at Colonus:* not to be born is best, next best to die soon after.[22]

The funerary rites and burial customs followed for the death of a child in such cultures are often quite different from those for a dead adult (as they typically were in ancient Athens). Since Robert Hertz's brilliant article (1960), it is almost a cliché to argue that rites for children are less elaborate, the pollution caused by their death less powerful, simply because they have played a less important social role; they have not fully entered into the community, and so can make the transition out of it more easily.[23] More may be involved, however. The burial of children within the house, for example, need not be regarded only as a sign that a child is too unimportant to receive a more elaborate burial. It may also be a form of sympathetic magic, a statement that the household welcomes children; or a mark of the parents' unwillingness to give up a treasured child completely.[24]

It seems, then, that more than demography governs the reaction to a child's death in high-mortality populations in general. How does Stone's stand up as an account of attitudes in early modern Europe specifically? Research on individual parts of the thesis may give rise to skepticism. On wet-nursing outside the household, for example, it has been stressed that the practice was not universal, but was subject to local fads and fashions. Where it existed, it was primarily a response to economic necessity among young mothers who had to work and could not care for their children (often to their considerable regret). These children might well be mistreated; their mortality was higher than the norm. But the neglect was on the part of their nurses, who often preferred to provide their milk to their own children first.[25] On fosterage, it has been emphasized that this complex institution served the interests of the children as well as those of the adults in the two households concerned. Elizabethan parents who placed their children in better-off homes secured them valuable patrons and an opportunity to achieve a place in society they themselves could not obtain for them; contemporary immigrants from West Africa place their children in English foster homes for similar motives.[26] As Aristotle observed long ago, mothers may love their children even as (and after) they give them up.[27] Linda A. Pollock has recently reviewed the thesis of parental indifference in an important book-length study (1983). After summarizing evidence against it from evolutionary theory and ethnology, Pollock examines primary sources, especially the diaries of children and adults and autobiographies, from the sixteenth to the twentieth century in Britain (and the United States). She turns up many examples of parents who seem to have cared deeply for their children, tried conscientiously to understand and adapt to them, and grieved painfully when they died. She concludes: ". . . most parents were only too clearly anxious and upset by the ill-health of a child. In fact, it appears that the high rate of infant mortality operated to increase their anxiety" (127, cf. 140). Once again, the argument that adults in high-mortality populations did not care that their children died fails to convince.[28]

It is to the credit of scholars such as Keith Bradley, Robert Garland, and Keith Hopkins that they know Stone's work, have considered it carefully, and have argued against applying it to the ancient world, without the benefit of much of the recent research I have referred to.[29] But Garland and Hopkins (and other commentators such as Donna Kurtz and John Boardman) are troubled by a seeming contradiction, the practice of exposure of newborns, sometimes called infanticide. In his book on the Greek way of death, Garland (1985) outlines Stone's thesis and then immediately adduces the practice of exposure as "evidence in its support" (80). Hopkins (1983) affirms that the Roman parent did not passively tolerate and pretend "not to care about the death of babies and young children," but then continues: ". . . nagging doubts remain. Even rich and educated Romans killed or exposed new-born babies" (225).[30]

Now, it is likely (though not beyond reasonable doubt) that the exposure of newborns, especially newborn girls, was widespread and even common at Athens. But (and this merits emphasis) this tells us nothing—at least nothing negative—about the Athenians' response to the death of the children they did decide to raise. Once again, studies of more recent populations are helpful. Infanticide is known to coexist with care of and affection for children both in societies studied by anthropologists—for a second time we may point to the Kalahari Desert San—and in pre-industrial Europe.[31] The key question is whether a child was wanted or not. Writing from a theoretical perspective quite different from Pollock's, Sheila Johansson (1987a, 1987b) draws attention to the widely varying rates of infant mortality from different places and periods in early modern Europe. Her explanation for these significant variations gives pride of place to social, economic, and ideological factors that influenced standards of parenting. One constant lies behind this complex of local conditions: the fact that infanticide was illegal (and harshly punished), which led parents to neglect or even mistreat unwanted children so that some or many more died than would otherwise have been the case. One implication of her argument (though Johansson does not bring it out) is that in societies that permit infanticide, children who are accepted into the family are less likely to be neglected or mistreated (at least to this extent) and are more likely to be mourned deeply when they die.[32]

Perhaps the motives and experiences of contemporary women who choose to abort their pregnancies can provide some insight here. "Every child a wanted child" is a slogan of pro-choice activists; it also reflects a reality for many women who decide not to carry a pregnancy to term. Thus, a study of more than three thou-

sand Belgian women who had induced abortions in 1979 found
that a "desire to have no children at all is rare, as 91 percent of the
women claimed to want children . . . in most cases they desired
two or three."[33] That dislike of or indifference toward children is
seldom a motive for abortion is borne out by other reports. For
example, in a group of sixty-two women undergoing abortion in
an urban center in the U.S. South in the late 1970s, 65 percent
indicated they wanted children in the future, while only 11 percent said lack of desire for any children at all led them to seek
abortion.[34] Significantly, follow-up studies seem to show that
many women who abort do in fact have children later and care for
those children like any other mothers. An account of 312 women
who had induced abortions in Hawaii in the early 1980s concludes: "Their subsequent births have been overwhelmingly intended and wanted and have occurred in a positive emotional atmosphere. At the time of these subsequent pregnancies, they are
indistinguishable from the control sample [of women who have
not had abortions] in attitudes and emotions, albeit slightly higher
in socio-economic status."[35] The thrust of this research is that contemporary women who seek abortion do not normally do so out
of dislike of or indifference toward children; and that the experience of abortion does not affect their attitudes toward other children, either already living or yet to be born, in any negative way.
On the contrary, it is arguable that many of these women choose
to abort when they do largely in order to provide a better environment for other children they have or will have in the future; they
postpone childbirth until they are better able, financially or emotionally, to raise a child.

Of course, no such surveys are available for classical Athens,
nor is there any other Athenian evidence that seems directly relevant to this argument (though poverty was one of the dangers ad-
vocates of population control such as Plato wished to avert; e.g.,
Pl. *Resp.* 2.372BC). But a few scattered comments indicate that
such considerations influenced parents in other parts of the ancient Greek and Roman world, and so may not have been utterly
foreign at Athens. Polybius's famous remark on the depopulation
of Greece charges that "many parents wish to have just one or two

children so as to leave them in affluence and bring them up to waste their substance" (36.17.5–7). A hostile witness; but what he denounces could be described as prudence on the part of parents who care for their children's well-being. The Stoic Musonius Rufus's diatribe against rich parents who do not want to raise all their children so that they may leave all their wealth to their firstborn points in the same direction (fr. 15). Among some Greeks and Romans exposure of newborns could coexist with, and even be caused by, care for other children.

Thus, recent research renders doubtful the hypothesis that children have not been deeply mourned in high-mortality populations; and evidence from contemporary Western society controverts the assumption that the decision not to rear some babies stems from indifference or hostility toward children as a whole. Neither line of argument can prove that the Athenians did care that their children died, but each removes a reason for believing that they did not.

In fact, the weight of the evidence seems overwhelmingly to favor the proposition that the Athenians loved their children and grieved for them deeply when they died. The death of the infant Astyanax is a staple of Athenian art as early as a geometric shard from the Agora dating from the late eighth century.[36] Nor is pathos aroused by the death of mythical children only. Both Herodotus and Thucydides choose the death of schoolchildren as an example of a crushing calamity; the incident recounted by Thucydides, the slaughter of the children of Mycalessus by Thracians, is called the most complete, most sudden, most horrible disaster that ever struck the city.[37] Seeking sympathy from an Athenian jury, a defendant tells of a similar loss: Parmenon's house collapsed, his wife and children died in the ruins. One would expect even a cruel arbitrator or an opponent to postpone a case in the circumstances ([Dem.] 33.20, 33–34).

Parents' concern may be judged by the precautions they took to prevent more foreseeable fatalities. Antiphon's comment is only one example of a sentiment that became a commonplace: "Suppose children are born; then all is full of anxiety, and the youthful spring goes out of the mind, and the countenance is no longer the same."[38] This anxiety found expression in many forms, from the amulets that were thought to avert disease and the evil eye, to the dedications made to healing deities on behalf of children.[39] When all precautions failed, parents' sorrow was often great. Xenocleia died of grief for her eight-year-old son.[40] Other bereaved parents are said to have wished they'd never had children at all.[41]

One of the most striking statements of a deep attachment to children comes from tragedy, part of a lament for a son killed in the Argive expedition against Thebes. "Seeing others who had children, I had a passion for children and was lost in longing," says Iphis (Eur. *Supp.* 1087–1088). The Greek is *paidōn erastēs,* the first a common word for the younger member of a homosexual couple, the second for his older lover; Iphis describes himself as in the grip of an overpowering desire for children, an emotion akin to sexual passion. The phrase is bold but not unparalleled in Euripides.[42] Childless both, Xuthus and Temenus journey to oracles of Apollo and of Zeus because of a passionate desire for children.[43] Similar reflections, if not such highly charged vocabulary, are common elsewhere in his tragedies. Heracles' comments in the play dealing with his mad murder of his own children may stand for many others: "Both the best of mortals and those who are nobodies love children; they differ in material things; some have property and some do not; but the whole race is child-loving."[44] His own tragedy would be much diminished if it were not; as it is, it is deepened by his abandonment by his own father, Zeus, a betrayal of a parent's role criticized both in this play and in Sophocles' *Trachiniae.*[45]

Of course, Euripides' characters can be quoted as evidence for almost every attitude.[46] But these sentiments are not confined to them, nor are they restricted to contexts of childlessness and loss. Socrates speaks of the common case of a man who values his son above all other things (Pl. *Lys.* 219D). Aristophanes provides a glimpse of a new father's joy, which is so intense that it makes him easy to deceive, and of tired veterans half-bragging, half-complaining, about their sons' birdbrained enthusiasms like late-night stand-up comics; take my son—please.[47] Another father commandeers his son from a nurse, feeds him from his own mouth, makes kissing sounds, and calls him a pet name, "daddy's little rascal."[48] This is Theophrastus's Ill-Bred Man—it was unseemly for a father to take on a slave woman's work. Nor does Theophrastus approve of the flatterer who buys a man's little children fruit and says, as he kisses them, that they're chips off their father's block.[49] But the behaviors, testifying as they do to fondness for children, are as significant as (and perhaps more widespread than) the philosopher's reaction. Writing as a rhetorician, Aristotle lists both *euteknia*, "having good children," and *polyteknia*, "having many children," as among the components of happiness, an idea reflected already in the archaic Athenian poet and politician Solon.[50] He is more original and no less revealing when he writes as a scientist.[51] Here we are told that nature herself wishes to provide for the care of the young of all species. In lower animals, the feeling she implants lasts only until birth; in others (such as birds), until the baby reaches its complete development. In more intelligent animals, the concern instilled by nature lasts until rearing is completed. However, in the most intelligent species, humans among them, there is intimacy and attachment (*synētheia kai philia*) between parent and child even after offspring are fully grown. Finally, though it is always easy to read too much into a work of art with no text or context, it is pleasant to think that a bearded figure tenderly observing the birth of Erichthonius on a red-figure stamnos is Hephaestus, as close to a father as the baby has.[52] Those who find this far-fetched will perhaps be more convinced by the many moving depictions of parents and children on Attic gravestones.[53]

It is the orators who supply the most reliable evidence for Athenian attitudes. Defendants swear oaths on their children's heads and bring them into court to win the jury's sympathy.[54] Concern for children is appealed to as a common bond.[55] Apollodorus began to get letters about problems at home, which led to a longing to see his small children and wife and mother again. Very likely he did not feel this emotion at all; this is the same mother whose chastity he impugns in another speech (to be mentioned in Chapter 5). Clearly, however, he thinks his audience will judge the sentiment appropriate and credible. "What is sweeter than these?" he asks. "Why would anyone want to live deprived of them?"[56] Mantitheus tells another jury that his father brought him up and loved him (*ēgapa*), "as all of you love your children" ([Dem.] 40.8). Another Apollodorus, adoptive father of one of Isaeus's clients, had a son whom he trained and cared for, "as was fitting" (Isae. 7.14). On the other side, it is a strike against Lampis that he was little concerned about his wife and children, and Aristotle advises likely lawyers to discredit opponents by claiming that they had used the rejoinder the Egyptian soldier made to King Psammetichus: he pointed to his genitals and said, "Wherever these go, I can get children and wives."[57] Perhaps the most interesting passage does not come from a forensic context at all, but from the funeral oration ascribed to Lysias (2.75). To show gratitude to the dead, the author instructs what is to be thought of as an Athenian audience, we should esteem their parents as they did, embrace their children (*aspazoimetha*) as if we were their fathers, help their wives as they did when alive. This is more than just a reference to behavioral norms or a compliment to a particular audience. Funeral speeches were advertisements for the community as a whole, a compendium of the achievements and moral standards it liked to claim as its own. Affection for children must therefore be regarded as one of its values. And one even slaves were thought to share: the *Oeconomica*, a Peripatetic work that goes under Aristotle's name, speaks of children as hostages for slaves' good behavior, as they fear they may lose them through sale (*Oec.* 1.1344b17).

A general comment is in order at this point. It might be objected that at least some of the evidence I have adduced need not testify to meaningful emotive feelings toward children, but may merely signify a realization of their practical value. A law sometimes ascribed to Solon (and therefore regarded as old and venerable) required Athenians to provide food and lodging for their parents when they were alive and proper burial when they died.[58] It was open to anyone to bring a prosecution under this law, and those who did so were exempt from the usual penalties imposed on plaintiffs who withdrew their case or failed to win one-fifth of the votes and from the usual limitation on speaking time. Law has a greater claim to represent popular attitudes in a direct democracy like Athens than in most societies; the impression that care of parents was of special importance to the community is confirmed by the inclusion of a question on the treatment of parents in the scrutiny those selected as archons had to undergo.[59] Children were a prudent investment in a society that knew no pension plans and in which burial and tendance of the grave were important responsibilities of one's descendants; and individual Athenians were well aware of it.[60] This line of thought has led to such observations as the comment that *anagkaioi,* "relatives," a derivative of *anagkē,* "necessity," implies duty, not affection, as the basis of kin relations.[61]

How to respond? It is of course important to recall that our perceptions of the emotional context of any interpersonal situation may be misleading. An example: Bernard Vernier, writing on a village in the modern Dodecanese, has argued that it is the traditional matches, usually arranged with calculations regarding land uppermost in mind, which are nostalgically regarded as romantic. In contrast, contemporary marriages, though they (ostensibly at least) allow a freer choice, may nevertheless be viewed as coldly commercial. This runs against our expectation. According to Vernier, it arises because the economic ramifications of marriage are now likely to involve money or other forms of property which do not have the sentimental associations of land.[62] More fundamental is the fact that few cultures make so rigorous a dichotomy between practicality and sentiment as contemporary North Americans sometimes claim to. That they were closely intertwined for the ancient Athenians is indicated by the word *tokos* itself, which means both "child" and "interest on a loan or investment."[63] This should not rule out an attempt to apply our own understanding to ancient phenomena, here as elsewhere, but it does suggest how difficult the task can be. And perhaps how futile too. How could we tell if many or most Athenians did in fact care for their children only because they brought them certain benefits? To quote E. P. Thompson: "Feelings may be *more,* rather than less, tender or intense *because* relations are 'economic' and critical to mutual survival."[64] The more parents need and depend on children, in other words, the more they will care for them, like them or not. It is certainly theoretically possible to differentiate this care from what some have come to consider the real thing, concern for children as unique human individuals, though many parents do not find it so simple. But I do not know how a historian would make such a distinction with any confidence, and I suspect an Athenian could not help.

Some distinctions can be made in this discussion, however. Fathers may not feel what mothers do, sons may not be regarded just like daughters. There are, for example, some signs that daughters were devalued by their fathers. As I have already indicated, they were probably refused admission to the family and exposed more frequently than sons, a father's decision;[65] differential exposure of females is generally associated with a higher valuation of males in other cultures.[66] Girls were apparently fed less well than boys, not only another sign of diminished concern but a potential cause of what has been called passive or deferred infanticide in societies in which all children are supposed to be reared.[67] Archaic and early classical Athenian tombs that identify themselves as sons' outnumber those for daughters by about five to one.[68] Relationships are explicitly recorded in fewer than one-third of Athenian epitaphs from this period; those so singled out may therefore be regarded as of special importance to the dedicants (usually fathers). The birth of a daughter could increase friction between husband and wife; at least it does so in one comedy.[69] Better to pretend it hasn't happened; one of women's tricks, says Mnesilochus in another, is to smuggle in a slave's newborn son in exchange for a legitimate baby daughter (Ar. *Thesm.* 564–565). The daughter's fate, to become a slave, is apparently of no moment even to her mother. (It is left to a slave in New Comedy to provide caustic comment. "Could you see your master's baby brought up as a slave?" asks Habrotonon the harpist. "You'd deserve death for that" [Men. *Epitr.* 468–470].) The birth of a son, on the other hand, was a relief. "Don't worry," Praxagora inventively informs her husband, "the neighbor's had a boy" (Ar. *Eccl.* 549).

Again, this is not to say that men could not care for the daughters they did decide to raise. Girls might be named Aspasia, "welcome," or Boulete, "wanted."[70] While about 60 percent of the Greek votive statues that can be identified by gender are of boys—

and this is probably an underestimate of their original predominance—those of girls are of equal quality.[71] Aeschines attacks his political opponent Ctesiphon because he took part in a public sacrifice on the seventh day after his daughter's death, before the full period of mourning was up (3.77–78). How will such a base and child-hating (*misoteknos*) man, who cared so little for his only daughter, have any concern for the citizens of Athens, he asks. Aeschines counts on his audience to recognize some emotional tie between father and daughter, as well as the niceties of religious observance. That with girls the tie might be especially tender is suggested by Iphis in Euripides' *Suppliant Women*: "There is nothing more joyful to an aged father than a daughter. Boys have greater courage, but are less given to sweet endearments" (1101–1103).[72] Creon refers to the joy another tragic father, Oedipus, takes in his daughters, and Oedipus's last thoughts in this play are for them (Soph. *OT* 1476–1477, 1522).

But fathers did not care for daughters in just the same way they did for sons. One comic prayer, which neatly sums up the difference in attitudes, is all the more interesting because it is presented as a woman's, from the disguised Mnesilochus again. "May my sexy (*eukhoiron*) daughter meet up with a rich husband, especially if he's silly and good-for-nothing. And may my little pecker (*posthaliskon*) have brains and sense."[73] It will be noticed that both wishes are really for males. The boy's is for himself: he is to be an intelligent man. The girl's is for a certain kind of husband—she is to get a stupid one. The essential fact of an Athenian woman's life, that it is defined by her relationship with a man (or men), could hardly be clearer. Compare Apollodorus's summing up for the jury in the case of Neaera ([Dem.] 59.122). We introduce sons to our phraters and fellow demesmen, he says; we give daughters to husbands. Men engage in civic life directly, women for the most part only through their menfolk.

Sexual innuendo is an undercurrent in another comic passage, from Aristophanes' *Wasps* (605–609). Philocleon, enumerating the benefits of the juror's life, comes to the sweetest of all. When he comes home with his pay, everyone comes to greet him. First is his daughter, who washes his feet and rubs them with oil and then bends down to kiss him, calling him "pappa" (*pappizous'*) and fishing all the while with her tongue for his money, which he carries for safekeeping in his mouth. This is kiddie porn; there is no mistaking the ribald image of the little girl French-kissing her old man.[74] An additional theme in this scene is the depiction of the daughter as a gold digger, a characteristic charge in a culture in which money was controlled mostly by men and was usually accessible to women only through them.

Aristophanes' scenes of fathers and daughters do not all have this edge. Trygaeus's daughters also use pet names for him because they want something—they're hungry—but he is portrayed as genuinely disturbed by their plight (Ar. *Pax* 110–149). Even the few passages showing fathers' affection for their daughters should be enough to indicate that the difference in attitude toward daughters is not simply to be summed up as a consequence of male hostility toward women. Nor is there animosity in a remark made by Xenophon's Socrates: "We wouldn't think a loose-liver worthy of trust, if at the end of our lives we wanted to appoint a guardian to educate our sons or protect our girls" (*Mem.* 1.5.2). There is, however, a clear sense that girls were not to be allowed an equal share in the broad range of activities the Athenians described as education, or in the community life for which it was in part a preparation.

Since in its political and legal structure Athens was a community of adult males, it is not surprising that Athenian fathers tended to reinforce and reproduce the prejudices that diminished daughters' roles. It is worth wondering, however, whether individual fathers didn't occasionally wish more for their girls than the *polis* provided. Some stories staged by the Athenian dramatists seem relevant. A number of kings are bidden to sacrifice their daughters for the public good.[75] Agamemnon chooses to slay his daughter Iphigenia, "the adornment of his house," at the altar as a charm against the winds that hold his Trojan expedition in the harbor at Aulis.[76] His bargain brings a usurper to power in the city and, for himself, death on his return. Contrast Demophon. Though aware that the death of a young girl is necessary to save the descendants of Heracles from Eurystheus's army, this king of Athens refuses; no one would willingly be so senseless as to give up children, who are very dear (Eur. *Hcld.* 408–414). In the end, the Heraclids are saved by the self-sacrifice of Heracles' daughter, an element likely invented by Euripides; it is her death which ensures Athens' victory in battle against the invaders. The Athenians of the classical period prided themselves on having provided refuge for the Heraclids.[77] Euripides' introduction of the girl (elsewhere called Macaria) would contribute to their self-esteem, in that it allowed their king to fulfill an obligation to outsiders without harming any of his own household or people. Both stories imply that heading a household and belonging to, even ruling, a community imposed different demands, which were hard to reconcile. Paradoxically, the point is made more strongly by the story with a happy ending, Euripides', since the resolution it provides for the dilemma is so obviously exceptional and unexpected.

That mothers are especially close to their children was almost a cliché, found in law-court speeches, in treatises on household management, in tragedy, in scientific accounts of procreation.[78] Lycurgus exploits this expectation in his prosecution of Leocrates. In Euripides' *Erechtheus,* another Athenian king is called upon to give up his daughter to save his country from invasion, and does so, at her mother's urging. "All women are fond of children (*philoteknōn*) by nature," comments Lycurgus. If this one could love her homeland more than her daughter, surely Leocrates should not have forsaken it (*Leocr.* 99–101).[79] Of particular interest is a portion of the important passage in which Aristotle discusses affection (*philia*) within the family (*NE* 8.1161b16). This is said to stem from the affection of parents for their children, for parents love (*stergousi*) children as being part of themselves, whereas children love parents as the source of their being; we would expect progenitor to be more attached than progeny, on the analogy of the relation between a hair or a tooth and the person it is part of. Moreover, parents know children better than children know parents. Finally, a parent's affection, which begins at birth, is of longer duration than a child's, which starts only when some time has passed and the child develops understanding or at least perception. For all these reasons, Aristotle concludes, parents love children more than children love them—and this is all the more true of mothers.[80]

The assumption leaves a trace in the epigraphic record too. Mothers are as prominent as fathers among those making dedications on behalf of children in the archaic and classical periods.[81] The gap in the conventional ages of marriage for men (about thirty) and women (about fifteen) guaranteed that there would be many more women surviving as single parents than men.[82] This would tend to increase the proportion of women making dedications of this kind; the one or two dedications on behalf of a woman (or man) and her (or his) children probably come from such households. But there is no reason to believe that this is so for most of the dedications. More likely, though they were planned by both parents (and perhaps paid for by the father), it was frequently felt appropriate that the mother be identified as the parent especially concerned with children's well-being. One of Lysias's clients, opposing Philon's election to the Council of 500 at the required scrutiny of his eligibility to serve, shows how an enemy could use the expectation of a mother's ongoing love and loyalty for an adult son (31.20–23). While she was alive, Philon's mother made accusations against him. When she was reaching the end of her life, she didn't commit herself to his care, but as she had confidence in Antiphanes, who wasn't even a relative, she gave him the money for her burial. (Nicostratus's mother, on the contrary, helped him out of a legal jam by laying claim to some of his property: [Dem.] 53.28.) The link was recognized in Athenian law, for adoption severed only a man's tie with his father, not that with his mother, and brothers and sisters who had the same mother could not marry, though homopatric siblings could.[83]

Mother love is an important motif in drama too. Both Megara, Heracles' wife, and Andromache, who was Hector's, deliver touching farewells to their young children. Megara recalls the inheritance Heracles playfully bestowed on each son in turn, and mourns the marriage plans she made for them. "Which shall I take first, which last," she concludes, "to lift up, embrace and kiss?"

(Eur. *HF* 462–489). Her last words have been condemned as rhetorical artifice;[84] yet they do express a difference between a father, who apportions his gifts according to set principles, and a mother, whose love is less logical. Andromache vividly describes her child's distress, but also lingers on the sweet scent of his skin.[85] This detail is an echo of the most moving of maternal farewells, Medea's (Eur. *Med.* 1021–1077). The central difference in her case, of course, is that Megara and Andromache seek to protect their children from others, while Medea intends to kill hers by her own hand. This is a step even Clytemnestra feared to take; according to Electra's farmer husband, she killed her husband but spared her children against Aegisthus's will lest she stir up bad feeling (Eur. *El.* 30).[86] That Medea braves it is a sign of both strength and weakness. A hero's act of daring, it is also a mark of her vulnerability as a woman and mother. Her most crushing blow against her husband Jason must hurt herself as well. It is also a final irony in a play that sees men and women reverse their roles; Medea gets her way with Creon and Aegeus in succession by playing on their affection and desire for children, while the chorus of Corinthian women declares it is best not to have children at all (Eur. *Med.* 1090–1115).

In the more homely vein of comedy, one of the women who plots to take over the Athenian Assembly intends to card wool for her scantily clad children as its meeting place fills up (Ar. *Eccl.* 88–92). Preparing wool was prototypically women's work, an association already used to good effect in an earlier comedy, *Lysistrata,* where women's expertise in this area is presented as a qualification for engaging in politics. The audiences for both plays, male or predominantly male, must have found the notion of wool-working as a claim to political participation ridiculous. As was often the case, however, Aristophanes' humor is double-edged here. Women's presumptions are not more absurd than men's complacency. There were indeed poor families in the postwar Athens of *Ecclesiazusae,* and, insofar as it was apportioned by gender, the blame for the hardships of the times must have fallen to the male citizens who made public policy. Simpleminded though she may be, this woman is not only concerned about her children's comfort (as a mother should be), she is doing something about it (as fathers ought as well).

When we turn to the attitudes of children themselves, we might well expect to find that their feelings for their mothers were more intense than those for their fathers, the product of more constant and more intimate contact and of closeness in age (or at least fostered by these factors). This seems to have been the Athenian assumption. It is the mother for whom children in a fragment of Euripides' *Erechtheus* are urged to feel a lover-like passion (*erate:* Eur. fr. 358N.[2]). The orators' use of the law requiring sons to provide *tropheia* (support) when they grow up is consistent with this. Not only was the legal obligation met, but the necessity to meet it could carry weight with a jury. Apollodorus notes approvingly that Lysias forbore to bring his girlfriends into the house out of respect for his wife and for his aged mother, who lived with him ([Dem.] 59.22).[87] Other speakers ask for acquittal on the grounds that they will otherwise be unable to support their mothers when alive or bury them properly after their death.[88] Why are mothers so prominent in such contexts? Again, one reason is simply that more mothers than fathers survived into their sons' maturity.[89] But in addition it looks as if speakers felt that an approach based on a mother's plight was particularly effective. However cynical a ploy, it must have been based on a considered judgment about a jury's sentiments. Moreover, it must often have met with success if the feelings expressed in the epitaph of Telemachus, buried in the first half of the fourth century, were at all common (*IG* 2[2] 7711). Telemachus is very much missed by his children and dear wife, yet it is his mother the inscription addresses. He is buried at her right side, not deprived of her love (*sēs philias*). Of course, the law, enacted by adult males, demanded *tropheia* for fathers too, and those who ignored them were rebuked,[90] but the obligation only rarely figures in emotive appeals (as in Aeschin. 2.179). Instead we find sons who court sympathy on the grounds that they must take their fathers' part, though it would be more natural for their fathers to protect them.[91] This is not merely a reflection of the legal capacities of men and women. There is a quite different emphasis: the son is to be pitied, not the father. Similarly, in funeral speeches and other contexts both parents are said to suffer when their children cannot support them; fathers are rarely singled out for sympathy, here or elsewhere.[92]

An interesting motif involving fathers and sons in particular suggests that proper filial behavior was often thought to pass down from one generation to another. This golden rule is expressed most explicitly in Isocrates' advice to Demonicus: "Behave toward your parents as you would wish your children to behave toward you."[93] Demosthenes provides a variant. Conon's actions, and those of his sons, are proof that he does not respect his own father, for if he did honor and fear him, he would make sure his sons treated him likewise (Dem. 54.23). Bad behavior breeds. This is a recurrent motif of comedy, where Pheidippides justifies his assault on his father, Strepsiades, by recalling the beatings the older man gave him as a child (Ar. *Nub.* 1399–1451). Not only there: A man charged with beating his father (according to a story told by Aristotle) defended himself by saying his father and his father's father had done the same, and his little son would carry on the family tradition (*NE* 7.1149b8). We need not believe this story, or even believe that Aristotle did. What is of interest is that the relationship of son to father is treated as an object of inheritance, like any family possession; this is not the realm of sentiment, however conventional. A fair presumption, even on the basis of this impressionistic presentation, is that emotional feelings between sons and mothers were thought to be warmer than those involving sons and fathers, both as children and as adults.

The value the Athenians put on a proper attitude toward parents is reflected in the interest in the subject they attributed to the gods. Lycurgus, prosecuting Leocrates for leaving the city during the crisis brought on by the battle of Chaeronea, notes that the gods preside over all human affairs, but most of all over duties to parents, the dead, and themselves (*Leocr.* 94). The gods are said to love whoever reverences his parents. If a man does not love them (continues the speaker in a passage from tragedy), let him not sacrifice together with me nor sail with me at sea (Eur. fr. 852N.²).

It was possible to speak of disrespect to parents as an attack on the gods, to lump those who were guilty with men convicted of impiety, even to exalt parents to the level of the gods.[94]

Respect, loyalty, obedience. These recur frequently among the qualities expected of children, especially toward fathers.[95] The speaker of a tragic fragment assures his mother that she will always be dear to him (*prosphilē*) for the sake of what is right and her birth pangs, but adds, "I love my father above all other mortals" (Eur. fr. 1064N.[2]). The concluding lines of the fragment, though obscure, seem to explain this preference by asserting that no man should be called a woman's, but a father's. The logic may be similar to that lying behind Apollo's famous denigration of the woman's role in procreation in Aeschylus's *Eumenides* (657–666). The sentiment is not altogether surprising in a male-dominated society, but the formulation is extreme. More characteristically, the prime importance of respect for the father is left implicit, expressed through the prominence he is given in discussions of family relations. So in Aristotle's *Politics* we are told that the father rules his wife *politikōs*, like a magistrate rules a fellow citizen (except that he has no set term), and his children *basilikōs,* like a king (1.1259a38-b18). Nothing, we gather, needs be said about a mother's authority.[96] In another work, Aristotle focuses on the proper relations between father and son, arguing that they are not those of a friendship between equals. He stresses the obligations of a son to his father—they far outweigh any claims the son may have—and says that no one can ever render his father the honor he deserves (*NE* 8.1158b11, 1163b15).

The subject was significant enough, and the view expressed by Aristotle sufficiently influential, to inform the comedy of Menander. In both *Samia* and *Adelphoi,* sons relate to a father (or foster father) on terms of equality, and as a result the relationship between them is endangered or even irreconcilably disrupted.[97] In another public forum, respect for a father did a litigant credit, as disrespect disgraced him. "I am now thirty," Lysias has a client claim, "but I have never yet had a dispute with my father, nor been subject of complaint from any citizen" (19.55). Mantitheus tries to persuade a jury that Boeotus's case amounts to slander against his father's reputation—a crime no true son would commit ([Dem.] 40.45–47). More than respect alone, loyalty and obedience also were demanded, notably by Creon in an angry exchange with his son Haemon. "Put everything second to a father's opinion. It is for this that men pray to have obedient children in their homes, to pay back evil to their father's enemy and honor his friend as he does" (Soph. *Ant.* 639–644). Mantitheus is relevant again: "While my father was alive, I thought it wrong to oppose any of his wishes" ([Dem.] 40.13; cf. 58.2, 58).

These passages should not mislead us into thinking that regard and respect were not a mother's due as well. Among the noble and reverend qualities that adorn and preserve the city (according to a speech modeled on Demosthenes) are sobriety, orderliness, and respect of the young for their parents and elders ([Dem.] 25.24). Not just fathers alone. Lycurgus tells an exemplary tale about the eruption of Mount Etna. One of the younger men stopped to help an aged father, though he could have made his escape; overtaken by fire, they were nonetheless the only two saved by the gods, while others who left their parents to their fate all died (*Leocr.* 95–97). A father provides a specific instance, but the moral includes both parents (as Lycurgus makes clear elsewhere in the speech, e.g., *Leocr.* 15). General reflections in tragedy and comedy also regularly refer to both parents.[98] For both as well, respect and obedience were enforced by physical punishment.[99] But it was perhaps more often the father who imposed it, especially on older boys; it is fathers from whom Socrates imagines truant boys fleeing, and, according to one view of the division of labor nature imposes on parents, it is fathers who train or educate, while mothers nurture.[100] This might be a consequence of a mother's indulgence of her sons, or perhaps a cause. On a lekythos by the Sandal Painter, a boy beaten by a man runs for refuge toward a woman, surely his mother.[101]

This mother might merit a son's gratitude. Others too. It is somewhat startling—a mark of the unconventionality of the Socratic circle?—to find that one of Xenophon's reminiscences of his teacher deals with the proper regard of Socrates' eldest son, Lamprocles, for his mother (Xen. *Mem.* 2.2). This short conversation begins in the Socratic manner with an inquiry about those who are ungrateful (*akharistous*). It has been observed that the Athenians, in conformity with the importance assigned to attitudes toward parents, usually labeled what we would call ingratitude toward them as something quite different, impiety, and that Xenophon in this passage "comes far nearer the modern emphasis on gratitude than does anyone before him, or for many years after him."[102] We should not exaggerate the unique character of this vignette; Socrates' closing remarks are conventional enough, urging Lamprocles to pray to the gods to forgive his mistreatment of his mother and making clear that his is just a special case of the neglect of parents. But the insistence on gratitude to a mother remains remarkable, and is not (in my view) simply a case of an *a fortiori* argument. Also noteworthy, and surely related, is the emphasis placed on a mother's distinctive gifts: she conceives and carries the child at risk to her life, feeds it from her own body, gives birth with much labor, and rears and cares for it, guessing what is to its advantage and what pleases it, without knowing what thanks she will get. (We are a long way from Apollo!) Many of these are processes governed by nature and specific to women; none involves close calculation. Precisely for such acts, Xenophon implies, repayment in kind is impossible for a young man (any man), and reckoning of the extent of obligation is out of place. Again, special recognition for the mother.

Good relations between the generations were highly valued. "How sweet is concord between parents and children!"[103] Lest harmony prove hard to arrange, advice was available. Some snippets from Euripides are typical indications of the importance of moderation and an even temper. "A father who is mean to his children heavily weighs down his old age": the Greek pops with *p* sounds, regarded as unpleasant by some rhetorical theorists.[104] "It is sweet for children to find a mild father and not to be hateful to him"; the reverse is a great misfortune.[105] Two success stories: Asked if his victory in the boys' *pankration* at the Panathenaea is his main mark of distinction, Autolycus blushes and says no, it is his father he is proudest of (Xen. *Symp.* 3.12–13). If imitation is really the sincerest form of admiration, the young Alcibiades tops even this, supposedly taking over his father's lisp, carriage, and clothes.[106] Unfortunately, as in the other relationships that are the subject of these chapters, bad feeling and conflict could not always be avoided, despite good advice and better intentions.[107] As Plato's Athenian stranger puts it, "A child in his present helplessness loves and is loved by his parents, and always seeks refuge in his relatives, his only allies—even though he is likely to be at odds with them at some future time" (Pl. *Leg.* 6.754B). In treating parent-child tensions I will continue to concentrate, as do our sources, on conflict between fathers and sons, especially as these, too, reached manhood. It is instructive that the series of rebellions in which the gods Uranus and Cronus are overthrown by their sons comes to an end when Zeus swallows Metis and gives birth to a daughter, Athens' patron deity, Athena.[108]

In other ways, however, myth (or our impression of it) may mislead. The importance of the Oedipus story on the Athenian stage and its vibrant afterlife in the Western tradition almost demand a consideration of sexual rivalry as a main source of friction between fathers and sons. Another myth of special relevance to Athens, the story of Hippolytus, his father, King Theseus, and his father's wife, Phaedra, appears to confirm the centrality of this issue. In addition, the structure of the Athenian family, in which the mother (married in her mid to late teens) might be as close in age to some of her sons as to her husband, seems likely to have exacerbated such antagonism. But crucial qualifications intervene. Oedipus's is an atypical tale in more than its impact: sex between mother and son is otherwise rare in myth, usually situated on the periphery of the Greek world, often presented as the revenge of Aphrodite for a slight, or as unintentional, or both.[109] Moreover, its combination of father-killing and mother-incest is unique, and even in Oedipus's case rivalry over Jocasta is not the motive for Laius's murder.[110] Similarly, is it pedantic to point out that Hippolytus is not in fact guilty of a sexual attack on his stepmother?

Sexuality and aggression are certainly linked in these stories of fathers and sons, but it is important for their interpretation to note that both sexual advances and hostile acts are initiated by the older generation. Hippolytus spurns his stepmother, Oedipus literally goes to great lengths to avoid killing the man he thinks is his father and arguably marries his mother, quite unwittingly, only because she comes with the territory, the city of Thebes. *In praise of older women* this isn't. Achilles' mentor Phoenix provides only an apparent counterexample. Though he seduces his father's concubine, his motive is not (explicitly at least) lust but the desire to take his mother's side in a family feud (*Il.* 9.447–451). Even that most sexually charged of unfilial acts, Cronus's gory castration of Uranus, is only partly explained by hatred of his father (Hes. *Theog.* 138); his action is undertaken at the behest of his mother, who masterminds the plot and even supplies the weaponry (159–168). Likewise, Zeus's mother, Rhea, is the brains behind his own coup against Cronus (453–506). Significantly, classical Athenian references to these stories never isolate the sexual element; in fact Agathon is made to say that they were the work of Necessity, not of the god Eros.[111] To summarize, then, sexual desire in these stories primarily characterizes fathers, mothers, and others of their senior status, and the sexual conflict that exists is between them as well; sons figure mainly as allies or adversaries of the parental protagonists (on which more will be said in Chapter 6), and their sexuality is, if anything, understressed (as in the case of Hippolytus). It may therefore be legitimate to say, as E. R. Dodds does in a celebrated discussion, that "the mythological projection of unconscious desires is surely transparent" in such stories, but it is more questionable whether the concerns expressed are those of sons (as Dodds believes) or those of fathers.[112]

It is more productive to consider another common cause of conflict—money.[113] This time bad feeling arises on both sides of the generation gap. At its simplest, money trouble amounts to grousing about the costs of raising children. It involves "no small expense" to bring up a child, educate him from childhood, and introduce him to the phraters;[114] introduction to the phratry, like many other ritual acts, would involve an outlay for a sacrificial victim and perhaps other fees, and the phraters could expect a feast, as they did on the occasion of a marriage. Property owners could owe money on their taxes on account of child-rearing (*paidotrophia*) and other household and civic expenses (Dem. 22.65).

By way of contrast, Gorgias was reputed to be the wealthiest of the Sophists because he had no wife or children and was therefore free of "this most unremitting and expensive of liturgies."[115] It was a relief when children became self-supporting, "pleasant to have a son who lives on his own means" (Anaxandrides fr. 24E.). We cannot do much more than guess how considerable these expenses really were. Theophrastus's Grumbler, when told he has had a son, retorts, "If you add that I've lost half my property, you'd be speaking the truth" (*Char.* 17.7). Diogeiton, trying to exculpate himself from the charge of embezzling his grandchildren's inheritance, apparently claimed to have spent five obols a day on food for two boys and a girl and seven silver talents and 7,000 drachmas all told over eight years (Lys. 32.20); his prosecutor allows him costs of 1,000 drachmas a year for the children, a *paidagōgos,* and a slave woman, but says this is more than anyone else in the city has ever spent (28–29). A generation later, Demosthenes says that Therippides remitted 700 drachmas a year from the profits of the slave workshop he held in trust as support (*trophēn:* Dem. 27.36). This is too small a sum to provide for thirty-two or thirty-three slaves, and so must have been meant for Demosthenes and his little sister. These are certainly ample sums in some circles—more than 300 drachmas a year for each child, say, twice what it would cost to feed a family of four[116]—though it is less easy to calculate the drain they involve for Athenian propertied families. One indication: Mantitheus's mother died when he was still young, and the interest on her dowry was sufficient to rear and educate him ([Dem.] 40.50). More significant than any objective reckoning anyway is the acceptance of the idea that children were a financial burden by jurors and other fathers or potential fathers.

In his autobiographical seventh letter, Plato offers insight into a son's point of view (*Ep.* 7.324B). "When I was a young man (*neos*)," he recalls, "I had the same experience many do. I thought that if I were to take control of my property soon, I would straightway play a part in community affairs." A number of issues, logically and legally distinct though they are, are intertwined here. *Neos* is a vague word, but it is normally appropriate for a man up to the age of thirty or so; this is how Plato uses it himself.[117] Thirty was the minimum age set for a number of important offices in the Athenian democracy (such as serving on the Council of 500 and on juries), some administrative functions in public festivals, and positions of responsibility in the phratry of the Demotionidae.[118] As mentioned above, thirty or so was also probably the most common age of first marriage for Athenian males in the time Plato describes, the end of the fifth century or the beginning of the fourth. Nothing would be more natural, then, than to regard leaving the ranks of the *neoi* at thirty as an important step. But Plato has in mind more than simply reaching a chronological milestone; his political ambitions seem to have depended, to some degree at least, on coming into his inheritance, perhaps as much because this economic indicator of maturity and responsibility would validate his involvement in decisions affecting others' welfare as because the money was needed to win influence.[119]

The more adventurous would look for ways to make money on their own, especially warfare, its economic importance never to be underestimated. A *neos* like Plato might be content simply to wait until his father died to get his inheritance. But it was also possible for a father to divide up his property while he was still alive, with one son agreeing to take him (and his wife) into his own household, often now to be based in the original family home.[120] A prudent father who took this route might decide to distribute only some of his property, not all. Outlining the dispositions Conon and Nicophemus made of their goods, one of Lysias's clients reflects that even if a man gave his sons what he himself had inherited from his father (and had not acquired by his own efforts), he would save a sizable portion for himself; "everyone wishes to have money and be courted by his children rather than to be without and beg from them" (Lys. 19.36–37). There was certainly no definite age at which such a full or partial handover of property had to take place. Here too, however, thirty or so seems a likely modal age for the recipient; the father of a man of thirty would probably be at least sixty, the age at which he would retire from the last of Athens' formal civic duties, service as an arbitrator (Arist. *AthPol* 53.4).[121] We seem to be dealing with a complex of social expectations, perceived biological restraints—the philosophers and their friends at least were convinced that marrying and having children at ages that were too young or too old had serious consequences for the health of parent and child and the well-being of the family[122]—and political regulations: a man becomes fit for a wide but interconnected range of social and political rights and responsibilities in his late twenties or early thirties. Ever since he was nineteen or twenty, the age of leaving the ephebate or some less formal equivalent, the *neos* has been on all fours with his father-in-law. When he takes on the additional roles of progenitor of children, participant in the deliberative bodies of the democracy, and manager of the household's property, he can be said to supplant him. A similar sequence is followed by the Sarakatsan shepherds: a father retires at sixty, and the eldest son, age thirty, marries and takes charge of family affairs.[123]

Of course, this is very abstract and only loosely accurate even as a model. "Retired" citizens often served as jurors. Sons married at many different ages, much younger than thirty in a few cases known to us from the orators.[124] Perhaps some lived with their parents, as an imitator of Demosthenes envisages.[125] Others might still depend on their fathers for support, especially among the elite; though the story that Pericles' sons and their wives resented his tight hold on a drachma is found in no source more reliable than Plutarch (*Per.* 16.4). In any event, since property at Athens seems invariably to have been shared out to all sons at the same time, and not, for example, to each as he married, the age proposed in my sketch could be accurate for only one son in each family at best. And of course we know too little of the day-to-day details of Athenian life to flesh out this sketch with any confidence. Where, to take up only one point, did adult sons with surviving fathers live between the ephebate and marriage? The poorer *neoi,* those without property or expectations, are the most likely to have left home early; their ties with their parents probably remained weakest. The sons of smallholders and craftsmen probably stayed at home, working in the family's fields or taking a hand in its workshop or hiring out as skilled or unskilled labor, a continuation of their lives since leaving school early in their teens. Among their better-off fellows, some must have done the same, like Pheidippides and Bdelycleon in comedy. Others moved out, as perhaps Callicles and Philostratus did.[126] What might have been the consequences of pursuing these different paths? Sharing a roof would likely exacerbate tensions at the same time that contributing to the household economy diminished them.

Much must be left to the imagination. But if the picture I've outlined gives roughly the correct impression, we may at least presume that tension between father and son over inheritance was accentuated by the links with a son's prospects in other areas, and guess that it was greatest in the well-to-do social circles where fathers had something to leave and sons had political ambitions. Naturally, we would expect these tensions to be reduced when a father gave up financial control of his household's property sooner rather than later. If a father was unwilling, his sons' resentment would increase to the extent that this recalcitrance posed a barrier to marriage or political activity, and all the more if the father's own powers were thought to be failing. (This was a danger Aristotle identified, though he set the optimum age for transfer of property and the time at which a man begins to lose vigor at about seventy, consistent with the later age of marriage he recommended.)[127] In extreme cases a son (or someone acting on his behalf) could seek to protect his interests through a *graphē paranoias*, a lawsuit asserting that the father was no longer competent to manage his affairs.[128] There is a story (alas, unlikely) that his son or sons brought such an action against the playwright Sophocles, who defended himself successfully by reading passages of his last tragedy, *Oedipus at Colonus*.[129] It is possible (one can hardly say more) that some cases were brought on by the conflict between traditional relationships of authority and respect imposed on children within the family and the impetus to play a more active role in the political life of the *polis*. But an impatient son would have to calculate whether success in such a lawsuit would outweigh the stigma he would likely incur in bringing it.[130] This must go some way toward explaining why examples are so rare—Sophocles' is the only one we hear of. Fathers, too, had a legal recourse, disowning an adult son (*apokēryxis*), but again little is known of this.[131]

The passage from Lysias quoted above (19.36–37) indicates

that Athenian fathers were well aware of the financial risks involved in giving up control of property to their sons. Psychologically, too, such a retirement might give grounds for unease, not necessarily restricted to fathers alone. Sons might also find that the passing of the old order inspired intimations of mortality. It is perhaps not out of place to support such speculation with a citation from a character in a modern novel, Saul Bellow's Wallace Gruner: "What I'm finding out is that when the parents are living, they stand between you and death. They have to go first, so you feel pretty safe. But when they die, you're next, and there's nobody ahead of you in line." [132]

Conflicts of this kind must have been of great importance to those involved, but how significant were they in the community as a whole? One valuable approach is to establish what have been called the demographic realities of the situation. In a series of important studies, Richard Saller has de-emphasized the practical effect of the Roman institution of *patria potestas,* demonstrating that at the age of thirty, only 19 percent of Roman men outside the elite would have had a father living, and at thirty-five, only 12 percent. [133] Saller's results are based on a computer simulation for which an age at first marriage of thirty was assumed for this stratum. These figures should therefore be roughly valid for Athens, which most likely was not very different in demographic character; there, too, only one or two of every ten men reaching the age of marriage would still have a father alive. This would seem to set the upper limit for the number of sons involved in the particular conflict I have been concerned to trace.

Yet even these demographic realities allow some room for interpretation. I'm reminded of that hoary subject, "the Jewish question"; many in the circles most directly affected prefer to call this "the Christian question." It depends on the point of view. While relatively few sons would still have a father when they reached the age of marriage, more fathers—still a minority, but quite a substantial one—would live to see at least one son married. Using the same life-table that underlies Saller's calculations, we may conclude that some one-third (33 percent) of men reaching thirty could expect to survive until sixty, and more than one-fifth (22

Children and Childhood in Classical Athens

percent) until sixty-five.[134] The number of families affected would be fewer since some would have no sons at all, others no sons who reached maturity. But adoption, a customary recourse, would supply sons in many instances. Two additional thoughts. First, since property was divided among all sons at the same time, division (and concern about it) would affect not only the oldest son (the one most likely to reach the age of marriage while the father was alive) but younger ones as well. Second, and more important, despite elaborate methodologies, the future was no easier for the Athenians to predict than it is for us. Many fathers, many sons, died younger than they anticipated. Their expectation of what life had in store would have included the possibility of tensions over property as both parties aged; examples of disputes were surely known to them in so small a community. Even this potential for disagreement would presumably have colored the relationship between father and son, though it is hard to know just how.

Once again, subjective impressions are a necessary supplement to the quantitative approach. The early handover of property and its consequences are among the themes of Aristophanes' *Wasps*, staged in 422.[135] The two main characters in this comedy are Philocleon ("Cleon-lover"), an old man who has given up control of his property, and his son Bdelycleon ("Cleon-hater"), with whom he lives. This father and son are dissimilar not only in their opinions of Cleon, the most famous Athenian proponent of a vigorous prosecution of the Peloponnesian War, but also in their natures. Bdelycleon is a sober, even straight-laced, young man; his father is a rascal, a self-described thief and coward (easier to like than to admire) who spends his time serving as a juror in the Athenian courts. He prides himself on the godlike powers the position gives him (619–627), and on the way he is free to abuse it, by doing harm (320–324, 340), awarding *epiklēroi* to whomever he likes (583–586), and convicting every defendant who comes before him (158–160).

As the play begins, Philocleon is under virtual house arrest at his son's orders, and the early action is taken up with his attempts to escape so that he can present himself for jury duty; he is aided by a chorus of old men, his fellow jurors and the wasps of the

112

play's title. Unsuccessful, he accedes to his son's suggestion to satisfy his need to sit in judgment by hearing an unusual form of domestic dispute, the case of a dog that has stolen some cheese (a thinly disguised reference to recent events in Sicily). Overcome by pity and fooled by Bdelycleon, he votes for the first time in his career for acquittal. "I'm finished!" he exclaims (997). Indeed the rest of the play, episodic after the *parabasis* (the chorus leader's address to the audience) like many of Aristophanes' comedies, features a rather different Philocleon, a new man. His rebirth is symbolized by a change of costume. After swearing that he will never give up his trusty old cloak while he is alive (1122–1124), Philocleon does in the end don the new Persian garment proffered by his son (1133–1153). He is still unquestionably an old man, as the text often reminds us.[136] But he has given up the severity of the elderly juror in favor of the sprightliness (and silliness) of youth, and exchanged the pleasures of passing judgment for the role of student, being instructed in the ways of polite society by his son. Not very effectively; acting out of turn at a posh party, he incurs the wrath of a fellow guest, who threatens him with a lawsuit. "You'll pay for this, and you would even if you were a young man."[137] Philocleon, no longer so enamored of the law, is content to act as young as he feels. "You're out of date!" is his response.[138]

The reversal of roles becomes still more explicit when Philocleon turns to chatting up a slave girl:[139]

> If you're a good girl now, I'll have you freed and keep you as my mistress, piglet—when my son dies. But now I'm not yet in control of my property, for I'm young (*neos*) and under a close guard. My kid watches me, and he's a bad-tempered skinflint.[140] He has no father except me, so he's afraid I'll be corrupted. There he is. . . . Take this torch, and I'll make a fool of him like a young man, just as he did to me once before [my initiation in] the Eleusinian Mysteries.[141]

A little later, Philocleon is threatened with a charge characteristically brought against a young man, *hybris;*[142] and in the finale he displays his new youth again by dancing the comedy off stage.

We should not be too hasty in generalizing from this or any other set of personages in Aristophanes. There is no reason to

113

think that the other elderly jurors, Philocleon's allies, also have given up control of their properties; their sons are apparently younger than his, and their keen awareness of the cost of oil confirms that they still pay for such things themselves (251–253, cf. 293–313). Nor is Philocleon's behavior to be attributed to his present position alone; accounts of earlier escapades indicate that he was never a solid citizen (354–357, 1200–1201). Nevertheless, the contrast between his attitudes and his son's is unmistakable; as is the link between control of property and responsibility (or irresponsibility) in other areas.

Wasps thus provides a dramatic illustration of the way household relations established early in life could change as children took on more of the roles and attributes of citizens. Of course, the case of fathers and sons was particularly apt to be treated in terms of reversals precisely because the shifts in their relative legal, economic, and political power were in fact the greatest. Tensions and transformations in other household relationships were less extreme, but as we will see in Chapters 5 and 6, still significant.

Five

Brothers, Sisters, and Grandparents

Brothers

lose and cordial relations between brothers was a widely recognized ideal at Athens. A fragment of Menander even speaks of a "passion (erōs) for concord" among brothers (Men. fr. 809E.). We may suspect that this was fostered in childhood. Certainly numerous *choes* portray boys playing together or otherwise sharing a scene, and though we cannot be sure that these represent brothers, it seems likely enough, especially in the depictions of children of different ages.[1] Nor can we tell whether the activities depicted on these *choes* were meant to reflect everyday life, the festival of the Anthesteria itself, or some ideal, but in any case the notion that brothers belong together is obvious. Ties with brothers also find more public and more formalized expression on tombstones and in dedications.[2] But the best evidence comes from speeches before Athenian courts, in which affective ties often carry as much weight as legal arguments.[3]

A speaker makes a point of saying that he and his half-brother by the same mother were brought up together from childhood, were very affectionate, never quarreled;[4] a kind of character refer-

Fig. 14. Brothers on a *chous*

ence (Isae. 9.30).[5] Another claims a man wouldn't conceal a mother's misconduct from his brother (Dem. 36.20). It was expected that brothers support each other in court, as Callicrates, for example, does in bringing suit on behalf of his brother Callicles.[6] This assistance might extend to more dubious maneuvering to avoid penalty, and to interpersonal policy by other means, illegal acts such as breaking and entering and theft.[7] So strong was this expectation that a speaker could dismiss a brother's testimony as unreliable or, conversely, argue that an incriminating statement by one brother against another must be true, or say that an opponent's guilt is so manifest that even his own brothers and sons would convict him.[8] When brothers on the other side are at odds, it is presented as *prima facie* evidence of guilt or at least moral depravity. Aristogeiton has so little to recommend him that his own brother, a twin at that, once brought a charge against him; Theocrines is so heartless that he took a bribe rather than prosecute his brother's murderer.[9] To take sides against your own brother, therefore, requires apology—even if he is only a half-brother (Antiph. 1.1, 5). Nor would one want to be blamed for setting brothers against each other (Isae. 2.29). Even a brother's neutrality demands explanation: Apollodorus astonishingly alleges that his brother Pasicles has failed to join him in prosecuting Phormion because he is in fact not his father's son, and should be called "adversary," not "brother" (Dem. 45.83–84). That Apollodorus should publicly insult his mother in this way is an indication of the persuasive force of the idea that brothers should stick together, and of the danger it poses to his case. Yet the very fact that Aristogeiton, Theocrines, and Apollodorus at one time or another fail or are failed by their brothers testifies to the fragility of this ideal.

This is nicely illustrated by Xenophon's Cyrus, who, in his deathbed advice to his sons, praises the power of the bond between brothers at some length, stressing the effects of growing up in the same household (*Cyr.* 8.7.14–19). He then rather spoils the effect by remarking that brothers are friends as a rule—but sometimes they aren't (8.7.24, cf. *Hiero* 3.7). Mythology supplies further indication of the range of fraternal relations, including memorable types of concord and discord both. The Spartan princes Castor and Polydeuces were so close that Polydeuces killed a man who slandered his brother (Plut. *Mor.* 483C). In a fight against Idas and Lynceus, Castor was killed and Polydeuces wounded. Rescued by Zeus, Polydeuces refused to accept immortality, and the two brothers were allowed to alternate every day among gods and mortals.[10] Their fraternal solidarity is stressed by comparison with their sisters, Helen (herself associated with divinity) and Clytemnestra. Both sisters betray their husbands, and so lack the loyalty their brothers demonstrate. They are forces of disunity within the new family they've established by marriage, just as Castor and Polydeuces are examples of how the original family of birth can be maintained. A second story, featuring rival brothers, also is set outside Athens, but was presented on stage by each of the city's three great tragedians. Oedipus's sons Eteocles and Polyneices fall out over their inheritance and each dies by the other's hand.

This pattern, in which ideals of solidarity and cooperation are frequently tested by fraternal rivalry, is perhaps characteristic of the Mediterranean culture area. Peristiany suggests that both the affection between brothers and the ill-feeling that results when the ideal is transgressed are particularly strong in this region.[11] He quotes a proverbial question, "Who but your brother would have gouged out your eye?" Aristotle cites a tragic tag with similar implications, "Difficult are the wars of brothers," and elsewhere notes that some oligarchies, concerned about such family feuds, forbid brothers (and other family members) to hold office together.[12]

A convenient compendium of sources of conflict is given in Plutarch's essay *On Brotherly Love* (*Mor.* 478A–492D). Though written in or just before the second century of our era, this work draws on examples from the whole range of Greek history down to Plutarch's own day. Enmity between brothers, according to Plutarch, may arise from rivalry for parents' affection, differences in ability or achievement, competition for honors or office, the instigation of wives and other intimates, the roles of younger and older, or childhood squabbles. (These are presented in an interesting progression: over care of animals, over quails or cocks, over contests in the palaestra, in the hunt or in horse races, and then over "more important matters.") Some of these factors were perceived to be at play by writers of the classical period as well. Even within the same household, Plato notes, some sons of the same mother and father may be unjust, others just (*Leg.* 1.627C). As for roles related to birth order, older brothers were expected to look out for their younger siblings, an obligation on which Eurydice relied when she entrusted her small sons (one Philip, the future king of Macedon) to the Athenian general Iphicrates and reminded him that he was their adopted brother (Aeschin. 2.28).[13] But insisting on the prerogatives of age, like challenging its authority, could give grounds for conflict. Sophocles' Polyneices regards it as shameful to give in to a younger brother (*OC* 1422–1423). In Menander's *Aspis,* Smicrines insists on the priority owed to his age (172, 255). When he addresses his younger brother as *pai,* "my boy," Chaere-crates throws the word in his face, referring to his slave girlfriend as *paida* to stress her youth and unsuitability (257–258).[14] This issue was interesting enough to figure in one of Xenophon's Socratic anecdotes. Socrates, stressing the importance of brothers, scandalizes an associate by recommending that he take the initiative in improving relations with his older brother (*Mem.* 2.3.15–16). But there is one other important root of dissension—Plutarch says most commentators make it their starting point—the division of the inheritance.[15]

Inheritance at Athens was partible. Though the firstborn son had certain privileges—*presbeia*—involving such things as claims to a family name or first choice in the division of property, in principle all sons shared equally in the estate. (Of course, this could not guarantee that all would remain equally prosperous.)[16] A small plot of land, therefore, might not only be inadequate to support more than the smallest family, its subdivision into two or more parts might impoverish all heirs.

That this was perceived to be a problem, and that solutions were not straightforward, is evident from a passage in the *Works and Days* of Hesiod, a poet living in Boeotia, just north of Attica, in the archaic period. Hesiod presents himself as a relatively poor farmer, offering advice to others like him. "There should be one son to feed his father's household," he says. "In this way wealth will increase in the house." But, he continues, "May you die old, leaving a second son. Zeus may easily provide limitless wealth for more" (376–379). It is hard not to feel that Hesiod is expressing a somewhat confused attitude toward what we would now call a family-planning strategy.[17] The depth of his concerns, though not necessarily their precise content, comes through clearer in his less explicitly didactic poem, *The Theogony.* Here we learn of Cronus and Zeus, both youngest sons, both put out to die, who survive to overthrow their fathers (37–182, 453–506); of Ceto's youngest, a terrible snake (333–335); of Gaea's, Typhoeus, who has (among other horrors) 100 snake heads (820–835). With these frightening figures we may contrast Nereus, eldest son of Pontus, gentle, kind, and just (233–236). The extra son represents a risk; his birth may have extraordinary impact, for good or for ill.[18]

Such traditional tales appear to reflect the concerns of parents. What of the brothers themselves? It is common for anthropologists and social historians to associate partible inheritance and fraternal discord.[19] Ancient examples abound. Hesiod himself was at odds with his brother over an inheritance, Histiaea suffered a civil war because of a brothers' quarrel about land (Arist. *Pol.* 5.1303b33), and Athenian disputes, sometimes very bitter ones, are mentioned in the law-court speeches. It is alleged, for example, that Thudippus assaulted his brother Euthycrates over the division of an estate; Euthycrates died a few days later (Isae. 9.17). Pantaleon is said to have deprived his brother of his patrimony (Lys. 10.5). But it is also important to recognize that the members of societies in which partible inheritance is practiced may take steps to minimize such strains. It has been suggested that enmity among brothers is likely to be greater when shares are given out at their marriages, largely because changes in the family's wealth or in the number of heirs over time may result in inequality. In this case, a father may mediate, watching over his sons to see that they do nothing foolish, as Democritus suggests, perhaps thinking of customs in his native Abdera (68 B 279D.-K.). Conversely, harmony among brothers is fostered by postponing division of the estate until the father dies—but this in turn increases bad feelings across the generations.[20] In other words, the consequences of partible inheritance are not inevitable, but resolution of conflicts among one group may exacerbate others.

Athenian brothers often went to some lengths to avoid conflict over division of property, one dividing the property and the other choosing his portion ([Dem.] 48.12), one agreeing to take a smaller share (as a speaker prides himself on doing: Lys. 16.10).[21] Still more striking is the reluctance of some brothers to dissolve the original household.[22] Some land might be left undivided; capital might be apportioned, but the land held in common; properties might not be divided at all.[23] It is not easy to estimate how common this was; Aristotle seems to regard it as old-fashioned.[24]

In the first of the cases just mentioned, we are explicitly told that the property remained undivided because one brother wished to remain unmarried; in the second it is probable that one of the three brothers involved died before he could marry and that another, who was blind, never wed. This need not mean, however, that properties remained undivided only when brothers did not marry. In [Demosthenes] 44, Meidylides offers his daughter to his brother, and it is possible that the estate would have remained intact if his brother had agreed to marry her. Furthermore, there may have been an economic inducement to leave estates undivided. In his speech *On the Symmories,* Demosthenes lists those holding property in common among the citizens exempted from paying for the costs of a warship (14.16). The lexicographer Harpocration's comment on this passage indicates that the excluded property might previously have been liable for liturgies (s. *koinōnikōn*). Whether joint ownership brought freedom only from the trierarchy or from liturgies in general (the strict construction of Harpocration's note) is not known. It would be surprising, however, if the burden shifted to other property owners in this way were not resented, and the problem of supplying warships (or funds for other public expenditures) for the community were not made more severe. Thus, just as the division of the inheritance to establish separate households might involve strains on fraternal solidarity, so, too, maintenance of an undivided estate might lead to tension with the community as a whole, or with some part of it. Thus Eucrates' son makes a point of telling jurors that he and his brothers have each performed liturgies for the *polis,* which therefore benefits as much as possible from their property (Lys. 18.21, cf. Isae. 7.5).

Brothers and Sisters

The relationship of brothers and sisters is of course a special case of that between men and women in general. At Athens, very special indeed. Relations between adult men and women were generally characterized by difference and distance. Government and politics, the law courts, and large-scale trade were reserved for

121

men; women did not vote or hold office, represent themselves in court, control significant amounts of property, even (among the elite at least) do the shopping. Furthermore, husbands and wives were so separated by age—men marrying at about thirty, women at fifteen or soon after—that they might almost be said to belong to distinct generations. But Athenian childhood presents a contrast, a time when boys and girls of the same family, more or less of an age, were often together, especially within the home and its environs. More surprising, perhaps, the close links established between brothers and sisters in childhood were often maintained in later life, and protected by Athenian patterns in the devolution of property. These bonds must be part of any complete picture of the relations between men and women at Athens.

"It's hard for women to get out," says Calonice in Aristophanes' *Lysistrata* (16). Calonice has a watchful husband; but in general an Athenian woman's place was in the home.[25] This was especially so for a young woman. "A woman who travels outside the house must be of such an age that onlookers might ask, not whose wife she is, but whose mother": Athenian etiquette according to a lost speech of Hyperides (fr. 205 Jensen). For an unmarried girl to go out in public was perhaps particularly unseemly. The speaker of Lysias 3 accuses Simon of breaking into his house and alarming his sister and nieces, who had lived such a respectable life that they would be ashamed to be seen even by their relatives.[26] We may count on some exaggeration here, but it does not sound as if an Athenian jury would have found it incredible for girls to be so sheltered.[27] Nor would an Athenian audience: Oedipus rebukes his sons for staying home like girls while his girls work to support him; Helen refuses to send Hermione to Clytemnestra's tomb because "it is not nice for girls to creep through the crowd."[28]

Even within the home, women had a special place. Larger houses at any rate had a room or suite of rooms in which women worked and otherwise spent much of their day, the women's apartments, the *gynaikōnitis*.[29] In two-story houses, the *gynaikōnitis* might be upstairs. This is the layout of Euphiletus's small house (*oikidion*: Lys. 1.9).[30] So, too, in Aristophanes' *Ecclesiazusae*, Praxagora imagines women regaling homecoming revelers with accounts of the beautiful women who await them upstairs (698) and, later in the play, a young man coaxes his girlfriend to run down and open the door for him (962).[31] This arrangement would provide privacy and protection. But in other houses—like the one in Lysias 3—the *gynaikōnitis* seems to have been on the ground floor, presumably to ensure easier access to water for cooking and washing.[32] The word *parthenōn*, which occurs in a few passages in tragedy, is probably an equivalent of *gynaikōnitis*, found in prose and comedy but not in tragedy.[33] It is interesting, however, that unmarried girls are mentioned each time the word is used. *Parthenōn* is otherwise applied to a part of a temple used for girls' choruses or young female participants in cult activities.[34] Just possibly, therefore, very grand houses like the palaces mentioned in tragedy had a still more secluded apartment for girls.[35] For the most part, however, we should imagine the *gynaikōnitis* as an area for both women and girls. But not for them alone: young boys shared the lives of girls and women too.

We have already seen (in Chapter 2) that women usually ate with their children, including boys. In general, caring for children was women's work. We may take Xenophon's Ischomachus as a spokesman for a widely held opinion: "Knowing he had created the woman and had imposed on her the nourishment of infants, the god gave to her a larger portion of affection for newborns than to the man" (*Oec.* 7.24).[36] Women must have loved children, runs the argument, they've made so many of them; and they look after them too. In contrast, says Aristotle, "No male creatures take trouble over their young" (*Gen. An.* 3.759b7). There is a similar, more-or-less unconscious, and thus revealing assumption in Plato's *Laws*. The Athenian stranger—who regards child rearing as one of women's three functions, along with domestic service and household management (7.806A)—speaks of children as under the care of *paidagōgoi* and teachers after they have left their nurses and mothers (7.808E). The implication is that children, including boys, are in the hands of women until they are old enough to require more serious attention. Much of the childcare assumed here would surely take place in the *gynaikōnitis*.

Vases and grave reliefs occasionally show boys and women to-

Fig. 15. A boy and a woman in the *gynaikōnitis*

gether in contexts that suggest the *gynaikōnitis*. A red-figure cup by the Sabouroff Painter bears several scenes that "depict life in the women's quarters (the boy is still with his mother)."[37] A red-figure pyxis, perhaps by the Aberdeen Painter, shows a large wool-basket, setting the scene in a *gynaikōnitis* where women play with birds and carry a dish and jewel boxes; a naked boy stands nearby and reaches toward one of them.[38] A grave relief from the fourth century depicts a woman working wool while a girl stands at the right with a cat and a young boy plays with a dog at her feet.[39] It is of course quite impossible to establish how long boys shared women's space in this way; no doubt there was a good deal of variation within the community, and not just along the lines of the divisions between richer and poorer. One intriguing piece of evidence suggests that in some cases boys might be quite grown up. Plutarch's account of the liberation of Thebes from Spartan domination in 379 includes a pretty story about Charon and his son. Summoned to a feast by the *tyrannos* Archias, Charon brought his son from the *gynaikōnitis* and entrusted him to Pelopidas (*Pel.* 9.5). Elsewhere in Plutarch we learn that the boy was about fifteen (*Mor.* 595B). Though the source is late and the story has no direct reference to Athens, it does give some idea of what later Greeks thought was possible in a classical city-state.[40] Most significant for my purpose here are scenes in which both boys and girls are present. An example is another red-figure pyxis, by the Leningrad Painter, on which one woman spins, others, too, are busy with wool-working, a baby boy sits on the ground, and another is carried piggyback by a girl.[41] A few *choes* also feature boys and girls together; these may be brothers and sisters or other close relatives, but we cannot be sure. At any rate, these vase paintings do show that boys and girls could associate at an age when I have suggested both were being raised in the *gynaikōnitis*. A girl shakes a rattle for a baby boy; two boys and a girl lean with both hands on a tortoise, which crawls toward a boy holding out a branch; a girl stoops to a little boy; a girl and a boy hold a hoop for a dog to jump through; a girl shows a *chous* to a baby boy (who is larger than she is).[42]

Grave reliefs also show the association of male and female children.[43] Here we may be more certain that brothers and sisters are

Fig. 16. A girl shakes a rattle for a baby boy

shown. Young Mnesagora holds out a bird to Nicochares.[44] A memorial for Chaerestrate and Lysandrus shows a girl giving a bird to a standing boy.[45] On another stele from the later fifth century, a boy and a girl face each other and clasp hands; a small child sits between them and puts his hands on the boy's knees.[46] The bearded Euempolus displays a bird to a boy and a girl—probably his children.[47] Demonice's fourth-century gravestone shows a girl with a bird and a ball, and a boy behind her.[48] On the stele of Nicandrus, a young boy holds a bird in his left hand and gives his right to a girl, a little smaller, who stands in front of him.[49]

One famous gravestone, which predates the classical period, deserves special mention. This is the grave stele parents erected for a youth (Megacles?) around 540–535.[50] It shows a naked youth standing with a smaller female figure. The inscription on the stele is mutilated, but it seems clear that the pair are brother and sister (*IG* 1² 981). The youth has an aryballos, a small oil flask associated with sport, hanging from his left wrist. It is not likely that young athletes were in the habit of parading about naked with their little sisters. The representation, then, is not naturalistic, and the great disparity in the height of the two figures may well indicate their relative importance rather than a great difference in age. It is interesting, therefore, that the youth's left arm is held over his sister's

Fig. 17. Grave stele of a youth and his little sister

head. His arm is bent and his hand holds a ball; it is possible that the pose is merely the sculptor's solution to a problem of composition. But the effect of the position of the arm is to portray the youth as his sister's protector.[51]

Many of the scenes I have referred to seem to show boys and girls at play, but the real explanation may not be so simple. Research on a large number of modern cultures has brought out the important role traditionally played by siblings in childcare. According to the broadest survey, of 186 societies, "nonparental caretaking is either the norm or a significant form of caretaking in most."[52] In more than 50 percent of the societies sampled, the mother's role is supplemented to a significant extent by others; in about one-quarter, it is older children (mostly siblings) who look after infants, and their role becomes still more important as their brothers and sisters grow. For example, girls in two villages in Java and Nepal have been found to spend an average of 1.7 hours a day doing childcare from as early an age as six, more than any other group except for women from ages thirty to thirty-nine.[53] Most of this childcare is decidedly informal, and is supervised (at a distance) by one or more adults; it may well take the form of play. But it is play which has a purpose, to distribute some of the burden of child-minding and so to give adults freedom to pursue other tasks. Naturally, much of it is set where these tasks are performed.

The wide distribution of sibling care of this kind raises the presumption that it was important at Athens too, with slaves often acting in the supervisory role. We can say no more than that this presumption is consistent with the iconographic evidence cited here. Our texts are mostly mute. One exception: Sophocles' Electra says she raised her brother Orestes herself. "You were never more dear to your mother than you were to me," she cries when she learns of his death, "nor did the household raise you: I was your nurse" (*El.* 1143–1148, cf. 603–604). Of course, this outburst, Electra's claim to have been the mother Clytemnestra was not, can tell us nothing about the childcare strategies of Sophocles' audience. But the warm emotions Electra recalls for her baby brother are not so irrelevant.[54]

The close relations established in childhood continued when

Athenian brothers and sisters grew up.[55] To return to gravestones, Archedice, daughter of the exiled tyrant Hippias, was honored by a famous epigram commissioned by her brothers (Thuc. 6.59.3).[56] Gnathon died despite the care of his sister, who nursed him when he was sick and set up his memorial when he died (*IG* 1² 975). Mnesarete's death left grief to her husband, mother, and brothers, a good reputation to her child; Archestrate's brought grief to her mother, brother, husband, and son.[57] But the brother of Callisto and Phile—they may have erected the monument—left them honor.[58] Again, the impression of consideration and concern is confirmed and supplemented by other sources. The expectation that brothers would assist sisters is exploited by Euripides for purposes of pathos. Iphigenia, begging her father, Agamemnon, for her life, asks the baby Orestes to join her in her plea by crying along with her (*IA* 1241–1248). Though small, she says, he is a help to those dear to him. The appeal underlines the desperate position Iphigenia is in. Neither of those she would otherwise have counted on can help her here: her father is an enemy, her brother still a nestling (*neossos*), a word used elsewhere in Euripides for children in peril.[59]

Brothers were not always so powerless. The tyrannicide Harmodius was partly motivated by an insult to his sister (Thuc. 6.54–56). Hipparchus, angered by the youth's rejection of a sexual advance, invited his sister to be a *kanēphoros* in a procession and then turned her away. The implication was that she was unworthy because of some sexual misconduct, a slur against her and her whole family that her brother was determined to avenge.[60] This attitude was not characteristic of the archaic period alone. "It is alleged that I followed Charippus's wife at their wedding procession and urged her to leave him," reports the speaker of Hyperides' speech *In Defense of Lycophron* (3–8). "Ridiculous! Her brother was there too. Would anyone listen to such remarks about his sister and not kill the speaker?"[61] Brothers provided assistance in more mundane material respects as well, serving as their sisters' *kyrioi* in the absence of a father, finding a husband for them, or taking them in when their marriages ended in divorce or death. A speaker says that the loss of property in dispute means that he and his family, though poor, will have to look after his widowed sister and her many children (Lys. 19.33). Ensuring that a fatherless sister married well, with an appropriate dowry, was an especially pressing concern, equal in importance, perhaps, to protecting her honor (itself important in guaranteeing a good match); each might be regarded as a test of male competence.[62] Anyone would choose to borrow rather than fail to pay the dowry to a sister's husband, we are told in one speech in the Demosthenic corpus (30.12);[63] it is unlikely that a rich man would defraud a sister of her dowry, we read in another (40.25).

As in relations between brothers, the reality did not always match the ideal. But those who failed to meet such standards could expect abuse. It is to Diocles' discredit that he didn't try to find a husband for his sister, though she was of marriageable age; Olympiodorus ought not to let his sister and niece live in poverty.[64] Timocrates shouldn't have "sold his sister into export"— married her to a Corcyraean (Dem. 24.202–203, cf. [Dem.] 25.55). Are these attitudes and activities merely dutiful responses to social pressures? To an extent, of course they are. But a few passages suggest that sisters could count on influence based on an intimate personal relationship. It is said to have been Apollodorus's great regard for his half-sister which led him to adopt her son as his heir (Isae. 7.14). Similarly, Plangon could promise Mantias that she would induce her brothers to adopt his son Boeotus ([Dem.] 40.10).[65]

Sisters were more restricted in their activities, but they reciprocated as they could. Elpinice is said to have persuaded Pericles to drop bribery charges against her brother Cimon.[66] The story, like others about Elpinice, is a vehicle for sexual innuendo, and therefore suspect; but it might be argued in its defense that it is precisely such able and aggressive women who attract slanders in male-dominant societies. Theotime made a dedication to Athena on the Acropolis which her brother had vowed.[67] Onetor's sister colluded with him to defraud Demosthenes; Diocles' sister pretended she was pregnant in an attempt to further his designs on her husband's estate; the sisters of others visited them in jail.[68] After the battle of Chaeronea, women are said to have crouched in the doorways of Athens, inquiring for the safety of their husbands, fathers, or brothers—"a spectacle degrading to them and to the city" (Lyc. *Leocr.* 40). To show less regard, once again, was unusual, even suspicious. Euphiletus's first clue that his wife was unfaithful came when she powdered her face before her brother had been dead thirty days (Lys. 1.14).[69] Her insouciance could be set against exceptional behavior at the other extreme, a woman who killed herself in grief at her brother's death (Lys. fr. 22 Thalheim). Sisters could help their brothers less directly as well, notably in the involvement of their husbands in the business transactions and lawsuits from which they themselves were normally excluded.[70]

This capacity of sisters to come to their brothers' aid is a fundamental aspect of Sophocles' dramatic treatment of the story of Oedipus. The theme is present in *Oedipus at Colonus,* in which the blind Oedipus refers to Antigone and Ismene, his sole supporters, as his sisters (535), and says that Creon is a bad brother because he brings up his sister Jocasta's shameful marriage (978–980), and Polyneices appeals to the bond between himself and his sisters (1275, 1405). It is central to *Antigone.* The heroine is equally loyal to both her dead brothers, to the extent that she disobeys Creon, her uncle and king, and ignores his order to leave the traitor Polyneices unburied, and then justifies her act in a strange and often-criticized speech valuing her ties with him over any others, including those with a husband or a child (904–920).[71] It is, I think, clear that Sophocles means his audience to find both Creon, who insists on the rights of the community, and Antigone, who exalts family feeling while rejecting a woman's traditional role within it, extreme in their views. The equivalence of the duties owed to the *polis* and the regard a brother demands, each presented as problematic when pushed too far, serves to stress how important the tie between brother and sister could appear.

There are enough references here to bickering and betrayal to prevent us from taking too rosy a view of this relationship. The dissolution of the household at a sister's marriage raised the question of her loyalty, a question that is a constant undercurrent in Greek myth. Althaea, who killed her son Meleager to avenge her brothers, shared the male mind with Medea, whose marriage to

Jason was made possible by the murder of her brother.[72] The solution followed by Zeus, to take his full sister Hera as his wife, was
an ideal, producing as it did children who were all female (Eilei-
thyia and Hebe, associated with childbirth and youthful beauty)
or all male (Ares, god of war), but one forbidden to mere mortals.[73] A more practical consideration was involved as well, since
as a rule a sister took some of the family's property with her in the
form of a dowry when she married; division of the inheritance
again. In this case, however, brothers' resentment would tend to
be reduced by two factors. First, sisters married young, usually
well before their brothers. The dowry they took with them was
compensated for materially by the fact that they no longer had to
be supported from the household itself from an early age, and socially by their importance in forming links with other households,
from which brothers might later benefit. Second, the amount of
the dowry was relatively modest, an issue that deserves some attention.[74]

Richard Saller has argued that Roman dowries were neither
very large (as dowries often were in early modern Europe) nor
merely minimal, a trousseau. They were "not intended to contribute substantially to the production or wealth" of a daughter's new
household, but rather served to "maintain the daughter in a style
appropriate to her new position."[75] Saller does not commit himself
on the size of Athenian dowries, but the introduction to his discussion leaves the impression that they were proportionately
larger.

A dowry may be considered large or small in any or all of three
ways: in relation to living costs, as a proportion of the estate from
which it is paid, and in respect to the shares of that estate which
go to others. According to all these criteria, dowries at Athens were
moderate, comparable to those at Rome. We have information on
some forty-odd dowries for daughters and other members of the
family's junior generation such as sisters, granddaughters, and
nieces from Athens or areas under Athenian influence in or just
after the classical period.[76] Our sources are varied: speeches written for litigants in lawsuits, *horoi* (boundary stones recording liens

on property pledged to guarantee all or part of a dowry), documents from the islands of Mykonos and Tenos, a few passages of New Comedy (all or nearly all from plays by Menander), scattered references in other literary genres.[77] Among them, the evidence of New Comedy is anomalous and problematic; I will defer discussing it until the last chapter. The other sources, different and often difficult though they are, produce quite a consistent picture.

In seven instances, we are told or can calculate both a daughter's or a sister's dowry and the value of the estate from which it is paid.[78] Two of these dowries, involving the estate of Ciron (Isaeus 8) and that of Philostratus ([Demosthenes] 42), do indeed come to a substantial amount, perhaps as much as one-quarter of the whole. But in neither case are calculations or conclusions straightforward. The dowry paid for Ciron's daughter amounted to 2,500 drachmas. Unluckily, the size of the estate itself is indeterminate. The minimum value, as given by the list of its component parts supplied by Isaeus, is 9,600 drachmas; however, it is evidently underestimated—perhaps significantly, depending on just how much money was out on loan. The case of [Demosthenes] 42 is still more complex. Here we may calculate (though without complete confidence) that Phaenippus holds property worth 4½ talents, and probably more, and that his mother's dowry was more than one talent. Since Phaenippus apparently inherited two estates, one from his father and the other from his mother's father, Philostratus, it follows that Philostratus's estate, which supplied his mother's dowry, was less than the total sum of his holdings. How much less it is impossible to say. In none of the other five instances does the dowry amount to as much as 15 percent of the estate, and in three it is well under 10 percent. Similarly, only in the case of the estate of Ciron does a daughter's share seem at all comparable to that left for sons. Among other examples, Diodotus (in Lysias 32) has two sons when he provides for his daughter; he is generous, but the estate is so large that even the relatively large dowry leaves plenty for male members of the family. Philostratus's generosity, on the other hand, may have been prompted by the fact that his daughter was (almost certainly) an only child. One of

Isaeus's clients enunciates the general principle: a father should endow his daughter well, but see to it that his son is not less wealthy as a result (Isae. 11.39).

The question of the relation of dowries to living costs is more problematic. We can only estimate the expenses of a young woman of the elite. But it is clear at any rate that our calculations must include more than mere food and lodging; they must allow for suitable clothes, cosmetics, attendants—what we might call "social subsistence"—and perhaps, too, for the upkeep of children. Some indication of the costs involved may be derived from the difference in the dowries left by the elder Demosthenes for his wife (8,000 drachmas) and his five-year-old daughter (12,000 drachmas, Dem. 27.4–5): the extra 4,000 drachmas may have been meant to support the girl for the ten years until her marriage, at something like 400 drachmas a year. Similarly, one of Lysias's clients says it's impossible to spend more than 1,000 drachmas a year on the maintenance and education of two boys and a girl (Lys. 32.28–29). Something like 500 drachmas a year thus sounds sufficient to support a wife. The next question is, what capital would yield 500 drachmas a year? Interest rates also are uncertain. But a husband who was unable or unwilling to return his wife's dowry on divorce had to pay interest on it at 18 percent—clearly a punitive rate (Dem. 27.17, [Dem.] 59.52). At the other extreme, a passage in Aristotle's *Rhetoric* sets 10 percent as a low rate of interest (Arist. *Rh.* 3.1411a18). A prudent investment must have brought in something between these extremes, perhaps the 12 percent mentioned several times in our sources and accepted as the "normal" rate in Billeter's standard study.[79] If we accept that figure, we can calculate that a young wife could be supported on the income from a dowry of about 4,000 drachmas. Fifteen of the dowries we know from the orators are at or below this level, only seven certainly above. Of the nine dowries from Tenos and Mykonos, only two are more than 4,000 drachmas (though two more may be). As for the *horoi,* of sixteen for daughters' dowries, thirteen record dowries of less than 4,000 drachmas, one records more, and two perhaps more.[80] It is true that some dowries are much higher than this; Alcibiades' wife brought 60,000 drachmas (and another 60,000 when a son was born), and (outside Athens) Alexander is said to have given a friend's daughter 300,000.[81] But most are between 2,000 and 6,000 drachmas; again moderate, and unlikely to be a source of bad feeling.

Sisters

Unfortunately, little can be said about the relations of sisters. But though selective exposure assured that sisters were fewer than brothers, it would be wrong to assume that this was because Athenians had only one daughter. Our ignorance, once again, is the consequence of our sources' systematic scanting of women.

Slim pickings: the heroic sisters of tragedy, Electra and Antigone, have in Chrysothemis and Ismene more male-defined foils. *Appha,* one of a family of pet terms for siblings, fathers, girlfriends, and (by slaves) young mistresses in Greek, was apparently reserved at Athens for use between sisters (Eustath. *Il.* 565.14). A fifth-century inscription records that two daughters of a citizen of Argos jointly made a dedication on the Acropolis (*IG* 1² 553). Another inscription, perhaps our single most informative text, is a portion of the epitaph of two sisters (*IG* 2² 5673). Written in the middle of the fourth century, it says that they enjoyed the same share of their father's wealth and regarded both their love (*philia*) and their property as common possessions.

The same share of the family's wealth: an unexpected commemoration. A student of the modern Mediterranean family observes that sisters rarely squabble over property, and adduces a number of explanations; of these, most relevant to Athens are the effects of patrilocal marriage, which may isolate sisters in different (not necessarily distant) parts of the community, and their exclusion as active participants from public competition.[82] Once again, however, we should recognize the role of conscious choice: Athenian fathers and brothers clearly thought it of some importance to dower daughters and sisters equally. "Polyeuctus could have given one daughter a larger dowry than the other one," says his son-in-law. "However, that isn't what he did" (Dem. 41.26). Similarly, when Mantitheus tells the Council of 500 that he gave each of his sisters the same dowry, he hopes to win their good will as a man who does what is proper (Lys. 16.10). Other examples, too, attest to the prevalence of this practice.[83] It was perhaps the sensibilities of the girls' husbands that *kyrioi* had most in mind, but the intention is clear enough in any case: the avoidance of rivalry and bad feeling.[84]

Grandparents and Grandchildren

We can make rough calculations of the chances of having a grandchild in classical Athens by using, once again, the life-table derived by Bruce Frier, and estimating an age of marriage of thirty for men and between fifteen and twenty for women.[85] Under these conditions, about 65 percent of the mothers of firstborn daughters and about one-half of their fathers could expect to see at least one grandchild by them. The odds for a firstborn son's parents, who had to wait so much longer for his marriage, were worse. About 40 percent of mothers and about 22 percent of fathers could expect to see a son's child.[86] This disparity goes some way toward accounting for the greater prominence of the mother's father in our sources, though as usual it would be wrong to see demographics as the sole explanation.[87] Even fewer grandparents would survive to establish a reciprocal relationship with their grandchildren. For example, fewer than six in every ten men who became grandfathers at sixty-five would still be alive when their grandchild reached five years of age. Of course, it was possible for individuals to improve their odds. Mantias urged his son to marry exceptionally early so that he could see his grandchildren, and he did in fact live until his granddaughter's birth ([Dem.] 40.12).[88]

This example underscores the value placed on grandchildren. Solon annoys the Lydian ruler Croesus by identifying as the most fortunate of men Tellus the Athenian, who had fine sons, lived to see children born and survive from each, and then went on to die a glorious death in battle (Hdt. 1.30). Several Attic tombstones of the classical period proclaim that a man or a woman had lived to see grandchildren, *paides paidōn,* a sentiment presumably prompted in part by the relative rarity of the experience, especially for men.[89] According to her moving grave epigram, Ampharete regarded her daughter's boy as the light of the sun while she was alive, and holds him on her knees now that they both are dead; this scene is depicted on her stele.[90] Another late fifth century grave stele shows an old man with a beard leaning on a staff, and a small girl; their hands clasp, their eyes meet—probably grandfather and granddaughter.[91]

The birth of a grandson in particular was as good a guarantee as one could expect of the continuation of the family (and maintenance of the family cult);[92] a daughter's son could make up for her father's lack of male offspring by being adopted into his grandfather's household, even posthumously.[93] It therefore deepens the tragedy of King Priam that Troy's war against the Greeks led not only to his own death and the loss of all his sons (*Il.* 24.255–260, 751–753) but also to the murder of his son Hector's child Astyanax. Most poignant is the version followed by the Attic vase painters, whose depictions of the sack of Priam's city include the horrific vignette of the old man being clubbed to death with his grandson's body.[94] Peleus, another king of legend, loses his only son, Achilles, in the same war and his only grandson, Neoptolemus, shortly after it. Euripides' play on the subject includes a vain attempt by Peleus to save Neoptolemus and then a lament over his torn corpse in which the heartbroken old man, struck down by the same fate that overwhelmed his grandson, pores over "the fingers I loved so! These cheeks! And these lips!"[95] But Peleus has a great-grandson too, the infant son of Neoptolemus and his concubine Andromache; he is more successful in providing him with protection and so in saving his line from extinction (722–726, 746–748). In a typically Euripidean irony, this elite Greek family will survive through an illegitimate son whose mother was once wed to Troy's greatest hero.

In the relations of grandparents and grandchildren, as in those of parents and children, we find sentiment and utility mixed, though not perhaps in the same proportions. Grandparents' maintenance was enjoined by the same laws that provided for parents.[96] In tragedy, old Cadmus, mourning Pentheus, his daughter's son, remembers how the young king (whom he calls "the dearest of men") protected him from insult (Eur. *Ba.* 1302–1325). "No longer will you touch this chin with your hand, no longer call me your mother's father and embrace me, saying 'Who wrongs you, who dishonors you, old man? Who troubles your heart?'" Now, says Cadmus, he will be driven out from his home without respect—a prediction fulfilled at the end of the play. But few grandparents could expect to benefit in these ways. In most cases, active assistance would flow in the other direction. Isocrates, anxious to please his grandsons, appeals to the rulers of Mytilene on behalf of their teacher of *mousikē* (Isoc. *Ep.* 8.1–2, 10). Many of the heroes of myth were reared outside their parental homes by their mothers' fathers—Athens' Theseus among them;[97] we may include here Cyrus the Great, whose legend in Athenian sources includes a stay with King Astyages in which the boy proves his mettle by his wisdom and moderation (Xen. *Cyr.* 1.3–4). Such attentions were supposed to be appreciated by the recipients. Euripides' Orestes recalls the nurture he received from his mother's parents, Tyndareus and Leda (Eur. *Or.* 462–465): "He raised me when I was small, and often kissed me as he carried me about in his arms, the son of Agamemnon; and Leda too. They valued me no less than their own sons, Castor and Polydeuces."

We cannot miss the emotive coloring here. Similarly, a historical Athenian, the speaker of Isaeus 8, recalls that Ciron, allegedly his mother's father, "naturally" never performed a sacrifice unless he and his brother were there. The boys went with him into the countryside for the Rural Dionysia, sat at his side at public spectacles, and visited his house for festivals, especially that for Zeus Ktesios. The speaker himself claims to have visited Ciron, attended on him (*therapeuein*), passed time with him (Isae. 8.15–16, 37). These are important passages, valuable evidence on just what a grandfather and his grandsons might do together. But they are not as straightforward as they may seem. The speaker's relationship with Ciron is itself one of the issues in this lawsuit, as is the strength of a grandson's claim in relation to those of other family members. Detail and tone are therefore chosen to convince a jury. So the mention of Zeus Ktesios, the deity who safeguarded a household's goods, is apposite in a court case over an inheritance, the reference to the Rural Dionysia an appeal to the importance of keeping a family's land in the proper hands. Whatever the merits of the speaker's case, however, these details must have sounded plausible; and the picture of affectionate relations he paints must have been expected to evoke similar images among the jurors. Such considerations pose a problem for Lysias, hired by Diogeiton's grandchildren when they prosecute him, their mother's father and their guardian, for defrauding them of much of their inheritance and throwing them out of the house they shared.[98] The speech begins with an elaborate apology for bringing this family squabble into a public court, and in particular for having to accuse a grandfather of shameful conduct (Lys. 32.1–3).

Was there a distinctive quality to the relations of grandparents and grandchildren? Many years ago, the British social anthropologist A. R. Radcliffe-Brown suggested that grandparents and grandchildren made up a common case of a "joking relationship," a mixture of respect and raillery, often reciprocal, marking relations that incorporate both "social conjunction and disjunction."[99] Grandparents and grandchildren are very different in age and experience, but are also closely linked by birth, and perhaps by a kind of natural alliance against the generation in the middle, which is likely to be in conflict with each. There is little trace of such a pattern of interaction in our sources, in which grandfathers so often replace fathers rather than supplement them. Grandmothers, however, do seem to have had a special reputation for indulging their grandchildren. Socrates says the Spartans make use of Hippias as children do of old women, "to tell stories in a pleasant way" (Pl. *Hipp. Ma.* 285E–286A).[100] Ancient scholars explain the words *tēthalladous*, "granny's boy" (found in Attic comedy) and *mammothreptos*, "reared by a grandmother" (known only from late sources) as referring to spoiled children.[101] Many wives survived their husbands (one estimate suggests there were 20 percent more widows than widowers) and many widows moved in with a child and his or her family; grandmothers may therefore have had a significant impact on the lives of children, though the bias of our informants characteristically slights them in favor of grandfathers.[102] This, like brother-sister ties, is an often overlooked element in the complex relationship of male and female at Athens.

Six

Outsiders and Alliances

Outsiders

I move on to those I have termed outsiders in the household, members who were not part of the family by birth, such as adopted children, stepparents, *xenoi,* slaves. This principle of organization may seem to slight central issues. Definitions of the family and the household—indeed, their utility as analytical categories—are now subjects of vigorous debate among anthropologists and social historians alike. Scholars have argued that defining the family in terms of kinship necessarily stresses reproduction at the expense of other important areas—production, exchange, power—and that households are often very fluid, losing, gaining, and regaining members seasonally or through the course of the life cycle, with much mobility among them.[1] Furthermore, the realities these terms represent interact in crucial (and unpredictable) ways. The boundaries of the household, the residential location, may vary in permeability with the availability of kin in the immediate neighborhood; and accidents of geographical location may be as important in determining which kin matter from day to day as genealogical propinquity.[2]

Such factors are certainly significant for classical Athens.

Households had occasional members, regular visitors, and perhaps apprentices, and also experienced the seasonal out-migration attested by the rural shelters referred to in leases.[3] Death and remarriage caused frequent changes too, bringing in new parents and children and more distant kin whose households had dissolved; sometimes the same forces would result in the return of those who had left home, daughters whose marriages had ended, for instance.[4] And residence could in some contexts carry no less emotional resonance than kinship; not surprising, perhaps, since *synoikein*, "to live together," is as close as ancient Greek comes to a word meaning "to be married." Mantitheus complains that he was driven out of the house of his fathers, in which he was born and brought up; a cruel wrong ([Dem.] 40.2). Stephanus is attacked for ejecting his own uncle from the ancestral *oikia*, Dicaeogenes for buying up the house his aunts had inherited from their father and demolishing it.[5] Part of the outrage Evergus and his accomplice provoke results from the fact that the home they invaded is one their prosecutor has lived in from his youth ([Dem.] 47.53). Thus kinship and place of residence are often intertwined; so those guilty of political crimes against the *polis* (or its rulers) had their houses razed, a punishment both practical and symbolic.[6]

Such complexities must bring into question the assumption implied by my plan of presentation, that the household's "outsiders" were particularly likely to introduce tensions. Yet our sources are unequivocal. Despite the incidence of adoption, and indeed its vital role in a high-mortality population that put much stress on the continuity of the family line, the loyalty and affection of adopted children were open to doubt, and not only by those who saw such children supplanting them as heirs. "After Menecles adopted me," a litigant says, "he showed the same concern on my behalf as a father would on a son's; and I cared for and respected him as if he were my father by birth" (Isae. 2.18). Not an outcome to be taken for granted; rather, a success worth stressing. The difference between ties stemming from birth and adoption allows Demosthenes to ring a change on the familiar theme of the Athenians' unique autochthony (*Epit.* 4). Immigrants are adopted children of their countries, while the Athenian dead are legitimate sons of their native land. The implications are made explicit in Lycurgus's prosecution of Leocrates: men do not hold adoptive parents in the same regard as real parents, and they feel less loyalty to countries they have adopted as well (*Leocr.* 48). A provision of Plato's *Laws* is noteworthy (*Leg.* 9.878E). Judges of children who have wounded their parents are to have children of their own—not adopted, but *alēthinoi*. The sense required here, "true, genuine," is unusual when *alēthinos* refers to persons, and the more common meaning in that context, "trusty," must be present as well.[7]

As for stepmothers, they faced pervasive prejudice. A proverb terms good and bad days "mothers" and "stepmothers" respectively; according to metaphor, a dangerous place to sail is a "stepmother of ships"; a second wife proves herself "a real stepmother" by plotting against her husband's daughter; a dying mother in tragedy asks her husband not to bring in a stepmother for their children lest she beat them; and a law that comedy fathers on Charondas levies political liabilities against the man who does.[8] One of Isaeus's clients claims that differences between a stepmother and a daughter are common; Diogeiton's daughter provides an illustration, alleging that her father is generous to his children by his new wife while she and hers go in need.[9]

Quite different problems were posed by the outsiders who were probably most interesting to the children born into the household: the free children who came to it for protection or nurture. Some were sent away from their own homes in times of crisis, as many Athenians evacuated their wives and children to Aegina, Salamis, and Troezen when the Persians invaded Attica, Mantitheus's father entrusted his children to the court of Satyrus of Pontus in the last years of the Peloponnesian War, and the democratic opposition found refuge abroad for theirs in the war's aftermath.[10] In other cases, their presence does not seem to have been prompted by peril at home; Andocides' cousin and contemporary Charmides, raised in his household from boyhood, is an example (Andoc. 1.48). In a famous study of mythical instances—Orestes, spirited out of Argos and raised at Strophius's house in Phocis; Achilles, entrusted first to the centaur Chiron and then to King Lycomedes on Scyrus—Louis Gernet (1955) stressed the elements of passage rites in such stories. Now Gabriel Herman (1987) has furnished another context. This is the institution of *xenia*, or "ritualized friendship," a bond of solidarity involving an exchange of goods or services between individuals (including boys) from separate social units, governed by a set of customary observances, which lasted for the lives of the friends (*xenoi*) and was often carried on by their descendants.[11] The practice of raising others' children in the household may be regarded as one facet of *xenia*.

The circulation of children has been studied in many other cultures, where it typically (though by no means always) takes the form of the absorption of the children of the poor into wealthier households. Thus, David Herlihy, writing on medieval Florence, estimates that the richest quarter of all households contained more than 40 percent of all children, quite apart from young servants.[12] At Athens, however, we are dealing with movement between households of the same social station, as *xenoi* normally were. There may have been an element of seasoning intended; it is pleasant to think of children as yet another of the raw materials taken into the household and then treated and transformed into something of social value.[13] More obviously, to place one's child in another's household was a striking symbol of trust. Not always justified. In Euripides' play, Hecuba asks if her son Polydorus, sent for safekeeping to King Polymestor of Thrace, still remembers her—a hint that this practice might not be free from tension (Eur. *Hec.* 992). Worse fears still are to be realized, for she soon learns of his murder. The circulation of children was also a means of encouraging the maintenance of ties of *xenia* in the next generation.

Certainly children raised together in this way, whatever the circumstances of their introduction, did form lasting bonds, attested in myth—where Strophius's son Pylades becomes "dearest of the dear" to Orestes, "like a brother"[14]—historical romance (in which the boyhood friends of Alexander the Great grow up to become his closest counselors), and history. Andocides explains his decision to give evidence on the profanation of the Mysteries in 415 by saying that he was persuaded by the appeal of Charmides. "I have never in all my life hurt you at all and have been most enthu-

siastic in doing everything possible on your behalf," said his boyhood housemate (Andoc. 1.49–50). As often, we must recognize
the force of such an appeal to an Athenian jury, even though we
may doubt that it was ever made. Another example may be afforded by Demosthenes' Samian friend Aristion; the orator's boyhood companion (*hetairos*) lived in his house for a long time and
served him as an emissary to Macedon.[15] Aeschines implies that
the relationship was sexual; probably innuendo, no more, but in-
dicative of the way such personal links, especially with foreign
friends, could be used against those involved. To whom would a
citizen be loyal—to his *xenos* or his *polis*? Herman has persua-
sively sketched the impact of such concerns on the behavior of
two important *xenoi*, Pericles and King Archidamus of Sparta, in
the Peloponnesian War.[16]

It is tempting to speculate on the effects of such constant
changes on the psychological and social development of children.
Did they tend to diminish the intensity of emotional ties? To increase levels of insecurity? One group is so pervasive in its presence and so important for our understanding of the dynamics of
ancient society as a whole that the temptation becomes undesirable (or at least impossible) to resist. Slaves were closely associated
with children. The word *pais* is commonly used for both child and
slave, and the two groups shared a number of social characteristics, liability to physical abuse in particular.[17] Their identification
posed a potential problem when boys reached the age at which
they took on the status and roles of citizens; as I remarked in
Chapter 3, certain conventions of male homosexuality at Athens
therefore marked young males off from the slaves to whom they
were previously so closely linked.[18] But little has been written recently on Athenian concerns about this relationship and its effects
on individual Athenians, subjects that are no less crucial than they
are challenging.[19] I take them up now. The context, once again, is
the interplay of continuity and change in children's links with others as they reach maturity and after.[20]

I begin with a few preliminary remarks on the dimensions of
the problem. Most who have treated the influence of slaves on children have focused on those most particularly and most intimately

involved with them—female nurses, male *paidagōgoi*.²¹ This is somewhat misleading. For one thing, it ignores young slaves, children born in the household or brought into it very young (few though these may have been). There is no evidence that the Greeks of the archaic and classical periods valued such slaves as playmates for their own children, as the Romans and later Greeks certainly did.²² Indeed, conventions guiding the iconography of slaves, who are usually shown smaller than free men and women, make it impossible to be sure whether slaves and their masters and mistresses on vases and grave reliefs are even close in age.²³ But friendship of a sort cannot be ruled out. And judging by a famous grave stele (from Aegina) that depicts a young boy mourning an athletic youth, his master, a slave's affection (however imaginary) was worth advertising.²⁴ Equally important, such specialized slaves were not found in every household, and some nurses and *paidagōgoi* were not slaves at all.²⁵ To consider only wet-nurses: Even among the relatively well-to-do, many mothers breast-fed their own children. Euphiletus, though he presents himself as merely the owner of a modest *oikidion,* is a friend of Harmodius, a member of the prominent *genos* of the Gephyraei, and can afford the services of the speech-writer Lysias; yet his wife suckles their son herself (though it is Euphiletus she plays for a sucker).²⁶ Cinesias, who is not portrayed as particularly poor, implies that his son has missed Myrrhine's breasts as much as he has since she joined the other Athenian women on the Acropolis (Ar. *Lys.* 881). Others had the help of family members, or hired a fellow citizen; Euxitheus's mother was only one Athenian woman forced by poverty to work as a wet-nurse (Dem. 57.35). Still others will have kept a wet-nurse only until their child was weaned—say, until the age of two—and then sold her off.²⁷ This evidence warns us not to exaggerate the prevalence of slave nurses and *paidagōgoi*. But it would be equally wrong to underestimate the extent of the interaction between adult slaves and children. Let us take another look at the evidence I've cited. First, it is significant that Euxitheus's enemies could accuse him of being the son of a slave: his mother did a slave's work. Hired citizen wet-nurses were probably not very numerous. There is more to say about the examples of Euphiletus and Cinesias too. Euphiletus owns a slave girl, who teases the baby, and Cinesias brings along a slave to whom he can hand over the baby when Myrrhine leads him on.[28] These may not be slaves for whom childcare is the sole responsibility, but they are clearly involved with children nonetheless. The relative rarity of what we may call professional wet-nurses and other specialized slaves should not lead us to conclude that there were in fact few adult slaves in constant contact with children, or that such contact characterized only a few households.

Slaves participated in almost every aspect of Athenian life—as domestic servants, farmworkers, craftsmen, laborers, miners, civil servants, police. In terms of their cost, distribution, and pervasive effect on society as a whole, they were rather like another necessary luxury, the automobile.[29] No Athenian child could have escaped contact with them at some time.[30] And the effects of slaves within the household must have been magnified by the form of the Athenian family.[31] Athenian men married late, and directed much of their energy outside the home. Many died while their children were still young; some probably spent little time with them. As a result, it must often have been slaves who provided a stable and continuous adult presence, especially a male presence, in the household.[32]

It is domestic slaves in general with whom I am concerned here. Within this group, there is one very good reason for stressing the role played by nurses and *paidagōgoi*, notwithstanding the need for caution in making generalizations: the ancient authorities do the same. These slaves were special as well as specialized, because they occupied positions of extraordinary trust. It is a *paidagōgos,* Sicinnus, who is chosen by Themistocles to lure the Persians at Salamis; Panthea, about to commit suicide on the death of her husband, gives her last instructions to her nurse.[33] And Plato can include the nurse and the *paidagōgos* with the mother and the father as members of the family who do their utmost to raise the child as well as possible (*Prot.* 325C).

Such slaves might be regarded with affection; the baby Perseus greets Silenus with friendly (or, infant) sounds "like a respected nurse" (Aesch. fr. 47a.770–771R.). Their services were often repaid. The household of the speaker of Demosthenes 47 includes his old wet-nurse, who had been set free by his father. "I could not see my nurse living in want nor my *paidagōgos*," he explains (Dem. 47.56). Other nurses, too, were freed.[34] A number of gravestones commemorate this class of slaves, most presumably erected by their owners or their charges.[35] In fact nurses and *paidagōgoi* seem to have expected some return for their care, just like parents themselves. To cite only instances from tragedy, Hypsipyle says she had no motive to wish the baby Opheltes dead; on the contrary, he would have been a "great help" to her, his nurse (Eur. *Hyps.* fr. 60.8–12 Bond). Orestes' nurse calls her pain "useless" when she learns of his death; Agamemnon's *paidagōgos* expresses similar disappointment.[36] Creon says Oedipus owes more to Thebes (although it exiled him) than to Athens because it was his nurse (Soph. *OC* 760).

Thus, emotional ties could arise between slave and child and continue between slave and adult. But, though *paidagōgoi* and nurses were privileged, they were still slaves. Moreover, they were not necessarily slaves with special qualifications for their work. Pericles (so the story goes) watched a slave break a leg and observed, "There's a new *paidagōgos*."[37] More reliably perhaps, we are told that Alcibiades' tutor Zopyrus was chosen because he was old and unfit for other work (Pl. *Alcib. I* 122B). Therefore, like other slaves, even nurses and *paidagōgoi* would generally be regarded as intellectually and morally inferior to free citizens.[38] A curious contradiction: the Athenians, who believed that association and imitation were essential elements of upbringing and education, entrusted their children to the care of individuals who were apparently quite unsuited to be models or mentors.[39] Two questions arise. Were the Athenians themselves aware of this contradiction? What were its effects on individuals and on Athenian society as a whole?

The answer to the first question is yes. Several sources decry the role played by slaves in the upbringing of children. Plato criticizes parents for being careless in choosing those to whom they entrust this task.[40] But more than the selection of a suitable slave is at issue. The practice itself comes under attack, sometimes in quite general terms. Xenophon praises the Spartan lawgiver Lycurgus for not resorting to slave *paidagōgoi*, as is the custom in other cities.[41] Xenophon is also critical of others for giving their children sandals (they soften the feet), changes of clothing (they pamper the body), and as much food as their stomachs will hold; the implication is that slave *paidagōgoi* also are likely to lead to weakness and dependence. Socrates remarks that it is a terrible thing (*deinon*) for a free boy to be ruled by a slave (Pl. *Lys.* 208C).[42] Menander's Sostratus says it would be best for a girl not to be raised by some aunt or *maia* but "freely" (*eleutheriōs*) with her rustic father (Men. *Dysc.* 384–389); the collocation with *eleutheriōs* suggests that *maia* here refers to a female slave.[43] Aristotle's *paidonomoi* are to see to it that children—who will be raised in the home up to age seven—have as little contact as possible with slaves, and so avoid seeing and hearing things unfit for free citizens (*Pol.* 7.1336a4). Sometimes, too, we hear more specific charges against these slaves. House slaves (*oiketai*) may undercut a father's authority and example (Pl. *Resp.* 8.549E).[44] *Paidagōgoi* have no more taste and judgment than children themselves (Pl. *Resp.* 3.397D). Nurses may refuse to follow orders, tell unsuitable stories, eat children's food, pass on alcohol through their milk.[45]

Now, there is nothing new in this list of references regarding the role played by slaves in raising and regulating children. What is perhaps surprising is that I should bother to recite it. After all, the late Professor M. I. Finley, the most insightful and influential authority on ancient slavery, dismissed such evidence as "anecdotal in the extreme, ranging from exemplary tales . . . to the persistent grumbling by moralists from Plato to Plutarch."[46] I think, however, that Finley underestimates the extent of the concern about slaves in the household; in particular, he ignores interesting and important evidence from a major focus for public concerns, Athenian tragedy. Some of the evidence is well known.[47] In Euripides' *Hippolytus*, Phaedra trusts her old nurse and is counseled to disaster. In his *Ion*, the *paidagōgos*, the old attendant of Creusa's father, takes a leading role in an intrigue that endangers her when it fails and would only have cost her her husband and her child if it had succeeded.[48] These slaves mean well; their masters' interests are their own; yet the result is ruin. I suggest that this theme is an unrecognized element—perhaps the only unrecognized element—in one of the most famous works of Greek tragedy, Aeschylus's *Oresteia*.[49] The trilogy may be read (among many other ways) as a critique of the influence of slaves, especially household slaves.

Agamemnon opens with the watchman on the roof of the palace.[50] We do not know whether he is a free dependent of the house of Atreus (as seems likely) or a slave; but he is certainly a man of low social status (as his use of homely language may perhaps be meant to stress, 36–37). Yet his station is exalted, both literally and figuratively: he appears high up in a position most often used for the epiphanies of the gods.[51] A striking paradox, this *coup de théâtre* introduces us to a world where other inversions and contradictions abound. Clytemnestra is a woman with a man's will (10–11). The herald must mix together fair and foul (648): fire and sea, bitterest of foes, joined in alliance to destroy the Greek fleet (650–651). And so on.[52] Of course, this kind of language, ironic and riddling, is not unique to *Agamemnon;* it is characteristic of tragedy in general. But here it seems especially appropriate and resonant, used as it is to develop a plot in which decisive actions lead to their opposites, in which seeming solutions cause new problems. Agamemnon sacrifices his daughter and is himself cut down; Troy's conqueror is conquered. Perhaps the most telling example comes at the close of the play. Clytemnestra has killed the king; she hopes that she has swept away murder, guilt, the fury from the house (1567–1576). But no sooner has she spoken than Aegisthus enters, with his own motives and claims, and it is at once clear that the murder of Agamemnon has solved nothing; the play ends in dissonance and discord.

The figure of Clytemnestra, who kills her husband and king while her lover Aegisthus plays a woman's role (1625, 1643–1645), is the clearest symbol of the extent to which the social and moral order of Argos is disturbed. But Cassandra, given a new prominence in the story by Aeschylus, also is important in this regard.[53] The long scene of which she is the center has a number of functions. Most important for the trilogy as a whole, she is an outsider who dies as an innocent victim of the murderous history of the house of Atreus, and so her fate stresses that the story Aeschylus tells has import beyond the royal house itself; like the watchman and the herald, Cassandra helps us see that *Oresteia* deals with a set of problems which affects the community as a whole and all those who come into contact with it.

For my purposes, however, what needs stressing is that Cassandra is a slave (emphasized at 953, 1035–1046, 1065–1067, 1226, 1326), destined to be one of "many slaves by the household altar" of Zeus Ktesios.[54] Of course, she is a very unusual slave, one who still has a god's gift of prophecy (1083). And unlike all those around her, unlike Agamemnon, Clytemnestra, the chorus, she has a reliable (if sometimes cryptic) knowledge of past, present, and future: Cassandra's visions include insights into the terrible feast of Thyestes, the impending murder of Agamemnon, the revenge of Orestes. Yet, no matter how divinely inspired, no matter how accurate, Cassandra's words have no effect; she can't change the course of events herself or persuade others to do so. That a woman, a foreigner and a slave, has more and more accurate understanding than others is of course a paradox, another indication that the time is out of joint; but that her wisdom leads nowhere is no more than we would expect. Announced in this way in *Agamemnon,* this theme is more prominent in *Choephori.* Much of our attention in *Choephori* is directed downward under the earth, where the libations carried by the chorus are poured for the dead Agamemnon; its first line is addressed to Hermes, lord of the dead, its first half takes place at the king's tomb.[55] The social status of the play's characters has moved downward as well. Compare the makeup of the choruses: in *Agamemnon,* its members are elderly but free male citizens of Argos; in *Choephori,* captives, female domestic servants (76–77, 84). There is another important difference too. The Argive citizens in *Agamemnon* are slow to understand what has happened and is about to happen in their city. The slaves of *Choephori,* in striking contrast, take a leading and decisive role in the action of the play.[56] In this they are joined by other household slaves, by Orestes' old nurse in particular. Yet

their actions are in the end as futile as the hesitation and indeci-
sion of the citizens of Argos, their deeds as profitless as the words
of the slave Cassandra—they cannot end the house's troubles.

Let us move quickly through the play, noting the prominent
part played by slaves. Electra asks the chorus to advise her how to
perform the rite for her father (87, cf. 100), since it shares her
hatred of the house (101); fate awaits the free man and the one
who is ruled by another's hand alike (103–104). When the chorus
then instructs her to remember Orestes (115), Electra continues
to ask for advice, on the form of the prayer she must use (118–
122). The chorus is later as quick as Electra to guess that the lock
of hair may be Orestes' (178). After the recognition scene, it warns
Orestes and Electra not to talk too loud, lest someone overhear
them (264–268), and later urges them to turn from lamentation
to action (510–513). Orestes duly makes a plan. He knocks on the
door of the palace and calls on a slave to let him enter (652–656).

This scene is curious, and has perhaps not received the discussion it deserves. Orestes' language is unusual: this is the first use
of *pais* in the sense "slave" in Greek, and in fact the only use of the
word in this meaning in tragedy.[57] That is remarkable enough. Still
more so is the fact that the slave called on so conspicuously is
given a line of dialogue to answer the summons.[58] Much has been
made of the lines that Pylades, silent until then, speaks just before
Orestes kills Clytemnestra. But the slave's reply is no less unexpected, and also requires explanation. I suggest that both the unusual use of *pais* and the slave's short speech are meant at least in
part to stress that, just as the chorus of slaves has replaced the
chorus of Argive citizens, Argos as a whole has lost its freedom
and been enslaved; slaves, it seems, are to be seen and heard every-
where. It is significant in this regard that Electra refers to herself
as *antidoulos*, "like a slave" (135), and that Orestes charges that he
was sold to Strophius though born of a free father (915).

To return to this rapid survey of the play. The chorus, "dear
slaves of the house" (719), wonders when it will be able to do
Orestes some service with the power of speech. Soon: another
slave enters, Orestes' nurse.[59] Here, too, I would argue, Aeschylus
is concerned to stress that a particular character is a slave (and

thus that Argos is now a community in servitude). The nurse is a feature of the tradition, but no other authority, as far as we know, explicitly made her a slave.[60] Stesichorus and Pherecydes called her Laodameia, Pindar—Arsinoe; either is a name a free woman, even a heroine of myth, could bear.[61] The chorus in *Choephori*, however, addresses the nurse as Cilissa (732)—though it is uncommon for slaves to be identified in this way in tragedy; the name, indicating as it does her ethnic origin, clearly shows the nurse's slave status. Cilissa has been sent by Clytemnestra to summon Aegisthus and his bodyguard. Here the chorus makes a critical contribution to Orestes' cause. "If you hate our master," it says, "tell him to come unattended" (770–773). As a result, Aegisthus is easy prey, and Clytemnestra soon dead beside him. The help of these slave domestics, the chorus and the nurse, has made revenge possible for Electra and Orestes. Once again, there is the hope that the bloodshed has come to an end, expressed this time by the chorus (931–971). But once again, this hope is soon dashed, as Orestes spies the Furies, who demand vengeance for his mother's murder (1048–1058). The slave women (*dmōai gynaikes*, 1048) take one last initiative: Orestes must go to Apollo at Delphi for help (1059–1060).

In *Agamemnon*, a slave outsider sees the truth, but cannot act to prevent disaster. In *Choephori*, slave domestics, one intimately linked with Orestes, the others Electra's associates, take it upon themselves to act vigorously; but again the play ends with no resolution, the curse unbroken, Orestes in flight. Only in *Eumenides* is a solution found, and in *Eumenides* there are no slaves.

At its outset, *Eumenides* is set at the oracle of Apollo at Delphi. There is much to remind us of the earlier plays. The Pythia scurries from the temple in terror, on her hands and knees; an aged woman whom fear has made childlike (*antipais*, 38), she recalls the Argive elders, childlike in their weakness (*Ag.* 72–82). Figures from the underworld, mentioned or invoked in *Choephori*, now appear on stage: Hermes, the ghost of Clytemnestra, the Furies themselves.[62] But at 235, the scene shifts to Athens, and we find ourselves in a different atmosphere; there are still important links with *Agamemnon* and *Choephori*, but now they involve contrast and change more than likeness. Whereas in *Agamemnon* the watchman was raised to the level of the gods, in *Eumenides* the Olympian gods Apollo and Athena have come down to earth and mingle with men. Whereas in *Choephori* our attention was focused downward, to the earth and beneath it, in *Eumenides* even men may rise above it in a fashion, as the great trial of Orestes takes place on a hill, the Areopagus. And unlike the murders of revenge, that trial does finally lay to rest the curse on the house of Atreus, and provide a model for the settlement of other similar disputes in the community.

It is important for my reading of the trilogy to consider the social status of those who are party to this resolution. Apollo and Athena are gods, Orestes an Argive prince. The jurors are free citizens of Athens: their status is stressed—forms of *politēs* and *astos* abound.[63] The Furies become *metoikoi,* free foreign members of the Athenian community (1011, cf. 1018). Thus, what the words and actions of slaves could not accomplish, free men and women, citizens and metics, bring to fulfillment. And slaves are not excluded only from the process through which the problems of the house are solved. They are absent even from the language of the play: there is not a single reference to slaves or slavery.[64] Even where a mention might be expected, such as in the chorus's recollection of Apollo's stay at Pherae, nothing is said (723–724). In the two earlier plays, Aeschylus has shown that the influence of slaves is inadequate to resolve conflicts within the *oikos,* and may even help to keep them alive. Now, order and justice are reestablished quite apart from slaves, in a world where they have no part. This is not an argument against slavery. Rather, it is a recognition that the house of Atreus, like other households, is a complex of relationships; for domestic slaves to know and do as much or more than the masters of the house is a sign of disturbance and disorder similar to (if not as serious as) women ruling men, and parents and children murdering each other.

Aeschylus's trilogy, then, reveals that concern for the influence of the household's slaves was not as limited as Finley thought; and the son and daughter of the royal house of Argos are among those shown to suffer from its ill effects. I move on to my second question. How were the Athenians in Aeschylus's audience marked by the association of slaves and children in their own households? Here again Finley holds out little hope: "There are too many variables that we cannot control. Modern psychology has been unable to reach any agreement in this field, and I remain a complete skeptic about the easy generalizations and causal statements of historians writing about a society that has long been dead and cannot be observed directly."[65]

No one will deny the difficulties. Yet the answer proposed by the eminent sociologist A. W. Gouldner (1965) is worth considering.[66] Gouldner makes two major points. First, he argues that "it makes a difference whether a child is reared, educated, and disciplined by those who feel they embody the standards that the child is expected to obey, or whether the socializing agent's authority is only a delegated moral competence, requiring and allowing him to speak on behalf of values manifestly not possessed by him" (1:86). The authority of the Athenian's slave *paidagōgos* or nurse, says Gouldner, is of the second kind. This has important consequences. Since the slave's control is not absolute, but is subject to "review and revision" by parents, he must be prepared to bend and compromise, and so protect himself from appeals to his masters and possible punishment. For the child, the task is harder because less clear-cut: "The child . . . must adjust to demands that are communicated indirectly and known only uncertainly" (ibid.). The result is that the slave exerts discipline only for flagrant—and public—misbehavior. And the child soon learns that it is public actions, not private convictions, that matter. Gouldner concludes (1:87): "It may be in some part through such early experiences that a child first comes to develop a special sensitivity to the responses of others and is first socialized to be a member of a shame culture."

Second, Gouldner notes that the slave may resent his position, and that his recalcitrance and hostility may be apparent to the child. The child is too young to understand the slave's position intellectually. Instead, he experiences the slave's conduct as "disorderliness," and this impression is reinforced by the pattern outlined above, the slave's willingness to conciliate and change to avoid appeals to his masters. The slave explains or excuses his conduct—especially if he is emotionally close to the child—by reference to parental authority. And so the child learns, verbally, of an idealized standard of conduct apart from what he sees around him every day. As a result, says Gouldner, he compares his own thoughts and actions with that ideal, and finds them wanting, or "disorderly." He thus finds himself associated with the slave and—Gouldner's major point here—learns "to define his own spontaneous impulses as evil and unruly . . . to equate the natural with the disorderly" (2:194).

Gouldner's "conjecture on socialization and metaphysics" (2:191) has attracted little notice.[67] Yet, though it is presented with little reference to the ancient sources, there are passages that could be used to support it. Plato's concern (mentioned above) that slaves explicitly or implicitly undermine parental authority might reflect an awareness of the kind of compromise Gouldner refers to. At least one fictional nurse—Hecuba in Euripides' *Trojan Women*—expresses real resentment that she must raise the children of her captors (191–196). And some slaves in comedy object to being ordered about by a young master (a beardless *meirakyllion*, not a toddler), though meanness with leftover food, and not youth, is their main cause of complaint (Epicrates fr. 5K.-A.).

Inevitably, however, so stimulating a hypothesis is as fertile in questions as in answers. Those concerning values are at the same time the most important and the most complex. The commonsense assumption is that most slaves shared some values with their masters, though they did not necessarily play the same roles in their lives, and rejected or resented others.[68] It is of crucial importance for an evaluation of Gouldner's theory to identify the values in question, and to estimate the depth of divergence in every case, but for ancient Athens, at least, this is impossible. However, some relevant distinctions can be made on the basis of the origins of household slaves. Some were house-reared, brought up in the same society as Athenian citizens, though in different circumstances. These, we would imagine, shared their masters' values most completely, just as British nannies, though working-class in origin, identified with the elite they served.[69] (And so they might

react the more strongly if they believed these values had been betrayed.) Of the others, some (perhaps most) were Greek, and
probably not too dissimilar from Athenians in their outlook.[70] But
their very similarity with their masters may have accentuated resentment at their position and so magnified the impact of minor
disagreements. It is the slaves from outside the Greek world whom
we would expect to have very different values. Yet, though Gouldner's account seems most appropriate to these, it is far from
straightforward even here. The first part of his argument demands
that children be aware of the differences, either through observation (unlikely to be a widespread phenomenon, I think, though
obviously not to be discounted altogether) or through a slave's attempt to exculpate himself from some unpopular directive in order to curry favor with or prevent trouble from his charge. Such a
tactic involves obvious risks—parents would expect better service
than that—and slaves would do well to think twice before entrust-
ing their safety to a young child's discretion.[71] Plato (in the passages noted above) seems likely to be more worried about faults of
stupidity and orneriness than about any principled or even conscious disagreements over values. In sum, I suspect that the values
of parents and slaves differed less often and less markedly than
Gouldner supposes, and (more confidently) that differences which
did exist relatively rarely came to the attention of children.

Oddly, perhaps, Gouldner makes no mention of material from
another much-studied slave society, the antebellum American
South. Not that the use of such comparative material is straightforward. Questions arise. Is our comparative evidence reliable? To
cite an example relevant to our present subject, the most recent
research indicates that the role of the black slave woman as a wet-
nurse for white children has been much exaggerated; something
like 85 percent of mothers in the middle and upper classes breast-
fed their children themselves.[72] Are similar social institutions
really comparable? That U.S. domestic slaves normally reproduced
themselves, especially in the nineteenth century, while many Athenian household slaves were brought in from abroad and bought
on the open market, might indeed cause crucial differences in
their relations with their masters' children. What about the social

formations of which similar institutions form a part? Capitalism and racism, so important for our understanding of the South, have nothing or relatively little to do with slavery in Athenian society. Finally, if our facts are reliable, if institutions and the societies they belong to correspond—just what can we use our comparative evidence *for*? It can of course refute generalizations, especially rash remarks to the effect that something is implausible or even impossible. But positive contributions? Data from one society cannot replace evidence missing from another; they can only and at best lead to hypotheses that may make sense of scanty or unsatisfactory sources, or provide a connection with evidence that might otherwise appear irrelevant.

But even such contributions should not be despised. Paul Cartledge has recently shown how valuable a careful consideration of the antebellum South can be to a discussion of one facet of ancient slavery, the infrequency of revolt.[73] The possibility exists, therefore, that we may learn something from the South about the relations of slaves and children and their effects. In what follows, I will discuss an argument developed by students of American antebellum slavery, only to conclude that it should not be applied to ancient Athens. I will then move beyond the evidence provided by comparative material to put forward a hypothesis of my own.

As early as Benjamin Franklin, there were complaints about the baneful influence of slavery.[74] Many came from abolitionists, slaves and ex-slaves, and travelers such as de Tocqueville or Fanny Kemble, and may perhaps be discounted.[75] But critics included masters too, such as a Virginia judge:

> A slave population exercises the most pernicious influence upon the manners, habits and character of those among whom it exists. Lisping infancy learns the vocabulary of abusive epithets and struts the embryo tyrant in its little domain.[76]

The judge, like many others, was troubled to observe young children giving orders to adults, even slave adults; a natural enough development, however, when even a newborn white baby was to be called "young massa."[77]

What happened to lisping infancy when its voice changed? It

turned to violence, thought Thomas Jefferson, perhaps the first to ascribe the quick temper of those who lived south of what has been called the Smith & Wesson line to the influence of slavery. Not the last. The link between slavery and violence has become something of a staple of scholarship on the Old South.[78] Put most simply, the argument is that arbitrary and casual brutality toward slaves in the Southern household conditioned children to use violence not only against slaves but in their relations with one another, and to pursue this pattern of behavior as adults. As Jefferson says,

> The parent storms, the child looks on, catches the lineaments of wrath, puts on the same airs in the circle of smaller slaves, gives a loose rein to the worst passions; and, thus nursed, educated, and daily exercised in tyranny, cannot but be stamped by it with odious peculiarities.[79]

A more elaborate formulation has been put forward by D. D. Bruce, Jr.[80] He suggests that the Southern family was regarded as an ordered and stable place of refuge in a society based on a fragile foundation. Southern children were treated with moderation and restraint; corporal punishment was relatively unusual. And they were taught to express their needs and wishes with similar self-control. But the presence of outsiders in the household, the same slaves whose resentments threatened the equilibrium and the very survival of the South's social institutions, introduced a sense of insecurity into this idyll. This insecurity could only be heightened by the frequent arbitrary and cruel punishments to which slaves were subjected. Such punishments brought violence into the house; they reinforced the notion that there were dangers within it; and they demonstrated to the children that violence was sometimes not just acceptable but even necessary. "To the extent that aggression and frustration are closely connected, Southern parents encouraged a resignation to violence by virtually building frustration into their children's view of the world" (66). Insecure, confused, the children felt anger and hostility; since there were few other means of expressing these emotions, the children (and then the adults) turned to a response that had some legitimacy, violence.

Did the presence of slaves in the Athenian household make its young citizen men more violent? Certainly some aspects of slave-child relations at Athens seem to parallel the Southern pattern. We hear of boys refusing to go when fetched by their *paidagōgoi,* even beating them up.[81] Of particular interest is Aeschines' explanation of the law forbidding *hybris* against another man's slave: it is to prevent citizens from getting used to violence and so acting violently against each other (1.17, cf. Dem. 21.46). And that they did act violently nonetheless is certain from any reading of the corpus of law-court speeches from the fourth century. Athenians, one feels, were full of anger, litigious, quick-tempered—yes, violent. Athenian culture as a recent writer remarks, was "not only face-to-face but scowling."[82]

But of course we know much less of Athenian slavery and Athenian violence than we do about such things even in the slave South. Speculation on Athenian society depends to a great extent on the strength of the link between the relationship of slave and child and violence in the comparative material. And it must be admitted that the link is far from sure: *violence* is a vague term, levels of violence are hard to quantify, factors other than slavery are numerous, their influence hard to evaluate. It is not surprising, then, that some authorities on Southern violence ignore the impact of slavery, or reject it altogether.[83]

We seem to have reached an *aporia,* one of those dead ends into which Socrates so loved to lure his companions.[84] Mindful of his fate, however, I would like to propose a way forward, though it involves leaving the relatively well-marked path we have been traveling. Though I hesitate to insist that the relationship of children with slaves led to a higher incidence of violence within the citizen body itself, I suggest that slaves and children were bound together in a sinister irony that did indeed result in intensified violence.[85] The positive aspects of this relationship, the warm emotional ties between household slaves and children that I have referred to in the first part of this chapter, had two paradoxical results: abuse of slaves as a source of humor on stage, and extraordinary brutality toward slaves in everyday life. Here again my argument will require a reconsideration of Athenian drama, not tragedy this time but Aristophanic comedy.

That Athenians could ill-treat their slaves needs little demonstration. The Athenian could not harm another man's slave—just as he could not harm any portion of another man's property—but it seems he was free to do as he liked with his own, short of murder.[86] Furthermore, torture of slave witnesses was allowed and even required in Athenian courts.[87] This is perhaps not very surprising. It is striking, however, that harsh treatment of slaves is a not uncommon feature of comedy. Aristophanes criticizes this form of humor in *Peace* (743–747). But he is not above using it himself. Some examples: the slave Xanthias envies tortoises their shells after his beating by Philocleon (*Vesp.* 1292–1296). Manes is pecked by the chorus's beaks in *Birds* (1313–1336).[88] The humor of one scene in *Lysistrata* (1216–1224) "lies entirely in the bullying and threatening of slaves by tipsy citizens and in the exaggerated manifestations of fear on the part of the slaves."[89] A list of tortures highlights Xanthias's turning the tables on his master Dionysus in *Frogs* (616–624); Carion is threatened more briefly in *Plutus* (874–876).

These passages presumably mirror a part of everyday life. But they are also supposed to be funny. Certainly slapstick—knockabout humor—is one possible source of amusement in such scenes. But consideration of another class of characters which sometimes comes in for rough handling provides an indication that there is more to them than that. Fathers, too, make up a group whose beatings were fit subjects for comedy. Pheidippides not only beats his father (*Nub.* 1374–1375); he shows how he has profited from Socrates' school by convincing the old man that he was right to do so (1399–1451)—this is the natural way of birds and other animals (1425–1429). We are given a glimpse of such customs in *Birds*. The chorus invites the audience to join it in Cloud-cuckoo-land, where it is a fine thing to beat your father (756–759); and we later (1337–1370) meet a parricide who takes the chorus up on its offer and is welcomed and decked out as a war orphan (though given some gentle words of rebuke for his crime).

There is an element of wish fulfillment here. Pheidippides is repaying his father for past beatings (1409–1429). It seems that these scenes could titillate and amuse because they evoked and released a complex of emotions on the part of the audience. Social norms insisted that a father was owed respect; yet for many Athenians feelings of respect probably coexisted with resentment or hostility, whether because of real or imagined conflict or neglect in childhood, disagreements about the disposal of family property, or simply generalized discontent that found a convenient focus in the father. Thus, depictions of and references to father-beating provided a safe outlet for personal emotions that came into conflict with the community's customary and conventional attitudes, all the more so in that they took place at a public religious festival.

My suggestion is that the beatings of slaves should be regarded as involving a similar mix of emotions. There is no reason to believe that all slaves in comedy were meant to be recognized as domestics, still less as *paidagōgoi* or nurses, so we cannot argue that they would arouse a conflict of attitudes in their capacity as individual characters. But they were certainly representatives of a social group among which, as we have seen, some members were regarded with sentiment and affection at the same time that most were despised and held in contempt. So: to laugh at the mistreatment of a father is to indulge deep-seated feelings at the expense of social expectations; to laugh at the mistreatment of slaves is to follow social norms (which are to apply to all slaves) despite personal inclinations (which suggest that the norms do *not* apply to some slaves). In each case, the tension between individual emotional responses and community values can be exploited for humorous effect.

What has this exercise in literary criticism to do with social history? Simply this: the same complex of conflicting attitudes may in part explain the casual and consistent cruelty to which slaves were subject—a cruelty in which elements of repression and social control seem to be reinforced by psychological processes. I have emphasized the contradictions involved in the Athenian use of slaves in child rearing, and stressed that one of their forms is to oppose emotive feelings about individuals to socially approved general principles. It is important to recognize that these emotional feelings for slaves, arising from personal experiences in childhood, must to some extent be overcome or denied as the child gradually joins the community and learns to accept the prevailing rationalizations of the existing order, involving as they do contempt and hostility toward slaves as a group. Acceptance of the dominant ideology requires a break with the child's own feelings and perceptions.

Such denials are by no means rare in any society. But they do not come without a price. In this case, I suspect that many Athenians were able to counteract their own feelings of affection and gratitude toward particular slaves only at the expense of doing violence to those feelings—by overdoing violence to slaves with whom they had had no early positive contact. They tortured and beat some slaves, degrading them to a level far beneath themselves and their fellow citizens. In a sense this compensated for the consideration given other slaves as if to equals—or even as if to parents. The closeness of childhood attachments to the household's slaves might pose problems for a society based on the dehumanization of slaves in general. Modes and models of behavior which stressed slaves' low status and lack of worth would have an obvious utility in counteracting attitudes of affection and esteem. For individual adolescents and adults, the denial of early positive associations with slaves would be more convincing when shouted—when slaves were treated with especial cruelty and brutality—than when merely expressed by more moderate discipline and control. Both sociologically and psychologically, this seems plausible; more it is impossible to claim.

Alliances

In one respect, at least, the discussion of affective relations within the household has so far been simple, even simplistic. As anyone who has spent as much time in a family as in a library knows, the relations of one group of persons within a household have consequences for all the others. Households are not made up of neatly defined reciprocal pairs relating only to each other in a precisely choreographed slow waltz; rather, household members engage in more of a square dance, with alliances constantly shifting, groups forming and reforming in response to the actions of others. I have already alluded (in the previous chapter) to the dialectic that may affect relations among fathers and sons, brothers and brothers, with respect to the inheritance of property and to the impact of spouses' relations on sibling solidarity. A quite different interconnection, relevant to the main subject of this chapter, has been posited by Richard Saller; he suggests that the important role played by slaves in childcare in the ancient Roman household contributed to the distance between husbands and wives, who no longer shared this practical day-to-day area of interaction, and to the willingness of wives to leave their children behind in their husbands' households upon divorce.[90] In an attempt to nuance the account of emotional life within the family given here so far, I will now briefly take up a further example of the complexities involved in a family's interactions, the interweaving of marriage ties with those between parents and children.[91]

Relations between husband and wife were thought to be cemented by the birth of children. Marriage at Athens was often spoken of as being contracted specifically "for the birth of legitimate children."[92] And just as marriages were made for children, children made marriages. As a proverbial verse ascribed to Menander puts it, "The greatest link of *philia* is the birth of children" (Men. *Monos.* 736). Euphiletus says he began to trust his wife and put all his affairs in her hands when she gave birth to a *paidion,* considering this the greatest tie of intimacy (*oikeiotēta* [Lys. 1.6]).[93] His wife did not perhaps warrant his faith in her—he is on trial for killing her lover—but the implication is clear nevertheless: a marriage might be considered fully consummated only when a child was born. One of the many slanders spread by Alcibiades' enemies has him playing unscrupulously on this perception to claim (and get) ten extra talents on top of an extraordinary dowry when his wife had a baby ([Andoc.] 4.13). Even a quarreling couple might be reconciled through their children. According to Mantitheus, it is much more common for a husband and wife who are at odds to come to an agreement because of the children than for them to hate their children on account of the wrongs they have done each other.[94] This provided an incentive for even those who had children already to have more if they married a second time.[95]

On the other hand, childless marriages were likely to end in divorce, quite apart from the relations between the spouses. As Menecles grew older, relates his adopted son, he became progressively more concerned that he had no children, so he approached his wife and finally succeeded in persuading her to end their marriage. He took the responsibility for their childlessness on himself and, considerate as he was, made sure she remarried someone who wasn't sterile (Isae. 2.6–9). Menecles' portrayal as a kind of fourth-century sensitive male may strike us as too flattering to him and too favorable to the speaker's case to be true, but there was good reason for him to behave tactfully, at least in public. A divorce in which a wife's fertility was in question might cause dishonor for her and difficulties for her family, reducing as it no doubt would her value on the marriage market. In an extreme case, from a part of the Greek world the Athenians regarded as less than civilized, Alexander of Pherae was killed by his wife and her brothers precisely because (on one account at least) he planned to divorce her on the grounds that she had borne him no children.[96] Aristotle provides a summary: childless marriages are the more easily dissolved; children are a benefit possessed in common by both parents, and common property holds people together (*NE* 8.1162a27). This tells against the hypothesis that "the harshness of child mortality" made women likely to put their husbands before their children.[97]

But it would be naive to suppose that the presence of children in the family always served to minimize conflict. They might be involved on one side or the other as well, often as passive participants in what E. M. Forster has called "that curious duel which is fought over every baby."[98] Pulls in one direction include the Athenian preference for reckoning descent through males, which resulted in men inheriting ahead of women of the same degree of kinship and in children staying in their father's family in cases of death and (probably) divorce.[99] Pulls in the other include the fact that the mother's kin were more likely than the father's to survive as a child grew older, and were in addition likely to be closer in age, and so more intimate. Naturally, special circumstances must weigh heavily in individual cases. So Pericles could claim membership in the influential family of the Alcmaeonidae only through his mother,[100] and Pheidippides, the young wastrel in the *Clouds,* is more influenced by the horsy—(h)*ippides*—part of his name, his inheritance from his wealthy mother, than by the peasant virtues his father tried to instill with the prefix *pheid-,* "frugal."

As they grew older, however, children might play a more active role. Regrettable. Another count in the indictment against Alcibiades was that he bought one of the women enslaved in the Athenian sack of Melos and had a son by her; the child's birth was "more unnatural than Aegisthus's," because his parents were such bitter enemies ([Andoc.] 4.22–23). Even in unions less ill-starred from the start, children were drawn into family feuds. Can we generalize about the likely lines of alliance? Myth, though it has been imaginatively exploited, is an unsatisfactory source of evidence, if only because it allows no clear conclusions.[101] Alongside the stories of Cronus and Zeus and their fathers we may cite other tales that pit children against their mothers. Alcmaeon is mentioned by Aristotle as someone who appears ridiculous because he is compelled by threats to act in a way that is not credible: he kills his mother (*NE* 3.1110a25). Yet his dilemma seemed real enough to others in Athens, being staged by both Sophocles and Euripides.[102] Amphiaraus, betrayed to his death by his wife, Eriphyle, cursed his sons with famine and childlessness if they did not avenge him. One did, Alcmaeon, who was hounded by the Furies until he found purification at the mouth of the river Achelous. His story recalls (once again) Aeschylus's *Oresteia,* still more relevant here because one of Clytemnestra's motives for the murder of her husband is his sacrifice of their daughter, Iphigenia, "dearest product of my labor pains."[103] A detailed study of the forensic speeches, our richest body of real-life material, is only a little more conclusive: ". . . there is perhaps a slight tendency for matrikin to appear as more supportive than patrikin, although the difference is certainly not statistically significant."[104]

There may, however, be something to learn from a genre that

takes its subject matter from everyday life: New Comedy is more one-sided. I will have more to say about it in Chapter 7, but a few Roman plays based on Athenian originals merit mention here. The slave Syrus states that mothers usually help their sons when they are at fault and back them up when their fathers treat them harshly; the young Clitopho, an Athenian, agrees (Ter. *Haut*. 991–993). There are other examples in New Comedy of cooperation between mothers and unmarried sons in conflicts with fathers; consider Terence's *Phormio,* in which Nausistrata leaves it to her son Phaedria to decide how to deal with Chremes, her husband and his father, over an old affair she's just discovered. Stage fathers and sons only rarely join forces against mothers in this way, arguably because conflict between mothers and sons was felt to be an unseemly subject.[105] Plautus's *Asinaria* is a telling exception. Demaenetus and Argyrippus are in cahoots in opposition to their wife and mother, Artemona. The joke, however, is that this is a family in which the woman wears the toga. Demaenetus wants to indulge his son in order to buy his affection, while Artemona (as he says) holds a tight rein and plays a father's part (64–83). The one character who most nearly measures up to Artemona as an authority figure is another woman, the mother of Argyrippus's girlfriend. In other words, *Asinaria* is a play in which women take over the role a man has abandoned. Demaenetus's interest in his son's girlfriend—like Argyrippus's discomfiture—is a signpost to the unhappy end such reversals can lead to. A son's marriage brought new sources of tension into the family (though not necessarily into the household). This is a theme of Terence's *Hecyra,* "The Mother-in-law." But although the old Athenian Laches opines that mothers- and daughters-in-law are agreed on only one thing—hating each other and opposing their husbands (198–204)—in fact the two women are not really rivals in the play, and young Pamphilus, when he believes himself forced to choose, opts for his mother over his wife.

How can we be sure that these attitudes and alliances are features of family life at Athens rather than Rome? True, the plays of Plautus and Terence are in large measure adaptations of Athenian drama. But the few instances in which we can compare their con-

167

tents with the originals (e.g., Plautus's *Bacchides* with Menander's *Dis Exapatōn*) reveal that treatments could be very free; and in a number of relevant aspects—the economic position of women, the father's legal powers—the Roman family differed markedly from the Athenian. Yet, paradoxically, it is just this distinction which may lead us to believe that the family situations envisaged in the Roman plays I have mentioned are indeed taken from Athenian exemplars. In her persuasive portrait of the Roman mother (1988), Suzanne Dixon argues that discipline and the inculcation of traditional morality were as much the province of mothers as of fathers among the Roman elite. She explains the sharing of this role largely by reference to the control over property which distinguished the Roman woman from the Athenian. Since the Roman mother, as an authority figure, was comparable (in fact, if not in law) to the father, we would expect Roman mothers and sons to find themselves in conflict; and, indeed, Dixon discusses some examples. It is the Athenian mother, "the object of patronising affection common to Greek New Comedy and Dagwood comics" (7), whom we find in these plays (except *Asinaria*). Such a mother would give a son no reason to rebel against her. And her willingness to take his side would be enhanced by demographic and economic realities: as we have seen, she could expect to outlive her husband, and would then be dependent for support on her son.

But we have moved a long way from classical Athens, and ought to return. It is perhaps best to leave the last word to a Clytemnestra less fierce than Aeschylus's, the weary matron of Euripides' *Electra*. These are, in fact, virtually her last words as well, addressed to her daughter Electra moments before her death, in response to the charge that she killed her husband and so must die. "My child, you always liked [*stergein*] your father. That's the way it is. Some favor the male side, others love [*philousi*] their mothers more than their fathers" (Eur. *El.* 1102–1104). Once again, we should leave a lot of room for individual preference, unpredictable as it is.[106]

Seven

Change: A Postscript on the Dowries of New Comedy

Change over Time

As the story goes, Mao Zedong, perhaps the greatest revolutionary leader of our time, was once asked to outline the long-term effects of the French Revolution. "A good question," replied Mao. "But it's too early to tell."

Though Mao has fallen out of favor, not least among Maoists, this book reflects some of his caution in commenting on historical change. It covers some two hundred years, from roughly 500 to 300 B.C. Yet that period, six or eight generations, is treated as a homogeneous unit; evidence from the early fifth century is pieced together with data from the late fourth to produce a picture that may resemble in its fidelity to real life some Cubist bravura—a still life in which apples are added to oranges—more than the most grime-dusky Old Master. In short, my neglect of change over time (however convenient for a small book on a big topic) may mislead.

As it happens, there is some good ancient evidence for change in the laws and customs concerning Athenian childhood and the family. Among the most important, Pericles' citizenship law, passed in 451/0 and then reinstituted after the Peloponnesian War, stipulated that only children of two Athenian parents could themselves be citizens of Athens, and thus greatly curtailed the (mostly aristocratic) practice of marrying into families of influential foreigners. Nor has skimpier evidence deterred modern scholars from a series of suggestions (not necessarily compatible) about shifts in attitudes and emotions, more slippery though they are, in the fourth century: that the political elite virtually abandoned the use of marriage even within the community as a means of forging political alliances, that opposition grew to the right of a claimant to marry an *epiklēros* against her will, that tomb organization and grave reliefs testify to an increased interest in (and appreciation of) the nuclear family group and family life, that family identification with an individual's actions grew weaker until inclusion of children and other kin in imprecations against public enemies became less common and razing of relatives' homes altogether ceased.[1] I have not ignored such speculation because I think it uninteresting or without value. Why would I, when I have done my share myself? Some years ago, I discovered that linked names, sons' names sharing an element with their fathers', became significantly more common at Athens at two points in time—the end of the sixth century and the last third of the fifth—and explained this as a consequence of a need to assert family solidarity in the face of the challenge of Cleisthenes' reforms and the crises of the Peloponnesian War.[2] My thoughts on the timing and context of these shifts were offered with considerable private satisfaction, for professional reasons—explaining change separates the high-status historian from the lowly antiquarian or the sociologist—and because I believe in the possibility of radical change (even change for the better) in all areas of political and private life. And my sketch seemed plausible enough; it still does.

But in making my foray into diachrony, I was uneasily conscious that the two factors I had identified as the motive forces for change—Cleisthenes' reforms and the Peloponnesian War—are two of the very few large-scale datable events we know more than a little about during the two hundred or so years this study covers. Worse, our ignorance of so much else makes them stand out all the more starkly. Worst of all, any classicist of average ingenuity can link most changes affecting any branch of social life to them with a fair chance of persuading many of those outside his special field and none of his fellow workers. (Naturally enough, our own scenarios please us, others' carry less conviction.) Thus, when Rühfel accounts for the depiction of wreathed crawlers on *choes* by appealing to the heightened mortality of the Peloponnesian War period, a skeptic might prefer to think that the fact needs no special explanation, since children of that age were never excluded from the Anthesteria at all.[3] Similarly, when Raepsaet and Decocq assert that these *choes* demonstrate a new pleasure in observing children, stemming from a desire to imagine childhood as a sort of paradise lost amid the brutal reality of war, a skeptic might recall that the contrast between the ignorance and innocence of childhood and the world's true perils is hardly a new one—examples may be multiplied among the similes of the *Iliad,* and Simonides uses the conceit to good effect in his lines on Danaë and the infant Perseus (543P.).[4]

I am inclined to take the same stance, selective skepticism, even in regard to change affecting children and childhood from one historical period to another. Leaving aside general (and fundamental) problems concerning periodization in history, I will confine myself to a few remarks on some influential generalizations about the Hellenistic era.[5] More than sixty years ago, Hans Herter (1927) insisted that the Hellenistic poets were the first to put naturalistically drawn children at center stage in their work, and that the art of the Hellenistic period swarms with accurate depictions of real children—because the Greeks of the time took special pleasure in their joyful behavior. Herter pointed to such poems as Callimachus's *Hymn to Artemis,* a portrait of a young girl with an indulgent father of gods and men, and Theocritus's *Idyll* 24; in this work, Pindar's tale of heroic Heracles, strangling snakes as soon as he is born, is modulated into a vignette of domestic life at Thebes (*Alcmena in the Family?*), and the merely mortal and very frightened Iphicles gets a fair share of his mother's (and the poet's) attention. The comparison with Pindar, however, cuts both ways; it illuminates what is distinctive in Theocritus's treatment at the same time that it raises questions concerning Herter's larger claim about Hellenistic society. How much here is owed to a poet's fancy for playing with the tradition, and how much to a new sensibility? Herter himself invoked the new political realities of the time, when "cabinets ruled and mercenaries waged war"; these turned artists away from the great affairs of state which had once engaged them toward "quiet and harmless things"—like the observation of children.

Now, it is certainly true that poets and others who wished to express their opinions on political issues of the day ran risks in the despotisms and class dictatorships of the Hellenistic world; even at democratic Athens, a playwright could be fined for reminding his audience of their misfortunes, as Phrynichus found out (Hdt. 6.21.2). But insofar as Herter's argument depends on the assumption that public and private were generally more widely separated spheres after the downfall of democracy, it is more questionable. We must always remember that we can say very little about any Athenians except the more prosperous ones. And some aspects of the new order imposed in the first instance by Macedon might be said to encourage their participation in public life rather than to inhibit it. Archons and other officials continued to serve. But the abolition of pay for officeholders and the expectation that magistrates provide public expenses from their own purses guaranteed that those who chose to compete for status in this way did so only with their peers; success was consequently all the more honorable. In addition, while the politically ambitious were certainly inhibited in acting as they pleased in interstate relations, property qualifications for the assembly and the withering away of the popular law-courts may actually have increased their leeway internally, at least as long as they did not act against the interests of the great powers. It may therefore be misguided to imagine this stratum, at least, as shrinking into domestic concerns. Nor do grants of political rights and honorary decrees to women, their occasional magistracies, and their participation in public athletic festivals bespeak a widening gulf between the home and the community. We would now hesitate to speak of this new visibility of women as a sign of decadence or "weariness with civilization"; yet this is how Herter seems to regard the parallel focus on children in art.

An opposing tendency is no less troublesome, however: to idealize the Hellenistic Greeks so that their humanity more closely corresponds to some conceptions of our own. In her useful overview of the social history of childhood in ancient Greece, Marieluise Deissmann-Merten asserts that the exposure of newborns became more problematic in the Hellenistic period, a reflection of the notion that a child (even if illegitimate) had a right to live.[6] Her evidence: mainly the incidence of exposure as a theme in New Comedy, especially a passage in Menander's *Samia* (130ff.). But while New Comedy is in the main trustworthy in its presentation of Athenian law concerning marriage, inheritance, and so on—its plots often hang on such details—it is less reliable as an indicator of the frequency with which exposure (and seduction, supposititious children, kidnapping) figured in Athenian life; it is precisely such out-of-the-ordinary occurrences which spice up the stage.[7] With regard to the passage in *Samia*, these lines do not make an explicit statement about a child's right to live (and neither does a scene in *Periciromene* in which grown-up foundlings ask their father why he exposed them: 774–776, 801). Rather, they involve a variation of a theme found also in tragedy, the irrelevance of the distinction between legitimate children and others in a world where no social criterion is of much significance given the gulf between the gods and ourselves.[8] The denial of the claims of birth is fittingly (and perhaps ironically) put into the mouth of Moschion, himself an adopted son.

My comments betray a tendency toward harangue. Let me clarify. I believe that it is very important to deal with change over time. Equally vital, however, is the recognition that identifying change in the distant past is not a simple task—to turn Mao around, it's often too late to tell—and confidence about the causes of change is admirably courageous, but seldom justified. These presumptions may account for the tentative tone of what follows: a consideration of the dowries of New Comedy.

Children and Childhood in Classical Athens

The Dowries of New Comedy

I noted in Chapter 5 that most of our evidence for the size of dowries at Athens in the fifth and fourth centuries is consistent with
the conclusion that they were moderate. Girls were dowered with
much less of the family's estate than their brothers inherited, but
with enough to support a socially acceptable standard of living for
themselves and their children. However, as the accompanying
table indicates, the dowries of New Comedy seem at first sight to
be larger than this.

In absolute terms, these dowries are quite substantial. Those
known for sure amount to at least 6,000 drachmas in almost every
case. The exceptions are *Samia,* in which Niceratus gives Moschion his daughter Plangon and all that he has—after his death.
Niceratus is poor, so this is tantamount to no dowry at all; but it
is possible that Moschion lost any expectation of a dowry by se-
ducing Plangon before their marriage.[9] At the upper extreme, the
text in the fragment of Menander's *Plocion* (402E.) is not absolutely secure, but the likeliest reading, given by Sandbach in his
standard edition, is that Crobyle, a very unattractive woman,
brought her husband an exceptionally large dowry of 60,000
drachmas, but proved a bad bargain even at that; the passage in
Coneazomenae is less certain still, and may not refer to a dowry at
all. Even the other dowries, however, are higher than all but the
most generous known from the orators. There is little basis on
which to make generalizations about the size of these dowries in
proportion to family wealth and the share reserved for others, especially sons. But at least one father, the misanthropic Cnemon in
Dyscolus, is prepared to give his daughter half his estate even
though he has adopted a son.[10]

Scholars are divided in their willingness to accept these dowries
as evidence for Athenian practice in Menander's time, the end of
the fourth century. Historians tend to regard them as "comic exaggeration."[11] For students of Menander's comedy such as Lionel
Casson, however, they are no more than we might expect from the
"milieu of the plutocrats."[12] Gomme and Sandbach conclude that
dowries of 18,000 drachmas "were perhaps . . . unusually gener-

The Dowries of New Comedy

Text	Dowry	Estate	Other Heirs
Men. *Aspis* 135–136, 268–269, 350	12,000 dr. (for a niece)	360,000 dr.	a daughter
Men. *Con.* 3	?18,000 or ?30,000 dr.		
Men. *Dysc.* 328–329, 737–739	6,000 dr.	12,000 dr.	an adopted son
Dysc. 843–844	18,000 dr.		a son
Men. *Epitr.* 134	24,000 dr.		
Men. *Mis.* 446	12,000 dr.		?a son
Men. *Peric.* 1015	18,000 dr.		a son
Men. *Sam.* 727–728	none		
Men. fr. 402E. (333 Sandbach)	60,000 or 96,000 dr.		
Com. Adesp. fr. 117E.	6,000 dr.		
POxy 2533.6–7	?12,000 dr.		

ous, but not . . . incredibly large."[13] Certainly there are plausible arguments for either view. It would indeed be comic for young men to strive and suffer in order to marry the girls they love only to discover that large dowries made their mistresses masters; there are numerous complaints about the power of a well-dowered woman, and they are not confined to comedy.[14] Then, too, the dowry in *Epitrepontes,* 24,000 drachmas, is regarded as a large one. On the other hand, it is a miser who thinks of 6,000 drachmas as a worthy prize in the unattributed comic fragment listed above (*Com. Adesp.* fr. 117E.); perhaps no ordinary man would judge such a sum significant. We might add that some wages had risen by the end of the fourth century, and inflation may have affected dowries too.[15] Even the sumptuary legislation of Demetrius of Phalerum could be brought into the discussion. Large dowries might well have replaced other, outlawed outlays among the status-conscious elite. Such a scenario might lie behind a passage of Plautus's *Aulularia*: old Megadorus urges others to follow his example and marry a poor girl without a dowry (474–495, 524–

536). Another character alludes to the *praefectus mulierum* (504), presumably one of the officials (*gynaikonomoi*) Demetrius appointed to watch women's conduct, including their displays of wealth; this may be an indication that the use of dowries to make an end-run around consumption controls had come to the authorities' attention.

I would prefer, however, to consider the question of the dowries of New Comedy in the context of the relationships within the family I outlined in Chapters 4 and 5. Very simply, I will entertain the hypothesis that dowries did indeed rise as a proportion of the family's wealth devoted to daughters, point out some of the causes and effects we might expect to be associated with this change, and discuss the evidence for these in New Comedy. I remind the reader to remain aware throughout that we are always at least one remove from Athenian society in the late fourth century. When Roman adaptations are in question, we are still more distant. As has been my practice throughout this book, I will therefore confine my use of these plays to those known or plausibly supposed to be by Menander or his near contemporaries and also set in Athens; and even these are meant merely to corroborate other evidence.

Unregulated (except in the case of *epiklēroi*) by any law, dowries belonged to the domain of custom; their amounts, too, were to some extent conventional, so that rich fathers might normally pay out a smaller proportion of their property than poorer ones within the same social circles. Nevertheless, we should not underemphasize an individual's motives to move outside the norm. Unusual husbands might be satisfied with less than the usual dowry, or even none at all, in order to display generosity or devotion or to secure a tie with a father they admired; fathers might decide to offer more to gain an advantageous match or even to marry off an unfavored daughter like Crobyle.[16] In addition, dowries probably were not completely sheltered from larger-scale market forces involving supply and demand. Fluctuations in the availability of husbands and wives must (eventually) have had an impact. Thus, dowries could be expected to rise if more women of marriageable age were available than men, since daughters would become harder to place and husbands a scarce commodity with a higher value. Such a surplus of potential brides might have several causes: a fall in women's rate of mortality (in turn, perhaps, to be explained by a higher valuation of daughters) or an increase in men's, a drop in women's age at marriage or a rise in men's. Though an isolated line from *Halieis* does speak of a daughter as "difficult to marry off" (Men. fr. 18E.), there is otherwise very little evidence for any of these. It is hard to imagine brides marrying much younger than the fifteen or so we assumed in Chapter 4 for the classical period; at any rate, Greek New Comedy provides no sign that they did, and the girlfriends of Roman comedy are fifteen or older.[17] As for the husbands of New Comedy, these generally seem as young as or even younger than other Athenians. Designations applied to Menander's married or about-to-be-married men include *meirakyllion, meirakiskos, meirakion, neaniskos*.[18] These terms are impossible to define precisely, but they are certainly more appropriate to a young man in his twenties than to a man of thirty or older.[19]

The lack of reliable statistical data prevents us from saying anything very convincing about demographic trends in the late fourth century. But New Comedy does afford some evidence for close relationships between fathers and daughters. I have already mentioned (in Chapter 2) the unusual circumstances of Menander's *Dyscolus,* in which the misanthropic Cnemon works in the fields in the company of his daughter. I explained this as a sign of the old man's miserly nature: he chooses not to buy or hire help. But the girl's presence might also serve to show affection; she is described as very distressed when her "dearest dad" (*pappan philtaton,* 648–649) falls down a well (673–674). Among fathers, Cichesias cries in recalling his daughter's kidnapping many years earlier, and faints (with joy?) when he learns she is alive (Men. *Sic.* 354–364). An exchange in *Epitrepontes* even implies that mutual respect was an ideal to appeal to. Pamphile insists that her father persuade her to give up her husband rather than command her to; otherwise, he would be a master and not a father (714–715).[20] But it is one thing to collect such passages, more challenging to prove that they represent a shift in attitudes. In Chapter 4, I noted earlier evidence for similar sentiments binding fathers and daughters, who did not threaten or supplant them. Even the easy intimacy between Pamphile and Smicrines is not unparalleled on the Athenian stage: Antigone admonished Oedipus almost a century before (Soph. *OC* 1181–1203). And, on the other side, some much-quoted denigrations of daughters in favor of sons come from New Comedy.[21]

The discussion so far seems to point straight to the conclusion that no reason for the proportion of household assets devoted to dowries to increase can be identified. But such a conclusion would be too hasty. If the men of Menander's time were indeed marrying younger, this might provide a quite different cause for large dowries. The younger the bridegroom, the more likely it was that his father was still alive, and that he had not yet come into his inheritance. Under these circumstances, dowries might increase in order to cover a larger portion of the new household's expenses. Consistent with this hypothesis is the fact that some young men with living fathers undertook such liturgies as supplying a chorus for a local festival (Men. *Sam.* 13). We should therefore take a look at the other side of the equation, the consequences of a rise in dowries.

It is the relationship between brothers and sisters we would assume to be most affected by an increase in the relative level of dowries. If dowries were not merely larger absolutely but also (as in *Dyscolus*) as a proportion of the family's wealth, sisters' shares might begin to rival brothers': a likely source of conflict. Like other Athenian brothers, those of New Comedy clearly recognize an obligation to help secure a sister a dowry and a suitable marriage.[22] Cleostratus even goes on campaign to Lycia in quest of booty for his sister's dowry; Gorgias, urged to look after his half-sister and keep her safe, is prepared to sell off his holdings to provide her dowry (until Callippides' kindness makes this unnecessary).[23] The duty might therefore be onerous, but, as Gorgias remarks, "It isn't possible to escape a relationship (*oikeiotēta*)" with a sister (Men. *Dysc.* 239–240). Resentment at this responsibility might appear only natural, especially if the burden were perceived as increasing. In fact, however, neither Cleostratus nor Gorgias expresses any.[24] Another brother, a character in Menander's fragmentary *Phasma*, seems concerned that his sister may be depressed at marrying a man who doesn't love her (91–92). Roman adaptations, too, show brothers and sisters who are as concerned and as caring as our other evidence indicates. Consider, for example, Eunomia's speech to her brother Megadorus: ". . . I say this to you out of loyalty, as a sister should. . . . Remember, we're closer to each other than anyone else, so we ought to give advice and confide freely" (Plaut. *Aulul.* 120–132). Later in the play, when her son asks Eunomia to intercede with Megadorus on his behalf, she is confident her brother will do what she wants (682–687).[25] There is nothing here to lead us to believe that larger dowries had disrupted links between brothers and sisters.

Nor do large dowries commonly figure as a cause of complaint for the stage fathers who must provide for them. An exception: Donatus, commenting on Terence's *Phormio* 646–647, tells us that a slave's remark—"it did no good not to raise a daughter, for now one has been found who's looking for a dowry"—was made by an elderly male citizen in the play's early third century original by Apollodorus of Carystus (Apollodorus fr. 22E.). Otherwise, though Menander's fathers (like those in the orators) allude to the costs of parenting, they do not identify large dowries as a major burden or indeed concentrate on daughters at all.[26] In two plays where the issue might be made to arise, *Epitrepontes* and *Periciromene,* men decide against raising newborns because of the expense; but it is a baby boy which Davus declines to rear, and the twins Pataecus exposes include a boy as well as a girl.[27] Once again, the predictable effects of larger dowries are not easy to discern.

Given the preamble, my conclusions are not very surprising. The internal evidence of the plays does not supply support (at least not strong support) for the hypothesis that the dowries of New Comedy represent a significantly higher proportion of the family's wealth than those known from other sources. They are large sums, certainly; but they are paid by men who can well afford them (at least in their own minds), and they are not so lavish as to cause resentment in other family members. Thus, another apparent indication of chronological development in the history of the

Athenian family turns out to be an illusion. I repeat, however, that I have no doubt that such changes did occur. Indeed, even in this case (as in many others in this book), the evidence is so inadequate and the argument from silence so unsatisfying that it would take very little to make me recognize the existence of variation over time—and change my mind.

List of Abbreviations

ABSA	*Annual of the British School at Athens*
ABV	J. D. Beazley, *Attic Black-Figure Vase-Painters* (Oxford 1956)
AJA	*American Journal of Archeology*
AJP	*American Journal of Philology*
AntCl	*L'Antiquité classique*
AntK	*Antike Kunst*
ArkhDelt	*Arkhaiologikon Deltion*
ARV²	J. D. Beazley, *Attic Red-Figure Vase-Painters*, 2d ed. (Oxford 1963)
AthMitt	*Mitteilungen des Deutschen Archäologischen Instituts (Athen. Abt.)*
BCH	*Bulletin de correspondance hellénique*
BICS	*Bulletin of the Institute of Classical Studies of the University of London*

CB	*Classical Bulletin*
CJ	*Classical Journal*
CP	*Classical Philology*
CQ	*Classical Quarterly*
CR	*Classical Review*
CW	*Classical World*
EMC	*Classical Views / Échos du monde classique*
GRBS	*Greek, Roman, and Byzantine Studies*
GVI	W. Peek, *Griechische Vers-Inschriften*, vol. 1, *Grab-Epigramme* (Berlin 1955)
HSCP	*Harvard Studies in Classical Philology*
JFH	*Journal of Family History*
JHS	*Journal of Hellenic Studies*
JRS	*Journal of Roman Studies*
Paralipomena	J. D. Beazley, *Paralipomena: Additions to "Attic Black-Figure Vase-Painters" and to "Attic Red-Figure Vase-Painters,"* 2d ed. (Oxford 1971)
QUCC	*Quaderni urbinati di cultura classica*
REA	*Revue des études anciennes*
REG	*Revue des études grecques*
RhM	*Rheinisches Museum*
RPh	*Revue de philologie*
SEG	*Supplementum Epigraphicum Graecum*
TAPA	*Transactions of the American Philological Association*
ZPE	*Zeitschrift für Papyrologie und Epigraphik*

Notes

Chapter One. *Characteristics of Childhood and Children*

1. Pind. *Nem.* 3.43–52; Hdt. 1.114–115, Xen. *Cyr.* 1.4.16–20 (and compare the boasts of the ten-year-old Cambyses, Hdt. 3.3); Plut. *Alcib.* 2.3; cf. Plut. *Them.* 2.1–2. Golden (1979) 25–28 provides a discussion of Greek idiom for designating age in years.
2. Hdt. 5.92γ; Arist. *HA* 7.587b5, Hippoc. *Septim.* 7.450L.; Stuart (1921).
3. See especially Pl. *Leg.* 7.788D–790A, Arist. *Pol.* 7.1334b29–1335b20. A political enemy's nature is explained by the allegation that he was raised in an *ergastērion,* a brothel or workshop (Dem. *Ep.* 4.1).
4. Pl. *Tim.* 26B, cf. *Ap.* 18B, *Leg.* 6.753E, 765E, *Resp.* 2.377AB, Eur. *Supp.* 913–917, fr. 1027N.², Antiph. 87 B 60D.-K.
5. Pl. *Lys.* 211D; Xen. *Ages.* 10.4.
6. Lys. 2.13, 14.17, 20.34–35, Isae. 7.33–34, Dem. 38.20, cf. Eur. *Med.* 1101–1105, Ter. *Andr.* 51–59.
7. The fullest discussion is Boll (1913); cf. Nash (1978) 4–10, Vílchez (1983).
8. Eur. *El.* 541–544, cf. 283–284, *Or.* 377–379.
9. Pl. *Alcib. I* 123D, 127E, cf. *Leg.* 11.929C, Hyper. *Lycoph.* 15.
10. Kassel (1951) gives a valuable account of the literary sources down to the end of the fifth century. See also Herter (1961b) 146–158, French (1977) 13–15, Mette (1982).
11. Arist. *HA* 7.584a23, 581b9; Aen. Tact. 40.

12. Cf. (for Plato) Sprague (1984).
13. Athenian boys were enrolled in a deme, the local, hereditary body that recognized them as citizens, in the eighteenth archon-year after their birth. I have elsewhere argued that since all boys born in the same archon-year were enrolled together, most were eighteen, but some, born late in the year, were still seventeen; see Golden (1979), especially 35–38.
14. For such expressions of envy, see Soph. *Ajax* 552–555, *OC* 1229–1232, *Trach.* 141–152, fr. 583R., Eur. *Med.* 46–48; Herter (1961b) 146–152.
15. Eur. *IT* 1249–1282; *Hym. Merc.* 17–396, cf. Soph. fr. 314.277–282R.; Pind. *Nem.* 1.33–59; Laager (1957), Woodford (1983).
16. Hes. *Op.* 127–131
17. E.g., [Arist.] *Probl.* 34.10.964a33, cf. Arist. *Gen. An.* 2.733b2.
18. Arist. *EE* 7.1240b33 (cf. 2.1226b23), *Mag. Mor.* 1.1185a3, *NE* 1.1100a1, 3.1111a26, 1111b8, *Phys.* 2.197b7.
19. Aeschin. 1.18, cf. 1.39, *Trag. Adesp.* fr. 515aK.-S.
20. Aesch. *Eum.* 38, Soph. fr. 314.161R., Astydamas II 60 F 2 Snell, Xen. *Mem.* 1.4.7, Pl. *Gorg.* 479A, *Leg.* 11.933B, *Phd.* 77DE, *Resp.* 1.330E, *Tht.* 166A, 168D.
21. Pl. *Lach.* 197AB, Arist. *EE* 3.1229a18. But see also Pl. *Leg.* 12.963E.
22. E.g., Xen. *Hell.* 4.4.17, Pl. *Cri.* 46C, *Phd.* 77E, *Resp.* 2.381E; Mary Rosaria (1917) 34–40. Is the lamp mentioned at Lys. 1.14 perhaps a night light to comfort the baby? Winkler (1982) argues that two other female figures, Akko and Alphito, were not bogies but flibbertigibbets in tales told to rouse children from idleness.
23. E.g., a stamnos by Painter of Munich 2413, about 450, Munich 2413, *ARV*² 495.1, 1656, *Paralipomena* 380; Schefold (1981) 51–55. A *chous* may show a boy running away from a silen's mask (van Hoorn [1951] no. 918 pl. 84).
24. A. L. Brown (1983) 26.
25. *Dis paides hoi gerontes*: see especially Ar. *Nub.* 1410–1419, Pl. *Leg.* 1.646A, [Pl.] *Ax.* 367B, Theopompus fr. 69E., *Suda* s. *dis paides*, Diogen. 4.18. For full references see Cantarella (1971), Gigante (1973) 86–87.
26. Aesch. *PV* 987–988, cf. *Ag.* 277, 479.
27. Ar. *Nub.* 537–539, Eupolis fr. 261K.-A., cf. Ar. fr. 604K.-A., Arist. *Pol.* 7.1336b20 (disapproving).
28. For children's complaints, see also Xen. *Mem.* 2.2.8, Pl. *Resp.* 10.604CD.
29. Xen. *Cyr.* 1.3.10, cf. Pl. *Leg.* 1.645E–646A; Xen. *Ages.* 1.17.
30. Know little: Pl. *Clit.* 408E, *Tht.* 197E, *Tim.* 23B, cf. *Euthd.* 294E. Gullible: Pl. *Gorg.* 499C, 502E, *Leg.* 2.664A, *Resp.* 10.598C, *Soph.* 234BC

(cf. *Leg.* 2.663B), 242C; similarly, the Peripatetic Clearchus thought children especially susceptible to hypnosis (fr. 7 Wehrli). Lack understanding: Pl. *Euthd.* 279D, cf. *Ep.* 8.355C, *Leg.* 11.929E, *Phlb.* 65C, *Symp.* 204B, [Pl.] *Ax.* 365B. Talk nonsense: Pl. *Cri.* 46D, 49B, *Phlb.* 14D. Lack judgment: Pl. *Gorg.* 464D, cf. *Epin.* 974A, *Leg.* 4.720A, *Resp.* 2.377B–378E, 8.557C, 9.577A.

31. Pl. *Ep.* 4.320C, *Phdr.* 279A, *Prot.* 342E, *Tht.* 177B; *Gorg.* 470C, cf. 471D; *Euthd.* 301C, cf. 279D, *Symp.* 204B.

32. Pl. *Clit.* 409DE, *Ep.* 8.355C, *Leg.* 4.710A, 7.808DE, 12.963E, *Resp.* 4.431C, 441AB, *Tht.* 171E.

33. Arist. *Gen. An.* 1.728a17; Arist. *EE* 2.1224a29, 7.1236a1, 1238a33, 1240b33, *HA* 7.588a31, cf. *NE* 1.1100a1, 3.1111a26, 1111b8, 6.1144b9, 7.1152b20, 1153a30, *Part. An.* 4.686b24, *Phys.* 2.197b7, [Arist.] *Probl.* 10.39.895a13, 11.30.902b10, 30.14.957a43; Arist. *Rh.* 1.1371a15, 2.1384b24.

34. Arist. *Aud.* 801b5, *EE* 1.1214b30, 7.1238a33, *NE* 7.1154b10, *Pol.* 7.1323a33, *Protr.* fr. 55 Rose, [Arist.] *Probl.* 30.14.957a43.

35. Arist. *NE* 10.1174a1; *EE* 1.1215b24.

36. Arist. *Mem.* 453b5, [Arist.] *Probl.* 15.3.911a3.

37. Arist. *EE* 2.1219b5, cf. *Pol.* 1.1260a14, 8.1339a30, [Arist.] *Probl.* 10.46.896a19.

38. *Il.* 15.362–364, cf. Arist. *Phil.* fr. 26 Rose (19c Ross).

39. Aesch. *Ag.* 394–395, Eur. fr. 271N.², Pl. *Euthd.* 291B; Rabel (1987). Later, Plutarch mentions children trying vainly to hold the rainbow in their hands (*Mor.* 766A).

40. Soph. fr. 149R., cf. Plut. *Mor.* 508C; Apost. 12.93, Diogen. 7.11, *Ep. Diogen.* 3.47, Zenob. 5.58; Carson (1986) 111–116.

41. Eur. *Med.* 1071–1075, 1402–1403, *Tro.* 757–758, cf. Pind. *Ol.* 6.55–56.

42. [Arist]. *Probl.* 4.12.877b20, 4.24.879a22.

43. Pl. *Leg.* 7.789E, *Resp.* 2.377A, cf. Arist. *Pol.* 7.1336a10.

44. Pl. *Leg.* 7.791E, cf. Aesch. *Cho.* 751, Eur. *Alc.* 189–190, *HF* 98–99, *Tro.* 749, Lys. 1.10–11, Arist. *HA* 7.587a28, Men. *Sam.* 239; Pl. *Leg.* 7.792A, *Resp.* 10.604C, Arist. *Pol.* 7.1336a35.

45. Aesch. *Sept.* 348, Ar. *Vesp.* 570, Eupolis fr. 112K.-A.; Men. fr. 1004E.

46. Arist. *Gen. An.* 5.786b16, cf. *Aud.* 803b19, *HA* 7.581b9, [Arist.] *Probl.* 11.14.900a33, 11.24.901b25. Higher-pitched pipes were called *paidikoi*, "childish" (Ath. 4.182C).

47. Pl. *Gorg.* 485B, cf. Ar. *Nub.* 862, 1381, Arist. *HA* 4.536b5.

48. E.g., *bau* (*Com. Adesp.* fr. 1030E.); *bry, mamma,* and *kakka* (Ar. *Nub.* 1382–1385, cf. *Eq.* 1126 with Schol.); *lollō* (?) (Hermippus fr. 86K.-A.); *tata* (Theophr. *Char.* 7.9[?]); Stephanopoulos (1983), Lambin (1984).

49. [Arist.] *Probl.* 10.4.891a27; 33.18.963b10; 4.28.880a20; Arist. *HA* 5.557a7, [Arist.] *Probl.* 1.16.861a16; Pl. *Leg.* 2.663B.
50. Callias fr. 31dE., cf. Diphilus fr. 73K.-A., *Hym. Merc.* 294–298.
51. [Arist.] *Probl.* 1.19.861b3, 3.7.872a2, 3.34.876a15, 4.4.877a1, 30.14.957a43.
52. [Arist.] *Probl.* 8.20.889a15, 10.45.895b30.
53. Arist. *EE* 3.1229a29, *Pol.* 7.1334b25; *NE* 3.1119b8, cf. 2.1105a1.
54. Pl *Leg.* 2.664E; Pl. *Resp.* 4.431C, cf. 4.441A, *Leg.* 2.653A.
55. Ar. *Thesm.* 505–506 (the honeycomb) with Schol., cf. Pl. *Ep.* 13.361A; Arist. *Pol.* 8.1341a16.
56. Pl. *Leg.* 2.664E, 672C, cf. Arist. *Pol.* 8.1340b29.
57. Pl. *Leg.* 7.808D, cf. Xen. *Cyr.* 2.3.9–10.
58. Fr. 35 Wehrli.
59. Ar. *Vesp.* 1183–1185; Pl. *Menex.* 236C, cf. *Leg.* 3.685A, *Tht.* 168E.
60. Lys. 14.25, Pherecrates fr. 155E., Plut. *Alcib.* 3 (= Antiph. fr. 66 Thalheim); on the dangers of acting older than one's age, cf. Eur. fr. 603N.², Men. *Monos.* 690, where the contexts are uncertain.
61. I follow Herter (1961b); *contra,* Dover (1974) 104.
62. Pl. *Symp.* 217E, cf. Phot. s. *oinos aneu paideutōn.*
63. Their innocence (and suggestibility) led to their use as mediums in later antiquity; Hopfner (1926).
64. Of the many words referring to young persons, most were used throughout the Greek world. There were local usages, however, such as *laispais* (said by Hesychius, *s.v.,* to be a Leucadian synonym for *boupais*), *kōraliskos* (a Cretan equivalent of *meirakion*: Hsch., Phot. s. *kōraliskon*), *kyrsanios* (Laconian dialect for *neanias:* Ar. *Lys.* 1248 with Schol.), and *korasion* ("little girl" in Macedonian: Schol. *Il.* 20.404). In addition, some states (Sparta for one) had technical terms for age classes of children and youths. The discussion here will focus on those terms known to be in use at Athens.
65. Cf. Golden (1985b) 91–97.
66. Gomme and Sandbach (1973) 213–214 on *Dysc.* 500.
67. Thus, LSJ s. *pais* and *teknon,* Chantraine (1968–1980) 848, cf. Deissmann-Merten (1984) 268–269.
68. Aesch. *Pers.* 177, 189, 197, etc.; *Cho.* 896; *Supp.* 600, 739, 753, 980.
69. Eur. *Hec.* 171; *Ba.* 1305, *Andr.* 714; cf. Thury (1988a) 305 n. 9. The orators seldom use *teknon,* reserving it for highly emotive contexts; but *pais* can be substituted for it even there, as at Aeschin. 3.156–157.
70. See Schol. and Stanford (1983) 91.
71. For alliteration, see, e.g., Soph. *OC* 1140, Eur. *IA* 690. For puns on *pais* and *paiō,* "I strike," see Aesch. *Eum.* 496, Ar. *Eq.* 451, 453, *Vesp.* 1297–1298, 1307, and Golden (1985b) 102–104; for *pais* and Paris,

perhaps Aesch. *Ag.* 394, 399, and Bollack in Bollack and Judet de La Combe (n.d.) 1.2.413 *ad loc.*

72. For examples of words for *children* used with unusual force in *Agamemnon*, see Rabel (1984), Golden (1985b) 95.

73. Ariès (1973) 1–22. For a review of criticisms of Ariès' conclusions, see Vann (1982). For their relevance to antiquity, see Strubbe (1982).

74. Manson (1983) 152, cf. Manson (1978) 264–275, Néraudau (1984) 19–61.

75. See Saller (1984a) and (1987b) 67, against Herlihy (1985) 3–4; Saller and Shaw (1984), Shaw (1984). Gray-Fow (1985) argues that both popular and legal terminology for children at Rome cut across recognized distinctions of age and status.

76. Ar. *Byz. fr.* 37–66 Slater. In late-fourth-century Athens (and perhaps earlier), an *ephēbos,* "ephebe," was a young man who had reached majority and then underwent two years of military service during which his civic rights were restricted.

77. Hippoc. in Philo, *Opif. Mundi* 36.105. The division into units of seven is a recurring theme; see, e.g., Solon 27W. and Boll (1913).

78. Antiph. *Tetr.* 2.4.6, Pl. *Leg.* 10.904E, *Lys.* 204E–205B (where Lysis is still known by his father's name); Lys. 32.19, Aeschin. 3.154, Reinmuth (1971) nos. 1, 9; Ar. *Ach.* 680, Thuc. 8.69.4, Isae. 4.26, Aeschin. 3.161, Pl. *Symp.* 198A; Sacco (1979), Cantarella (1988) 49–52.

79. *Meirakion* and *neaniskos:* Ar. *Eq.* 556, 731, *Plut.* 975, 1016, Antiph. *Tetr.* 2.4.5–6, Lys. 3.10, 32.9, 19, Pl. *Euthd.* 277CD, Men. *Georg.* 67, 69. *Pais* and *paidion:* Isae. 11.37, Pl. *Crat.* 392BD, Arist. *NE* 3.1119b6. *Paidion* and *paidarion:* Pl. *Gorg.* 485B. Note, too, that *paides* are younger than *paidiskoi* at Sparta: Xen. *Hell.* 5.4.32, *Lac.* 3.5.

80. Cf. Bryant (1907) 74–76 and Roesch (1982) 307–354.

81. Arist. *AthPol* 42.1, 56.7, cf. Dem. 21.154, Aeschin. 2.99, 167, Pl. *Menex.* 249A. An exception: at Soph. *Trach.* 557, Deianira describes herself as *pais et' ousa,* "still a *pais,*" at a time when she was already (though very recently) married to Heracles, apparently to bring out her youth and vulnerability.

82. Pl. *Symp.* 222B (reflecting a Homeric adage), [Pl.] *Ax.* 365B, 366D, 367A, Arist. *NE* 2.1105a2, *Pol.* 8.1340b30, [Arist.] *Probl.* 11.24.901b27. It is used of an older boy at Antiph. *Tetr.* 2.2.11 for pathos and to emphasize that he was the unwitting agent of harm.

83. Xen. *Mem.* 2.2.5, *Oec.* 7.24; cf. Hdt. 1.111, 3.153.

84. *IG* 12.5 677.2, Syros, ?second century A.D.

85. Men. *Sam.* 254; Aesch. fr. 47a.787, 813R., cf. Theoc. 15.12, 42.

86. Pl. *Phd.* 116B, cf. *Ap.* 34D. Gorgo, a girl of eight or nine, is called *paidion* in Herodotus's Ionic dialect (5.51). Children old enough to be in school are *paidia* at Hyper. *Euxen.* 22.

87. *Meirakion* and *meirakiskos:* Pl. *Thg.* 122D, 131A, Men. fr. 530b.6, 9E. *Neanias* and *neaniskos:* Pl. *Charm.* 154D–155A. Note, too, that some manuscripts read *neaniais* and others *neaniskois* at Pl. *Resp.* 1.328D.
88. E.g., [Dem.] 53.19, 59.18.
89. Pl. *Pol.* 270E; Arist. *Gen. An.* 2.744a26.
90. Aesch. *Cho.* 750–760, cf. Pl. *Resp.* 5.460D and, for a list of a baby boy's material needs, Plaut. *Truc.* 902–908.
91. Arist. *Col.* 798a30, *Gen. An.* 5.779a27, 780b1. But note that their hair is said to be reddish at *Col.* 797b24. The reason is in each case the same, a shortage of food.
92. Arist. *Gen. An.* 5.778b21, *Somn.* 457a4, cf. *EE* 1.1216a6.
93. Arist. *Gen. An.* 5.779a13, *HA* 5.537b13, *Insomn.* 3.461a13, 462b5, [Arist.] *Probl.* 3.34.876a20.
94. Arist. *Part. An.* 4.686b10, cf. *HA* 2.500b34, *Inc. An.* 710b10.
95. For feeding bottles, see Kern (1957), Herter (1964), Bartsocas (1978); a sixth-century example of a potty-stool is in the Agora Museum in Athens, Rühfel (1984b) no. 19, cf. a cup by the Sotades Painter, about 450, Brussels, Musées royaux A 890, *ARV²* 771.1, Rühfel (1984b) no. 18; for cradles, see van Hoorn (1909) 17–21; walkers are mentioned by Soranus, *Gyn.* 2.45.114, and perhaps depicted on a *chous,* van Hoorn (1951) no. 855 pl. 42.
96. For the translation "swaddling clothes," see Hsch. s. *spargana,* Phot. s. *sparganōmata,* LSJ s.v., Mary Rosaria (1917) 17, Deissmann-Merten (1984) 290–291.
97. Pl. *Leg.* 7.789E; Soran. *Gyn.* 2.14–15.83–84, 42.111, Rousselle (1983) 71–73.
98. E.g., Étienne (1977) pl. 1–4; Plut. *Lyc.* 16.3.
99. E.g., Conze (1893–1922) no. 59 pl. 27, no. 274 pl. 63, no. 276 pl. 64, no. 306 pl. 73.
100. Cf. van Hoorn (1909) 6–16. Is there anything in Greek art to correspond to the "apron designed for children who are not yet toilet-trained" identified in a Hittite figurine from Nuzi (Canby [1986] 65)?
101. Whatever their purpose, such strictures appear to have no measurable long-term affect on physiological or psychological development; Chisholm (1983) 71–91, cf. Doumanis (1983) 52–53 (on the five months of swaddling practiced in rural villages of modern Epirus).
102. Cf. Rühfel (1984b) 9–16.
103. By Palion of Paros, about 450, Rühfel (1984a) no. 36.
104. London BM 628, about 435, Conze (1893–1922) no. 696 pl. 119, Rühfel (1984a) no. 51.

105. Athens NM 3289, about 380, Conze (1893–1922) no. 338 pl. 86, Rühfel (1984a) no. 64.
106. Rühfel (1984b) 100–107, especially 106–107, Kahil (1965) and (1977).
107. See, e.g., van Hoorn (1951) no. 100 pl. 507, no. 463 pl. 264, no. 1007 pl. 252.
108. Soph. *Ajax* 558–559, 1409–1411; Mills (1980–1981) 134. The newborn Ion would have been unlikely to reach out pathetically to the mother who abandoned him, and as a boy reveals a rather mature grasp of Athenian political realities (Eur. *Ion* 961, 585–632). See also Eur. *Andr.* 722–723; Kassel (1951) 66–69.
109. See the convenient table in French (1977) 18.
110. Cf. Pl. *Crat.* 414B, Arist. *Mem.* 453b6.
111. Hippoc. in Philo, *Opif. Mundi* 36.105, Solon 27.1–2W., cf. Ar. *Ran.* 422, *Com. Adesp.* fr. 572, 573E., Plaut. *Men.* 1116. Pollux, writing about horses, says that the tooth was called *gnōma* and the period itself *gnōristikos,* "capable of knowing" (1.182); cf. Quint. 1.1.15 (quoting Greek authorities).
112. Rogoff et al. (1975).
113. Arist. *HA* 5.544b20, 7.581a9; Eyben (1972), Durling (1986).
114. Lys. 10.4–5, cf. 26.21, 30.7.
115. Pl. *Resp.* 5.450C. The series *genesis, trophē, paideia:* cf. Pl. *Alcib. I* 122B, *Cri.* 50E, 51C.
116. Arist. *Aud.* 801b5, *HA* 4.536b5, [Arist.] *Probl.* 11.1.898b33. Exceptions: [Arist.] *Probl.* 11.27.902a5.

Chapter Two. The Child in the Household and the Community

1. See Golden (1981) and, for debate on the prevalence of rejection, Isager (1981–1982), Schmidt (1983–1984), Engels (1984), Gallo (1984), Patterson (1985), Ridgway (1987) 405–406. Oldenziel (1987) reviews the scholarship on exposure in the context of cultural and intellectual history.
2. Golden (1986) 252–256.
3. Hsch. s. *stephanon ekpherein.* Hippias is said to have raised revenue by requiring new fathers to give measures of wheat and barley and a silver coin to the priestess of Athena on the Acropolis ([Arist.] *Oec.* 2.1347a17). The practice may be historical, whatever its origins.
4. For names as a means of socialization, see briefly Golden (1986) 246–249.
5. See Golden (1986) 249–252.
6. Young children might be identified by the name of the father alone;

e.g., Pl. *Lys.* 204E, *IG* 2² 2345.73 ("son of Euphronius"), cf. Pl. *Parm.* 126B. Identification by the mother's name was usually an insult, a slur on one's legitimacy or one's father's worth; see, in tragedy, Soph. fr. 564R. (reading *mētros*), Eur. *El.* 933–935, fr. 1064N.², cf. Soph. *El.* 365–367. A few classical gravestones for women bear only the mother's name (*IG* 2² 10205, 10892, 11568, 11793, 12138, 12575); it is possible that these are unmarried girls whose fathers died before them, but more likely those not recognized by their fathers. (Skinner [1987] suggests that women referred to each other by their mothers' names in private life, but there is no evidence for this from classical Athens.) Exceptional instances occur in Plato's *Alcibiades I,* where Socrates addresses Alcibiades as "son of Cleinias and Deinomache" (105D) and later refers to him as "Deinomache's son" (123C). The contexts may be sufficient cause: a reference to the nobility of Deinomache's family, a challenge to Xerxes' mother and wife. See also Pl. *Ep.* 2.313A, where Dionysius is addressed as "son of Dionysius and Doris."

7. What follows is a summary of Golden (1986) 257–267.

8. On the nature of the *genos,* see Bourriot (1976) and Roussel (1976), summarized in R.C. Smith (1985).

9. Andoc. 1.125–127, [Dem.] 59.55–61.

10. On phratry membership, see most recently Flower (1985) 234 (all males members), Golden (1985a).

11. The one known exception is Thrasyllus, introduced by his adoptive father, Apollodorus, at the spring Thargelia (Isae. 7.15). There was a special reason for haste in this case: Apollodorus was a sick man who feared that he would die without an heir.

12. Very young: Andoc. 1.125–126, Isae. 8.19, *IG* 2² 1237.118, *Etym. Mag.* s. *Apatouria,* Dem. 57.54. Three or four: Schol. Pl. *Tim.* 21B. Seven: Ar. *Ran.* 422. Late: Isae. 6.21–22, cf. Lys. 30.2.

13. *IG* 2² 1237.5–8, 28–29, 53–54, 60–61.

14. It is possible that this practice was peculiar to the Deceleieis, but the references to the introduction of both older and younger children suggest that it was widespread.

15. Shares from each sacrifice were given to the priest (slightly smaller in the case of the *meion*) and to (? some of) the phraters, who might make up a fairly sizable group; *IG* 2² 1237.5–8, Schol. Ar. *Ran.* 798, Harpoc. s. *meion kai meiagōgos,* and, for the size of the phratries and their subdivisions, Flower (1985). Phrastor, a *genētēs* but a poor man, introduced his son at an early age, but he was sick and probably afraid of dying childless; besides, his father-in-law, Stephanus, may have paid his bills ([Dem.] 59.50). The nature of the *koureion* seems to preclude the participation of girls, and it is possible that no special

sacrifice was made on their behalf; cf. Labarbe (1953) 359 n. 4 (but see, *contra*, Zoepffel [1985] 375–376).

16. Hsch., *Suda* s. *Koureōtis*; van Hoorn (1909) 38–51. Boys entering the ephebate dedicated a lock of hair as well; Phot. s. *oinistēria* (on the authority of Eupolis, fr. 146K.-A.), Eustath. *Il.* 907.18, Hsch. s. *oinistēria*, Ath. 11.494F, cf. Theophr. *Char.* 21.3, Plut. *Thes.* 5.1, Eustath. *Il.* 165.4, 1292.66.

17. Crete: Koehl (1986). Thera: Davis (1986). Sparta: Xen. *Lac.* 11.3, Plut. *Lyc.* 22.1.

18. Davies (1969) makes a strong but not conclusive case for 366/5; cf. Brun (1985) 312–314, and, *contra*, Cawkwell (1973).

19. Labarbe (1953) asserts that the historical present in Isae. 6.22, 27, is meant to emphasize just how soon after the rejection of Alce's son Euctemon threatened to marry and the very short time between the boy's final acceptance and Philoctemon's death (388). But the tense may simply highlight an important point—Euctemon's outrageous threat, Philoctemon's untimely death—an expressive and vivid use much like the common forensic use of deictic iota; cf. Lys. 1.6, Dem. 32.5.

20. Hippoc. in Philo, *Opif. Mundi* 36.105, Solon 27.2–3W., Arist. *HA* 5.544b26, 7.581a11; Hopfner (1938) 225–232, Eyben (1972), Durling (1986).

21. Cratinus fr. 183K.-A., Thuc. 2.46.1 with Schol., Lys. fr. 6.35–40 Gernet (*Theoz.*), Aeschin. 3.154, cf. Pl. *Menex.* 249A. Xen. *Mem.* 2.1.21 may be an informal example of this usage.

22. Isae. 8.31, 10.12, fr. 25 Thalheim, [Dem.] 46.20, 24, Hyper. fr. 192 Jensen.

23. *Anecd. Bekk.* 255.15; *Etym. Mag.*, Harpoc. s. *epi dietes hēbēsai*, Schol. Aeschin. 3.122, cf. Dion. Hal. *Ant. Rom.* 2.26.

24. See Hopfner (1938) 228–229, Eyben (1972) 695–696.

25. Cf. Labarbe (1957) 66–67.

26. See, e.g., Rhodes (1981) 69.

27. Pelike, Eucharides Painter, 500/490, Oxford Ashmolean Museum 563, *ABV* 396.21, *Paralipomena* 173, Rühfel (1984b) no. 13; Theophr. *Char.* 9.5, 30.6, cf. Men. *Dysc.* 967.

28. Rawson (1986) 30–31.

29. [Dem.] 43.82; for depictions of boys and young men assisting at sacrifices, see Rizza (1960), Rühfel (1984b) 84–91.

30. See Oepke (1934), Rühfel (1984b) 107–114. For children in general as wedding guests, see Ar. *Av.* 128–134, *Pax* 1265–1304, and the nuptial *lebes* by the Marsyas Painter, about 340, Leningrad Hermitage inv. 15592, *ARV²* 1475.1, *Paralipomena* 495, Rühfel (1984b) no. 62.

31. Apostol. 8.16, Eustath. *Od.* 1726.18, Hsch., *Suda* s. *ephygon ka-kon . . .* , Zenob. 3.98.
32. See, e.g., the *lekythos* by the Amasis Painter, about 540, New York Metropolitan Museum 56.11.1, *Paralipomena* 66, Rühfel (1984b) no. 63, and cf. *Suda* s. *epaulia.* The *pais amphithalēs* may also have been present at the bride's unveiling; Oakley (1982).
33. See, e.g., the late-sixth-century pinax, Paris Louvre L4, *AthMitt* 53 (1928) no. 37 pl. 11; and the loutrophoros by the Kleophrades Painter, about 480, Paris Louvre CA 453, *ARV²* 184.22, *Paralipomena* 340. For earlier depictions, see Ahlberg (1971) 97–101. For funerals and family solidarity, see Humphreys (1983) 104–118.
34. Brauron: Rühfel (1984b) no. 66A; cf. Brauron Museum 1153, Kahil (1983) pl. 15.17; other unpublished votives from Brauron discussed by Walbank (1981) 280; Athens Acropolis Museum 581, van Straten (1981) pl. 18 (a family sacrifices a sow to Athena, 500–480); Athens Kanellopoulos Museum, van Straten (1981) 119 no. 9.1 (a family sacrifices a pig to a hero, fourth century); Athens NM 1407, van Straten (1987) 160 pl. 2 (a family sacrifices a sheep to Asclepius, fourth century). For a comic account of a family sacrifice, see Ar. *Ach.* 241–262.
35. Thucydides says that the Ionians took their wives and children abroad to certain festivals, but implies that this was unusual (Thuc. 3.104.3).
36. Cf. Pl. *Lach.* 187E. A fourth-century votive relief shows a father introducing his son to Heracles; Athens NM 2723, van Straten (1981) pl. 28. On another, a woman and her five children sacrifice to Heracles; Athens EM 8793 = *IG* 2² 4613.
37. See Zeller (1987) 541–548 for a review of the anthropological literature. Schildkrout's study of urban Nigeria (1978) suggests that women whose public movements are restricted (as at Athens) often use children as their agents.
38. White (1975) 137 (on modern Java).
39. Amphora, Princeton Painter, 540/530, Stuttgart Württembergisches Landesmuseum inv. 65/1, Rühfel (1984b) nos. 9A, 9B.
40. Votive tablet, about 560, Athens Acropolis Museum 2525, Rühfel (1984b) no. 8.
41. Szemerényi (1977) 388. A Boeotian terracotta shows a woman teaching a girl to cook; ca. 500, Boston Museum of Fine Arts 01.7788, Rühfel (1984b) no. 20.
42. Pl. *Resp.* 5.467A, cf. *Leg.* 6.769B, *Prot.* 328A. Note also (1) the older boys working in a bronze sculptor's foundry, cup, Foundry Painter, 480/470, Berlin Staatliche Museen 2294, *ARV²* 400.1, Boardman (1975) pl. 262.2, 3; and (2) the boy and youths working on metal

vases, hydria, Leningrad Painter, 475–450, Milan Torno C 278, *ARV²* 571.73, 1659, *Paralipomena* 390. And cooks in New Comedy are said to learn their trade *ek paidos* (Sosipater fr. 1.7E.). In each case, these may be apprentices or wage workers outside the home.

43. White (1975) 144–145, Nag, White, and Peet (1978) 297.
44. Lys. 20.11. For boys looking after chickens, see the *chous,* van Hoorn (1951) no. 66, Klein (1932) pl. 10C (Athens NM 1654), cf. Plato Com. fr. 20E.
45. Dem. 18.258–259. Aeschines is said to have helped his mother administer Oriental rites as well, but Demosthenes inconsistently refers to him as both boy and adult (18.259, 19.199).
46. For the case against her working, see Fitton Brown (1984) 73. The text says that Cnemon works alone. But it also says that he sees no one, and since he obviously sees his daughter, his working alone may exclude only the help of those outside his family, not his daughter's.
47. Hdt. 6.137.3, Arist. *Pol.* 6.1323a5, cf. Timaeus 566 F 11 in Ath. 6.264D. Menon was put to death for keeping a free boy from Pallene at work in his mill (Din. *Demos.* 23). Was the charge *hybris*—in this case, treating a free boy like a slave? Or was this a simple case of kidnapping, as perhaps in Men. fr. 204E.? Many vases show young women fetching water from fountain-houses; see the catalogue given by Dunkley (1935–1936) 198–204. These may be scenes of everyday life, but the girls are probably slaves; though citizen girls may well have done this chore occasionally at least, it is noteworthy that the citizen women who do it in comedy (Ar. *Lys.* 327–329) are old, and so are freed from many of the usual restrictions, and that they complain of being jostled by slaves.
48. Though Solon forbade securing loans on the person at Athens (Arist. *AthPol* 6.1, 9.1, Plut. *Sol.* 15.3, cf. 13.2), some evidence may be thought to show that Athenians, including children, were sometimes sold into slavery in the classical period in order to pay off family debts. However, of the passages usually cited, Lys. 12.98 refers to children sent abroad and living outside Athens (those at Athens faced *hybris,* not sale); Isoc. 14.48 (whether genuine or not) refers to Plataean children whose parents have not yet taken up residence at Athens; Men. *Heros* involves a boy and a girl who are thought to be the children of a manumitted slave, and so not citizens (hyp., 20, 36, Gomme and Sandbach [1973] 390–391); Ter. *Haut.* concerns a young girl who, though the daughter of Athenian parents, is given up for exposure and reared by a Corinthian woman, and pledged by her as security as any slave foundling might be (603, 793–795).
49. Cf. Jameson (1977–1978) 129–130.
50. Murray (1983a), (1983b).

51. *IG* 1³ 131, Isae. 5.47, Dem. 23.130, 136, 58.30, Aeschin. 2.80, Lyc. *Leocr.* 87, Din. *Demos.* 101, Pl. *Ap.* 36DE; Arist. *AthPol* 24.3, 43.3, 62.2; Schmitt-Pantel (1980).
52. D'Arms (1984).
53. Xen. *Symp.* 1.8; cf. the young man on the cup, Painter of Würzburg 487, about 470, Vienna Kunsthistorisches Museum 2152, *ARV²* 836.15.
54. Arist. *Pol.* 7.1336b22, cf. Pl. *Leg.* 2.666A.
55. Ar. *Eccl.* 678–680, cf. *Pax* 1265–1304 and the paroemiographers' explanation of the proverb *Abydēnon epiphorēma* (Zenob. 1.1, Diogen. 1.1; for a different explanation, see Ath. 14.641A). Iphigenia joined in the paean with her father's guests (Aesch. *Ag.* 243–245), but the presence of a girl may reflect the heroic age (or what was believed about it) rather than classical Athens; cf. Cic. *Verr.* 2.1.26.66. A similar explanation may account for Oedipus's claim that he never ate apart from his daughters (Soph. *OT* 1462–1465).
56. Isae. 3.14, cf. [Dem.] 59.24, 33, 48, Pl. *Symp.* 176E, Nep. *Praef.* 6–7. Wives might join husbands at (or after) dinner in their own home if no guests were present (Xen. *Hell.* 5.4.7, Thebes). A family dinner in New Comedy includes a father, mother, aunt, aunt's father, and an old woman; a young man is apparently present as well, but no children are referred to (Men. fr. 923E.).
57. One version of the anecdote in which Themistocles, prosperous in exile, tells his children that they would have been ruined if they had not been ruined (by being forced out of Athens), is set at a meal; Plut. *Them.* 29.7, cf. *Mor.* 185F, 328F, 602A (where Themistocles' wife is present too), Ael. Arist. *Or.* 20.9.
58. See Harrison (1968) 61–81, Simantiras (1975). Women could not make agreements for more than the price of a *medimnos* of barley, enough to feed a family for about two weeks; the classical text that mentions this restriction may mean it to apply to children as well, but it may also be read as excluding children from any contracts whatever (Isae. 10.10, cf. Dio Chrys. 74.9, Harpoc. s. *hoti paidi*). In either case, there will have been nothing to prevent children from shopping, but the *paidia* said to buy fish at Alexis fr. 125.9E., Men. fr. 399E., and the *paides* sent to the market at Theophr. *Char.* 18.2, are likely slaves.
    Generally considered unfit for war (e.g., Lyc. *Leocr.* 53) and sent away (see Chapter 6) or behind the city's walls (Thuc. 2.14.1, Dem. 19.125, cf. Plut. *Mor.* 849A) in times of crisis, Greek children might serve as hostages along with adult citizens (Thuc. 1.115.2–4, 2.72.2, Isoc. 8.92, cf. Hdt. 1.64.1–2). On one fourth-century occasion, the Mantineans left boys and old men in the fields to supervise agricultural work while the other males were at war (Xen. *Hell.* 7.5.14–15);

a reference to the tithe extracted from the sale or ransom of Athenian children and women seized when the Spartans occupied Decelea in Attica during the Peloponnesian War indicates the risks (Dem. 24.128). There were times when some Greek children were more active—for example, in providing supplies, including ammunition, during the Carthaginian siege of Selinus and later throwing stones and roof tiles at the enemy (Diod. Sic. 13.55.4–5, 56.7). At Athens itself, children and women joined in rebuilding walls immediately after the Persian Wars (Thuc. 1.90.3, Diod. Sic. 11.40.1). Plato recommends that children go on campaign as soon as they are old enough to understand what is in store for them as adults, fetching and carrying to make themselves useful and awarding prizes for valor (Pl. *Resp.* 5.466E–468B). However, the young men "below the age of service" who served with over-age citizens in Myronides' campaign in the Megarid in 459/8, though described in the funeral speech ascribed to Lysias in terms appropriate to boys, were probably ephebes or the fifth-century equivalent (Lys. 2.50–53, cf. Thuc. 1.105.4).

59. Arist. *Pol.* 3.1278a4 (or, reading *ek prostheseōs,* they are citizens "with a qualification"); cf. *Pol.* 1.1260b20, 3.1275a14.
60. Hyper. *Euxen.* 22, cf. Andoc. 1.130.
61. Arist. *Protr.* fr. 57 Rose (= 3 Ross), Plut. fr. 131 Sandbach, Diogen. 6.46, cf. Callim. fr. 75.9 Pfeiffer; Macar. 5.94, cf. Dio Cass. 52.14.2. Related proverbs: Apost. 1.60, 11.48, 12.48, Macar. 1.57, Zenob. 3.52, etc. Occasionally, others are said to be at risk (Plut. *Mor.* 714E, Ath. 5.214A).
62. Jurors: Arist. *AthPol* 63.3, Dem. 24.150, Poll. 8.122. Councilors: Xen. *Mem.* 1.2.35, cf. *IG* 1³ 14.9–11, Arist. *AthPol* 30.2; Hansen (1980) 167–169, Develin (1985).
63. Cf. Patterson (1981) 164–166 (on the use of *metekhein* to express membership in both family and *polis*).
64. Land: Eur. *Hcld.* 826–827, Dem. *Epit.* 5, Pl. *Menex.* 237E–238B, cf. Aesch. *Sept.* 16 (Thebes). *Demos, polis, patris:* Lys. 13.91, Dem. 18.205, Pl. *Cri.* 50E, Antiphanes fr. 196E., cf. Pl. *Ep.* 7.331CD, Isoc. 6.108 (Sparta).
65. Children: Thuc. 2.44.3, Arist. *Rh.* 1.1361a1. War orphans: Cratinus fr. 183K.-A., Thuc. 2.46.1, Aeschin. 3.154, Pl. *Menex.* 248E, Arist. *AthPol* 24.3, *Pol.* 2.1268a11, Goldhill (1987) 63–76. Orphans of the democrats: *SEG* 28.46, Stroud (1971). Dowries: Aeschin. 3.258, Plut. *Arist.* 27. *Tropheia:* Lys. 2.70, 6.49, Pl. *Resp.* 7.520B, Lyc. *Leocr.* 53.
66. Revolution or counterrevolution: Lys. 20.4, Thuc. 8.74.3, and note Xen. *Hell.* 1.3.19 (a Byzantine successfully defends himself at Sparta on a charge of betraying his city by pleading that he could not bear

to see children and women starve). Invocations: Dem. 19.240, [Dem.] 25.101, Aeschin. 2.23, 152, Lyc. *Leocr.* 2, 141, Din. *Demos.* 65, 99, 109, *Phil.* 2. Oaths: Dem. 19.292, Aeschin. 3.120. Exhortations: Thuc. 7.69.2, cf. Aesch. *Pers.* 403–405, Xen. *An.* 3.4.46, *Cyr.* 4.1.17.

67. [Dem.] 59.110–111, Aeschin. 1.187, Lyc. *Leocr.* 141. (Daughters are invoked in the first instance, as the case of Neaera is said to concern their status; sons in the second, which involves allegations that Timarchus prostituted himself as a boy.) For children's familiarity with political figures, see Arist. *Rh.* 3.1408b24.

68. Antiph. 2.2.9, cf. 2.3.7, 2.4.10. A Spartan boy was exiled for accidentally killing another boy with a dagger: Xen. *An.* 4.8.25.

69. Cf. Harris (1988) 45–47.

70. Antiph. 6.19, 22, [Dem.] 47.70 (cf. 73), cf. Pl. *Leg.* 11.937AB. MacDowell (1963) 102–109 is skeptical even as to homicide cases. Unfortunately, we cannot determine the age or status of the *paidion* (perhaps) called to testify at Din. fr. E21.

71. Most of the evidence is post-classical. See, however, the early fourth-century votive relief dedicated to Apollo, Rome, Barracco Museum 41, Rühfel (1984b) no. 67.

72. Ar. *Nub.* 861–864; 400–350, Berlin Staatliche Museen K92, Rühfel (1984b) no. 46, cf. Athens NM 3329 (man, woman, and child), Athens NM 1408, van Straten (1987) 169 pl. 17A, 17B (a fourth-century family group).

73. Parke (1977) 107; cf., among other recent writers, Rühfel (1984b) 131–134, Raepsaet and Decocq (1987) 10.

74. Philostratus and Athens: Bowersock (1969) 4–6. Age: *IG* 2² 1368.130, 13139. Wreathed crawlers: van Hoorn (1951) no. 248 *undecies* pl. 388i, ?no. 278 pl. 13, ?no. 367 pl. 504, no. 669 pl. 17a, 17b, no. 851 pl. 438, cf. no. 640 pl. 93; Stern (1978) 33, Rühfel (1984b) 163–168.

75. For this theory, see Rumpf (1961) 213–214, Simon (1983) 95. Some *choes* are found in the graves of older children; Green (1971) 189 n. 4.

76. Karouzou (1946) 136; e.g., Keuls (1985) 303, van Hoorn (1951) 33–35.

77. Hesychius (s. *limnomakhai*) refers to boys boxing in the precinct of Dionysus in the Marshes at an unspecified date and Rühfel (1984b) 147 connects this notice with a *chous* to argue for boxing competitions at the Anthesteria. But the older boys in the *chous* in question face each other with their hands open and do not wear boxing thongs; they must be wrestlers (van Hoorn [1951] no. 368 pl. 132).

78. Cf. Metzger (1957) 75–76, Rumpf (1961), Pickard-Cambridge (1968) 11 n. 1, Green (1971) 189, Kyle (1987) 45–46.
79. Hani (1978); Deubner (1932) 118–121.
80. Aristodemus 383 F 9 in Ath. 11.495E, Proclus *Chrest.* 92, cf. Plut. *Thes.* 23.2–3. Schol. Nic. *Alex.* 109, who calls the participants *paides amphithaleis,* does not necessarily contradict this; the youths may have been chosen from those with both parents alive. See Kadletz (1980), Rutherford and Irvine (1988).
81. Cf. Vidal-Naquet (1981) 156–162.
82. Ar. *Eq.* 729 with Schol., Plut. *Thes.* 22.5, Eustath. *Il.* 1283.7, *Suda* s. *eiresiōnē;* Deubner (1932) 198–200, Merkelbach (1952). The frieze: Rühfel (1984b) no. 48. Chirassi Colombo (1979) discusses the Pyanopsia, Oschophoria, and Apaturia in the context of rites for another marginal group—women—in the same month.
83. Loutrophoros, about 520, Eleusis, Deubner (1932) pl. 5.2. The suggestion by Mommsen (1898) 31 that children were initiated but excluded from the special rite of the Epopteia is based on an unnecessary emendation of Himerius 69.7. For the possibility of boys (or youths) being initiates in Corybantic mysteries, see Pl. *Euthd.* 277D; in the cult of Sabazius, Rühfel (1984b) 118–120.
84. The only classical references are Harpoc. s. *aph' hestias myeisthai* (cited from Isaeus) and (probably) *IG* 1³ 6 C 25–26 and *Hesperia* 49 (1980) 264 lines 41–42. Statues of boys found at Eleusis probably depict *paides aph' hestias* rather than ordinary initiates; Mylonas (1961) 203 and pl. 80.
85. See, e.g., Robertson (1975) 51 (girl), Boardman (1977) 41 (girl *arrhēphoros*), Simon (1983) 67 (boy).
86. Puppet shows: Pl. *Leg.* 2.658C. Musical contests: Pl. *Leg.* 3.700C. Spectacles: Pl. *Leg.* 10.887D. Spur on competitors: Pl. *Ep.* 4.321A. Cf. Pl. *Leg.* 7.817C, Theophr. *Char.* 9.5, 30.6.
87. Pl. *Gorg.* 502BD, *Leg.* 2.658BD; Ar. *Eccl.* 1146, *Pax* 50–53, 765–766, Men. *Dysc.* 965–967, *Sam.* 733–734, cf. Ar. *Nub.* 537–539, Eupolis fr. 261K.-A., Plato Com. fr. 206E., Arist. *Pol.* 7.1336b20, Plaut. *Pseud.* 1081–1083.
88. Sutton (1981). To say no more, postponement of introductory material to the end of the day seems most impractical pedagogically. For a different (and more plausible) account of the function of satyr plays, see Seaford (1984) 26–33.
89. Jory (1967), with the corrections of J. and L. Robert, *REG* 81 (1968) 462–463; Sifakis (1979a).
90. *Peace:* Carrière (1977) 31–36 (but see D. Bain, *CR* 29 [1979] 138). *Frogs:* Sommerstein (1980) 15. See Chapter 3 of this book for boys in festival choruses.

91. Aside from *choes*, we may cite the skyphos by the Brygos Painter, about 480, Boston Museum of Fine Arts 10.176, *ARV²* 381.173, Rühfel (1984b) no. 37, which shows "one of the first, one of the only, real children in vase painting" (Beazley [1918] 90).

92. See, e.g., Dale (1954) xx, Stanley-Porter (1973) 69.

93. Cf. W. M. Calder III, *CP* 78 (1983) 87, and, for theatrical families, Sutton (1987).

94. Goldhill (1987) 71–75.

95. I reserve discussion of another function of these cults—as a locus for the interaction of girls—for Chapter 3.

96. I translate the text printed by Stinton (1976) and Henderson (1987a), but take Artemis (not Athena) to be the foundress, with Sourvinou (1971) and Walbank (1981).

97. Brelich (1969) 229–311.

98. *Arrhēphoroi*: Paus. 1.27.3, Harpoc. s. *arrhēphorein* (perhaps reflecting Dinarchus), *Anecd. Bekk.* 202.3, *Etym. Mag.* s. *arrhēphorein*, cf. *Suda* s. *epiōpsato. Aletrides*: Schol. Ar. *Lys.* 643, Eustath. *Od.* 1885.15, cf. Hsch. s. *aletrides. Arktoi*: Schol. Ar. *Lys.* 645 (L.) (*epilegomenai*; but see further discussion in Chapter 3). *Kanēphoroi*: Philochorus 328 F 8, Hsch., Phot. s. *kanēphoroi, Anecd. Bekk.* 270.31, Schol. Ar. *Ach.* 242.

99. Thuc. 6.56.1, Arist. *AthPol* 18.2, cf. Pl. *Hipparch.* 229C, Arist. *Pol.* 5.1311a36; Lavelle (1986b).

100. Cf. M. Piérart, *AntCl* 40 (1971) 784–785, Loraux (1981) 177, Lloyd-Jones (1983) 92, and, for another example, Ar. *Lys.* 567–586.

101. Harpoc., Hsch. s. *dekateuein, Anecd. Bekk.* 235.1, say the *arktoi* were about ten; *Suda* s. *arktos ē Braurōniois* and Schol. Ar. *Lys.* 645 (L.) say, in almost the same words, that they were no older than ten and no younger than five. Kahil estimates the age of the *arktoi* shown on *krateriskoi* of distinctive shape found at the sanctuary of Artemis at Brauron to be from seven to ten or a little more ([1965] 22) or from eight to thirteen ([1977] 86). See Perlman (1983), who argues, however, that *arktoi* were from ten to fourteen or fifteen years of age.

102. Cf. *Anecd. Bekk.* 202.3, *Etym. Mag.* s. *arrhēphorein*. However, Van Sichelen (1987) argues that *arrhēphoroi* were chosen annually.

103. Lloyd-Jones (1983) 92–93.

104. See Walbank (1981) 279–280 for examples of *kanēphoroi* in different rites.

105. Cf. C. Sourvinou, *JHS* 91 (1971) 174–177, Walbank (1981) 276, Robertson (1983) 280, Cole (1984) 238.

106. Burkert (1966) 14, Brelich (1969) 290–291.

107. Robertson (1983) 241, 265–276.

108. *Suda* s. *khalkeia, Etym. Mag.* s. *arrhēphorein* and *khalkeia;* Robertson (1983) 276–280.
109. Kahil (1983) 240, Cole (1984) 239–240.
110. Schol. Ar. *Lys.* 643, Hsch. s. *aletrides.*
111. Hsch. s. *ergastinai, IG* 2² 1034 (98/7).
112. Philochorus 328 F 183, Plut. *Thes.* 23.3. A young man in comedy falls for an unmarried *deipnophoros* for Artemis at Ephesus (Men. fr. 286aE.).
113. Redfield (1982), Jenkins (1983), Seaford (1987).
114. Eur. *Med.* 231, 238–240, cf. Soph. *Trach.* 141–150, 529–530, fr. 583R. Sourvinou-Inwood (1987) 136–147 argues that girls fleeing amorous pursuers on Attic vases reflect a panic associated with marriage.
115. Cf. Parker (1983) 79–81, who stresses that children's cult roles are to be explained as often by social status as by purity.

Chapter Three. The Child and His or Her Peers

1. Arist. *EE* 7.1236a38, *NE* 8.1156a31, 1157a28, 1158a6, 9.1165b25.
2. Xen. *Cyr.* 1.3.14, 4.2.10, cf. 5.1.2. Others had hunted with him in their youth; cf. Xen. *An.* 5.3.10, *Cyn.* 2.1.
3. Isoc. 15.93 (*ek meirakiōn*), cf. Apollodorus fr. 13E. (IIIa p. 204); Dem. 29.23.
4. Xen. *Hell.* 2.4.20, cf. Isoc. 15.207 (for the assumption that schoolmates kept tabs on one another in later life), and Arist. *Pol.* 5.1313b1 (where tyrants are said to be concerned lest schoolfellows' familiarity and trust pose a threat to their regimes).
5. See the bibliography assembled by Karras and Wiesehöfer (1981) 58–62; illustrations are available in Klein (1932), Schmidt (1971), Beck (1975), Schmidt (1977).
6. *Paidia,* "childish pastime," was often contrasted with *spoudē,* "serious business"; e.g., Xen. *Symp.* 1.1, Pl. *Leg.* 1.647D, 5.732D, 7.796D, *Pol.* 288C, *Resp.* 10.602B.
7. Herondas 3.5–6, 65, Poll. 9.113–114, 125, Hsch., *Suda* s. *khytrinda.*
8. Ar. *Av.* 388–392; Lambin (1977).
9. Plato Com. fr. 153E.; Pl. *Phdr.* 241B with Schol., *Resp.* 7.521C, Poll. 9.111–112; Taillardat (1967) 168–169.
10. Pl. *Phd.* 110BC; *Leg.* 1.644D, 7.803BC, cf. already Heraclitus 22 B 52D.-K.; Sprague (1984).
11. Eur. fr. 272N.²; Theophr. *Char.* 5.5, and cf. 14.10—the stupid man forces children to wrestle and run about.

12. Ael. *VH* 12.15, Plut. *Ages.* 25.5, Val. Max. 8.8 *ext.* 1, Sen. *Tranq.* 17.4; Diog. Laert. 9.3.
13. In addition to the passages already mentioned, see, e.g., Ar. *Nub.* 763, Plut. 816, 1056–1057, Telecleides fr. 1E.; Sprague (1984).
14. Pl. *Resp.* 4.424E–425A; *Leg.* 7.797A–798C.
15. Pl. *Leg.* 1.643BC, *Pol.* 308D, *Resp.* 7.536D–537A. Egyptians: *Leg.* 7.819BC.
16. Anon., *Anth. Pal.* 6.280, Theodorus, *Anth. Pal.* 6.282, Leonidas, *Anth. Pal.* 6.309; Rouse (1902) 249–251, Elderkin (1918) 455–456, Daux (1973) 225–229.
17. E.g., Plut. *Mor.* 229B (Lysander), 330F (Dionysius), Ael. *VH* 7.12 (Lysander and Philip of Macedon).
18. Pliny, *NH* 34.19.55. School scenes include the famous "school cup" by Douris about 490–480, Berlin Staatliche Museen 2285, *ARV²* 431.48, 1653, *Paralipomena* 374, Rühfel (1984b) nos. 24a and 24b, and another cup by the Akestorides Painter, about 460, New York Metropolitan Museum 22.139.72, *ARV²* 781.1, Rühfel (1984b) no. 26, cf. Pl. *Lys.* 206E.
19. Pl. *Resp.* 2.374C (*ek paidos*); on the games, see Poll. 9.94–98, Taillardat (1967) 149–161.
20. *Helkystinda* and *ephelkystinda*: Eustath. *Il.* 1111.24, Poll. 9.112, cf. Pl. *Tht.* 181A, [Arist.] *Probl.* 8.9.888a19. Cockfighting: Pl. *Leg.* 7.789B.
21. Xen. *Hipp.* 5.10; cf. *Cyr.* 1.6.32, and, for children's arguments about cheating, Pl. *Alcib. I* 110B; for guessing games, see also Ar. *Plut.* 816, 1056–1057, Pl. *Lys.* 206E, Beck (1975) 52.
22. Cup, Painter of Munich 2660, about 460, New York Metropolitan Museum 17.230.10, *ARV²* 784.25, *Paralipomena* 417, Rühfel (1984b) no. 28.
23. Van Hoorn (1951) no. 108 pl. 200, cf. no. 244 pl. 197a, no. 402 pl. 199, no. 629 pl. 196.
24. Van Hoorn (1951) no. 854 pl. 147.
25. O. Raum, *Chaga childhood* (London, 1940), 256–258, as reported by Schwartzman (1978) 104–105.
26. *Etym. Mag.,* Hsch. s. *drapetinda;* Lambin (1975) 173–175.
27. Schwartzman (1978) 25, 124–133.
28. Cf. Elkin and Handel (1984) 172–173, Valsiner (1988) 292–294.
29. Ar. *Pax* 1300, *Thesm.* 291; Henderson (1975) 109, and, for the reading *posthaliskon,* Taillardat (1961).
30. Arist. *Gen. An.* 1.728a10, cf. [Arist.] *Probl.* 4.26.879b19, 30.1.953b36.
31. For boys' use of "the finger," a vulgar sexual gesture, see Ar. *Nub.* 653–

654, and cf. *Ach.* 444, *Eq.* 1381 with Schol., *Pax* 549, Phot. s. *katap-ygōn,* Poll. 2.184.

32. Ar. *Thesm.* 478–480. Solon's law: Lys. 1.30–32, 49, Dem. 23.53–55, Plut. *Sol.* 23.1.

33. Lys. 1.12–13, and, for a young man and a slave girl, (?) Xenophanes 21 B 42D.-K.

34. See, e.g., Ar. *Plut.* 242–244, [Andoc.] 4.31, Lys. 19.10, Isae. 10.25, Aeschin. 1.42, 94, Diphilus fr. 42.26–27K.-A., and, for the phrase, *Anecd. Bekk.* 25.15 (= *Com. Adesp.* fr. 848E.).

35. Hydria, Harrow Painter, about 480, Maplewood, N.J., Noble, *ARV²* 276.70. Another interpretation: Keuls (1985) 260. Both interpreta-tions depend on the identification of an object in the older man's hand as a money pouch. This is unfortunately far from certain; Pin-ney (1986).

36. See especially Dover (1978), and, for refinements and additions, Buf-fière (1980), Golden (1984), Cohen (1987).

37. Boys: Aeschin. 1.13–16. Adults: Ar. *Eq.* 876–880, Aeschin. 1.29–32; Dover (1978) 23–39.

38. Cohen (1987) 6–8. The suggestion is modified, but not improved, by Cantarella (1988) 66–67.

39. Dover (1978) 84.

40. E.g., Xen. *Mem.* 4.1.2, *Symp.* 8.23–41, Pl. *Euthd.* 282B, *Hipp.* 229CD, *Lys.* 205B, *Symp.* 184DE, Dem. 61.2, 6, 34–57; Dover (1978) 91, 153–164. A cup by the Akestorides Painter (about 460, Munich, Bar-eiss, *ARV²* 1670) may show a boy reciting before an older male ad-mirer; Immerwahr (1973) 144, cf. Immerwahr (1964) 21, 23.

41. For the association of homosexuality with public life, see, e.g., Eu-polis fr. 104K.-A., Ar. *Eccl.* 112–113, *Nub.* 1093–1094, Plato Com. fr. 186E., Pl. *Symp.* 192A. A cup by the Splanchnopt Painter, about 470, Würzburg Martin von Wagner Museum der Universität 488, *ARV²* 893.25, which depicts two boys of similar ages and (?) a money pouch, may refer to a difference in social and economic standing; cf. Keuls (1983) 226–229, and note 35 above.

42. Cf. Golden (1984) 318–319.

43. Dover (1978) 137–148.

44. The Aristotelian *Problems* regards adult fondness for passive homo-sexuality as the consequence of indulgence around the time of pu-berty (and not before it), and seems neutral in its tone ([Arist.] *Probl.* 4.26.879b37).

45. Two Greek words, *gymnasion* and *palaistra,* were applied to locales for physical exercise, sometimes without obvious distinction. In general, however, palaestrae (often privately owned) were less elaborate—

they lacked a running track—and gymnasia (usually public) were larger; Delorme (1960) 253–271.

46. For sexual advances in gymnasia and palaestrae, see, e.g., Ar. *Vesp.* 1023–1028, Aeschin. 1.135, Pl. *Charm.* 153A, 154AC, cf. Theophr. *Char.* 27.14 and the vases cited in Golden (1984) 317 n. 44. For the law, see Aeschin. 1.138, cf. Plut. *Sol.* 1.3, *Mor.* 152D, 751B, Hermias Alex. *in Pl. Phdr.* 231E; Kyle (1984) 99–102.

Some Greek cities had palaestrae (and possibly gymnasia) for boys alone, perhaps another measure to hinder unsupervised sexual liaisons with older males, but there is no evidence for this at Athens; Delorme (1960) 124–129, 178–182.

47. Ar. *Nub.* 961–983; Aeschin. 1.187, Pl. *Lys.* 208C, 223A, *Symp.* 183CD, Alexis fr. 289E., cf. Pl. *Leg.* 7.808CD, the vases listed in Beck (1975) 65 (under "literary and humane education"), and those discussed in *AntK* 23 (1980) 40–43. An unusual variant shows Heracles being led to school by a tattooed Thracian woman; skyphos, Pistoxenos Painter, 470–460, Schwerin Staatliches Museum 708, *ARV*² 862.30, *Paralipomena* 425, Beck (1975) no. I.37 pl. 25. We may compare the grown-up hero's subjection to Omphale.

48. Pl. *Phdr.* 255A; *Symp.* 183CD. Another example of children's capacity for exerting peer pressure is the saying "Pigs follow their mother," applied to mamma's boys and misfits (Schol. Ar. *Plut.* 314).

49. Pl. *Charm.* 161D. The enemies Plato mentions may be family foes. However, a child's ditty aimed at those with weak eyesight—"look up a dog's bum and three foxes' bums too"—indicates that Athenian children could make enemies on their own (Schol. Ar. *Eccl.* 255, cf. Ar. *Ach.* 863).

50. Much of the evidence is presented in Beck (1964), especially 72–141. Beck (1975) provides an excellent portfolio of illustrations from vases and other media, Beck (1986) a bibliography.

51. Encouragement and regulation: e.g., Plut. *Sol.* 22, cf. Pl. *Cri.* 50D, Alexis fr. 304E. (= Vitruv. 6 *praef.* 3), Aeschin. 1.9–12.

52. Xen. *Cyr.* 1.2.2–3, Arist. *NE* 10.1180a24, *Pol.* 8.1337a24, cf. Isoc. 7.37.

53. Niceratus: Xen. *Symp.* 3.5, cf. 4.6. Apaturia: Pl. *Tim.* 21B, cf. *Trag. Adesp.* fr. 515aK.-S. Of course, this does not mean that everyone thought they paid *enough* attention: Pl. *Euthd.* 306DE, cf. *Theag.* 122B.

54. Cup, Sabouroff Painter, about 460, Amsterdam Allard Pierson Museum 8210, *ARV*² 838.27, Beck (1975) no. X.1 pl. 349 (where the boy is identified as a girl), Immerwahr (1973) 144. Xenocrateia: *IG* 2² 4548 (but different interpretations are possible; e.g., Guarducci [1974] 58–59).

55. Plut. *Them.* 10.3, cf. (elsewhere in Greece) Hdt. 6.27.2, Thuc. 7.29.5, Ael. *VH* 7.15; Immerwahr (1964) 17.
56. Pl. *Leg.* 7.794C, Arist. *Pol.* 7.1336b36, cf. [Pl.] *Ax.* 366D, Plaut. *Bacch.* 440, *Merc.* 289–304, Quint. 1.1.15–16.
57. Arist. *Pol.* 8.1337b22, cf. Xen. *Lac.* 2.1, Pl. *Clit.* 407BC, *Theag.* 122E, and, for vases showing all three aspects of education, Webster (1972) 57–59. *Grammata* probably included basic arithmetic, the Greek letters doing double duty as numerals.
58. Pl. *Leg.* 7.809E–810B; Booth (1985).
59. Cf. Beck (1964) 80–83.
60. Dem. 18.257; Arist. *Pol.* 4.1294b21 (on Sparta).
61. Pl. *Prot.* 326C, cf. Xen. *Cyr.* 1.2.15, 8.3.37, Lys. 20.11, Isoc. 7.44–45, Dem. 18.265. *Mousikē:* Ar. *Eq.* 188–189, cf. *Ran.* 727–730, *Vesp.* 959, 989, Men. fr. 495E. (= Quint. 1.10.18), and, for concerns about the cost of schooling, Theophr. *Char.* 22.6, 30.14 (contemptuous). Better-off boys took lessons in horsemanship (expensive: Xen. *Hipparch.* 1.11–12) and dancing (Sophocles, Ath. 1.20F).
62. Ar. *Eq.* 188–189, cf. *Vesp.* 960–961; Pl. *Leg.* 3.689D, cf. Apost. 11.53, Diogen. 3.18, 6.56, *Suda* s. *mēte nein mēte grammata.*
63. Pl. *Resp.* 8.562C–563A; Arist. *Rh.* 2.1398b26, cf. Xen. *Cyr.* 1.6.20.
64. Beatings: Ar. *Nub.* 972, Xen. *An.* 5.8.18 (cf. 2.6.11–15), *Cyr.* 1.3.16–17, 2.2.14, Pl. *Leg.* 3.700C; cup, Splanchnopt Painter, about 450, Melbourne 1644.4, *ARV²* 892.7, Beck (1975) no. VI.15 pl. 273. *Paideuō:* Soph. *Ajax* 595, Xen. *Mem.* 1.3.5.
65. Apollod. 2.4.9, Diod. Sic. 3.67.2, Paus. 9.29.9, and, for depictions on Attic vases, Beck (1975) nos. I.38–41 pl. 26–29. See Xen. *An.* 2.6.12 for an indication of such hostility.
66. Herondas 3.59–61; gem, Berlin Staatliche Museen 6918, Beck (1975) no. VI.18 pl. 275.
67. See skyphos, Bari R 150, Beck (1975) no. VI.19 pl. 276a (*paidagōgos* with stick threatens boy).
68. Paus. 6.9.6 (Astypalaea), Hdt. 6.27.2 (Chios).
69. Hyper. *Epit.* 8, cf. Isoc. 12.198, 15.289–290, and Xen. *Cyr.* 1.2.6 (where it is implied that Athens' schools do not live up to this ideal).
70. E.g., Soph. *OC* 919, Eur. *Cycl.* 276, cf. Thuc. 1.84.4, 2.41.1, Pind. fr. 198a.
71. Writing: Muir (1984). Memorization: Xen. *Symp.* 3.5 (cf. 4.6), Pl. *Leg.* 7.810E–811A, *Prot.* 325E, cf. *Crit.* 113B, Aeschin. 3.135; Treu (1981), Debut (1983).
72. Asclepiades, *Anth. Pal.* 6.308.
73. Nolan amphora, Ethiop Painter, about 450, Boulogne-sur-Mer 667, *ARV²* 666.15, Beck (1975) no. V.10 pl. 228; lekythos, Klügmann Painter, about 430, Salonika University, *ARV²* 1199.20, Beck (1975)

no. V.11 pl. 229; cup, Splanchnopt Painter, about 450, Melbourne 1644.4, *ARV*² 892.7, Beck (1975) no. VI.15 pl. 273; cf. Queyrel (1988) 97–101.

74. *IG* 2² 1138.6, 11, cf. 2318.320–324 (restored), 3061, Dem. 21.10, 64, Arist. *AthPol* 56.3.

75. Antiph. 6.11, *IG* 2² 1138.6, 11, 3063, 3065–3068, 3070, Arist. *AthPol* 56.3.

76. Aeschin. 1.11, Arist. *AthPol* 56.3, cf. Pl. *Leg.* 6.764E.

77. Lys. 21.1–5; [Andoc.] 4.20–21. The authenticity of Lysias's speech is not assured, and the year in question was an unusual one. But the story of Alcibiades' outrage recurs in another near-contemporary source, and must have seemed plausible to a fourth-century audience (Dem. 21.147, cf. Plut. *Alcib.* 16.4).

78. Choragi commemorated victories with tripods, statues, and so on; see Isae. 7.40, Harpoc. s. *katatomē, IG* 1² 769, 2² 3039–3043, 3054–3055, 3061, 3063, 3065–3068, 3070, *BCH* 91 (1967) 102–110, *ArkhDelt* 25 (1970) 143–149 nos. 1–4, 6–8.

79. P. Cartledge, *Hermathena* 134 (1983) 84.

80. Pl. *Leg.* 8.836A. For quarrels involving the love of boys or young men and their private and public ramifications, see, e.g., Lys. 3, Thuc. 6.54–59, Arist. *AthPol* 18.2.

81. Hug (1956) contains a good summary of the evidence for the involvement of children in ancient athletics. Kyle (1987) provides a general account of athletics in archaic and classical Athens. For children and sport in Athenian art, see Rühfel (1984b) 53–61.

82. Cf. Klee (1918) 43–51.

83. Paus. 6.2.10–11. Other very young Olympic victors (in boxing): Paus. 6.3.1, 6.7.9. Robbins (1987) suggests that Pytheas of Aegina won the *pankration* at Nemea at the age of twelve.

84. It is sometimes said that boys in games on the Olympic model held in Naples in the first century A.D. were aged seventeen to twenty; but this statement is based only on a restored portion of a mutilated inscription (*IOlympia* 56.10; see Crowther [1988], Frisch [1988]).

85. For example, Ebert (1965) argues that *ageneioi* began to compete at the Pythian Games during the third century.

86. *IG* 7 1765, Thespiae, first century A.D. (where these age classes must be based on only the lower limit for *paides* at Delphia and Isthmia); Phot., *Suda* s. *Panathenaia* (but both texts are corrupt).

87. Xen. *Hell.* 4.1.40, Plut. *Ages.* 13.3, and cf. (for size as an indicator of age in an official context) Arist. *Rh.* 2.1399a35.

88. Diog. Laert. 8.47–48, cf. Paus. 6.14.2–3 and 6.2.2 (where a similar story is told of foals). Sogenes of Aegina may have won the pentathlon (presumably for *ageneioi*) at Nemea while still a boy in the early fifth

century (Miller [1975]); that the Athenian *pais* Leagrus won the Olympic pentathlon for men in 480 is unlikely, despite Francis and Vickers (1981). Their weight gave boy victors such as Aesypus an advantage in horse racing (Paus. 6.2.8).

89. Kyle (1987) 40–48 provides a brief account of these and other festivals.

90. Aeschin. 1.10–12, Pl. *Lys.* 206DE with Schol.; *IG* 2² 2980 (early second century, torch race), cf. 2971 (late fourth century, chariot race, but perhaps not at the Athenian Hermaea). Adult men were excluded from the Hermaea, once again to discourage sexual advances (Aeschin. 1.12).

91. Robert (1939) 238–244.

92. The most recent discussion is by Johnston (1987).

93. A fifth-century fragment of a list of victors at an unidentified Athenian festival includes first- and second-place finishers from three age classes, *paides, ageneioi,* and *andres* (*IG* 1² 846). Runners-up among *paides* and *ageneioi* in boxing seem to have received equal prizes, smaller than men's.

94. See, e.g., Paus. 6.7.8 (classical period), 3.11, 4.11, 6.3, 8.1 and 5 (undated). It is interesting to note that the name of an Olympic victor praised by Pindar turns up on a list of words used to teach pupils in fourth-century A.D. Egypt how to read and write; Debut (1983) 265.

95. Paus. 6.17.2. See also Ebert (1972) no. 53 (a statue of a boy victor set up by the people of Magnesia on the Maeander, fourth or third century) and no. 54 (from the people of Phocis for a boy athlete, about 300).

96. Cf. Ebert (1972) no. 31, for Mykon (the "only one of the Ionians to defeat the boys at the Pythian Games in boxing," about 400).

97. See the catalog in Kyle (1987) 195–216 (nos. A17, A18, A23, A41, A67), with the comments of N.B. Crowther, *EMC* 32 (1988) 237–238.

98. [Dem.] 58.66. For the phrase "a wreath for the city," cf. Ebert (1972) no. 12 (Theognetus of Aegina, boys' wrestling champion at Olympia, early fifth century) and no. 19 (restored; Pherias of Aegina, boys' wrestling champion at Olympia, early fifth century).

99. For what follows, see especially Young (1984) 133–162.

100. Meals: *IG* 1³ 131.11–18 (about 440–432), Pl. *Ap.* 36DE. Money: Plut. *Sol.* 23.3, Diog. Laert. 1.55 (where the money prizes are said to be reductions from previous levels [cf. Diod. Sic. 9.2.5]). But though some form of award may go back to Solon (or even earlier), it is generally accepted that Athens did not issue coinage until after

his term of office; thus, these money prizes cannot date back that far. Cf. Kyle (1984) 94–98.

101. Cf. Kyle (1987) 123, 148–149.
102. Pind. *Ol.* 8.54–59 with Schol. A similar case might be built on *IG* 2² 3125, which on one reading commemorates a winner in the *pankration* for *ageneioi* at Isthmia about 430 and his grandson, who repeated the feat, but neither the interpretation of this inscription nor the social status of the family is known for sure.
103. Hirsch-Dyczek (1983) 13.
104. Pl. *Leg.* 6.771E–772A; Eur. *Andr.* 595–600, Plut. *Comp. Lyc. et Num.* 3.3–4.
105. Women sponsored winning entries in equestrian events at the Panathenaea in the Hellenistic period. None of the known victors was an Athenian. For the athletic activities of Spartan girls, see Scanlon (1988).
106. Lys. 32.14–15, cf. Eur. *Hipp.* 857–859, *IA* 115–123, Theophr. in Stob. *Flor.* 2.31.31; Immerwahr (1964, 1973), Beck (1975) 58–60, Cole (1981).
107. Cup, Painter of Bologna 417, 460–450, New York Metropolitan Museum 06.1021.167, *ARV²* 908.13, *Paralipomena* 430, Beck (1975) no. X.3 pl. 350; Pomeroy (1977) 64 n. 8.
108. Phiale, Phiale Painter, 450–420, Boston Museum of Fine Arts 97.371, *ARV²* 1023.146, *Paralipomena* 441, Beck (1973) no. X.56 pl. 391a.
109. Amphora, Andokides Painter, about 530, Paris Louvre F203, *ARV²* 4.13, Arrigoni (1985) pl. 21a; amphora, Priam Painter, 515–500, Rome Villa Giulia, *Paralipomena* 146.8 *ter,* Arrigoni (1985) pl. 22. See Arrigoni (1985) 105–107 (citizen girls), and, for another view of the Priam Painter's vase, Moon (1983) 110–113 (nymphs).
110. Plut. *Mor.* 142D, 381E, 982B, Pliny, *NH* 9.12.37; Pomeroy (1978) 19, Arthur (1980) 58–59. For tortoises and girls at Athens, see the *choes,* van Hoorn (1951) no. 653, Klein (1932) pl. 15C (London BM F101) and no. 482 pl. 338.
111. Poll. 9.125, Eustath. *Od.* 1914.56 (cf. *Carm. Min.* 876cP.).
112. Texts are available in Page (1942) 486–489 and West (1977). I accept the identification of Erinna as a woman poet (though not necessarily a young one) with, e.g., Pomeroy (1978) and Arthur (1980) against West (1977).
113. Bowra (1936) 326–330; Schmidt (1977) 127.
114. Cf. West (1977) 105.
115. Osborne (1985a) 130–138.
116. Lefkowitz (1986) 45–46 discusses the place of friends in such stories; Sourvinou-Inwood (1987) 137, 144, notes that girls who are

the objects of erotic pursuit on Attic vases often have companions. Similarly, girls in myth are commonly carried off at festivals of Artemis precisely because these are female affairs; the intrusion of men is therefore more shocking and the break with girlhood more abrupt. For examples, see Perlman (1983) 126–127 (who believes, however, that the stories perhaps arise "from the custom of initiating matches during public festivals").

117. Aesch. fr. 43R.; Lambin (1986) 66–71, Seaford (1987) 115.
118. See Calame (1977) (summary at 2.144–146).
119. Eur. *Hcld.* 777–783; for choral dances at the Oschophoria, see Calame (1977) 1.231. Whether choruses of Athenian girls took part in the festival for Apollo which the Athenians reorganized on Delos is uncertain (Thuc. 3.104, cf. Callim. *Hymn.* 4.278–282); silence concerning girls at Arist. *AthPol* 56.3, Xen. *Mem.* 3.3.12, tells against it. Choruses of unmarried girls in tragedy were presumably made up of males, just as males played other female roles.
120. Plut. *Mor.* 839C; hydria, Kleophon Painter, about 430, Tübingen E112, *ARV*² 1147.61, Rühfel (1984b) no. 56.
121. E.g., Chirassi Colombo (1979) 39.
122. Ar. *Thesm.* 690–691, 733–734, Schol. Luc. *Dial. Mer.* 7.4 Rabe, Schol. Theocr. 4.25c Wendel, cf. Cic. *Verr.* 2.4.45.99. See Golden (1988c) 5–8 (with the other literature listed at 5 n. 20).
123. Schol. Ar. *Lys.* 645 (R.), *Suda* s. *arktos ē Braurōniois*, cf. *Anecd. Bekk.* 444.30, *Suda* s. *arkteusai.*
124. Schol. Ar. *Lys.* 645 (L.); Papadimitriou (1963) 118–120.
125. Ritual tasks: *Suda* s. *proteleia;* for other prenuptial rites, see Burkert (1983) 63 n. 20. Identification of the stoa: Sourvinou (1971) 175, Kahil (1977) 96 n. 59, Lloyd-Jones (1983) 93 n. 34. Widespread participation: cf. Simon (1983) 86, Perlman (1983) 128, Osborne (1985a) 165 (but note that nothing can be concluded on the basis of the numbers of dedications, which need not be by "bears").
126. Races: especially Perlman (1983). Spinning: P.B. Benbow, *Epinetra* (Ph.D. diss., Harvard 1975), as cited by Cole (1984) 239 n. 32. Iconography: Kahil (1965, 1977, 1983).
127. My comments on the Brauronia necessarily go beyond the evidence. Even the connection of the four-year sacrifice (Arist. *AthPol* 54.7, Poll. 8.107) and the procession (Ar. *Pax* 872–876 [misunderstood by Schol.]) with the "bears" is supposition.

Chapter 4. Parents and Children

1. So, e.g., Barker (1946) 38. For the meanings of *oikos* and *oikia,* see MacDowell (1989).

2. As, e.g., by Reinhold (1976) 28–47.
3. The answer that follows is a revised version of Golden (1988a).
4. Finley (1981) 159.
5. Ariès (1973) especially 29, Pinchbeck and Hewitt (1969) especially 301–302, Shorter (1976), Stone (1977). Cf. also Mitterauer and Sieder (1982) 60–61.
6. See, e.g., Frier (1982), especially the life-table at 245, and Frier (1983).
7. Woman of seventy-three: *SEG* 20.621 (Egypt). The only exception I know of is *SEG* 26.1555 (Commagene), for a child of one, but neither the reading nor its reliability is certain; see Wagner (1976) 212 no. 67, cf. *REG* 90 (1977) 429–430 no. 531.
8. For summaries and citations of evidence, see Kurtz and Boardman (1971) 55, 70, 92, 188–190, Bremmer (1983a) 96–100, Morris (1987) 57–71 (emphasizing variation over time).
9. Pl. *Lach.* 180B, cf. *Resp.* 10.615C, Arist. *EE* 7.1240a31.
10. Thuc. 2.44.3, cf. Hdt. 3.119, Soph. *Ant.* 909–912, Eur. *Alc.* 290–294, *Hyps.* fr. 60.90–96 Bond; Beekes (1986).
11. See the discussion in Chapter 6.
12. Cf. also Manson (1975) 147, Pomeroy (1975) 101.
13. Konner (1977) 315.
14. LeVine (1977) 23. Cf. Segalen (1986) 174 (on preindustrial France): "A whole range of popular prophylactics and remedies surrounded the most dangerous moments of the infant's life. . . . such practices bear witness to the loving anxiety of women who were powerless in the face of catastrophe."
15. Campbell (1964) 154, cf. Doumanis (1983) 52–57 (on rural Epirus).
16. LeVine (1977) 23, Scheper-Hughes (1987a).
17. On funerary rites in the Greek world, see Kurtz and Boardman (1971) 142–161, 200–217, Garland (1985) 21–37, 104–120.
18. For example, the Sarakatsani "will sometimes agree that the measure of God's punishment is hard, particularly when the life of a small child is taken" (Campbell [1964] 323); cf. Danforth (1982) 54.
19. On weeping and lamentation as ritual, see Alexiou (1974), Huntingdon and Metcalf (1979) 24–28.
20. Cf. Schiff (1978) xii, Scheper-Hughes (1987a) 148.
21. See Barrett (1984) 179.
22. Soph. *OC* 1224–1228, cf. Theog. 425–428, Hdt. 5.4.2, Eur. fr. 449N.[2], Alexis fr. 141.14–16E., Arist. *Eudemus* fr. 44 Rose (6 Ross).
23. Hertz (1960), cf., e.g., Parker (1983) 41.
24. For such explanations, see Binford (1972) 219.
25. On wet-nursing, see Sussman (1982).
26. McCracken (1983); Goody (1984); cf. Sanford (1975).

27. Arist. *NE* 8.1159a28, cf. *EE* 7.1239a38.
28. Similar conclusions result from a study of nineteenth-century American diaries (Rosenblatt [1983] 58): " . . . the classical literature [on grief] seems to say that child deaths increase the intensity with which parents invest in surviving children. . . . And the diary data seem inconsistent with the idea that high death rates lead to less parental valuing of young children." A study of the practice of a seventeenth-century English doctor reveals numerous cases of extreme grief and depression among bereaved parents, especially mothers (MacDonald [1981] 80–85). Herlihy (1985) 125–127 stresses the care for children in medieval families. Some of Pollock's arguments are put forward, apparently independently, in a well-documented article by Wilson (1985); her use of sources is criticized by Johansson (1987b) 345–347, who, however, does not make what seems to be a significant distinction between memoirs and diaries. Bellingham (1988) 349–350 offers an even-handed critique.
29. Bradley (1986) especially 216–220, Garland (1985) 80–86, Hopkins (1983) 222–226.
30. Cf. Kurtz and Boardman (1971) 331, deMause (1974) especially 25–32, Sagan (1979) 210.
31. Howell (1979) 62, 119–120; e.g., Wilson (1988) 783 (on nineteenth-century Corsica). On Rome, Dixon writes, "Parents who possibly exposed unwanted babies . . . became attached to those children they did rear" ([1988] 26); cf. Néraudau (1987) 195 n. 1.
32. Cf. Scheper-Hughes (1987b) 14: "What is altogether rare in preindustrialized, 'infanticide-tolerant' societies is the 'classic' pattern of child abuse found in near endemic proportions in the industrialized world: the so-called battered child syndrome."
33. Vekemans and Dohmen (1982).
34. Moseley, Follingstad, Harley, and Heckel (1981).
35. Steinhoff (1985) 127; cf. also Bracken, Klerman, and Bracken (1978).
36. The shard was first published by Brann (1959). The identification of the figure shown on this and other early pots with Astyanax is not secure; see Laurens (1984), especially 206–219. But this does not affect the point made in the text, that the death of a young child as a result of warfare evoked pathos.
37. Hdt. 6.27.2, Thuc. 7.29.5. Taking place as they do in schools, these deaths threaten the cultural continuity of the community as well as its simple survival; Longo (1980–1981) 143.
38. Antiphon 87 B 49D.-K. Cf. Eur. *Alc.* 882–888, *Med.* 1090–1115, fr. 543N.², Men. fr. 418, 649, 1133E., *Monos.* 641, Plut. *Sol.* 6.1–3, Plaut. *Mil. Glor.* 719–722 (from a Greek original of the early third century).

39. Amulets: Juvenal 5.164 (with Courtney's note) and F. Eckstein and J. H. Waszink, *Reallexikon für Antike und Christentum* 1 (1950) 397–406 s. *Amulett*. Dedications: see *IG* 2² 4351, 4400, 4403, 4412, 4429, fourth-century dedications to Asclepius. Beer (1987) discusses statues of sitting children dedicated to Asclepius and others, from Cyprus, Etruria, and Greece.
40. *IG* 2² 12335, about 360. A luckier mother boasts that she died "without having grieved for any of her children" (*IG* 2² 5673, mid fourth century).
41. Pl. *Alcib. II* 142BC, Eur. *Rh.* 982, *Supp.* 786–793, 1087–1091.
42. Cf. Dover (1980) 1: "The word [*erōs*] is not used, except rhetorically or humorously, of the relations between parents and children."
43. Eur. *Ion* 67 (*erōti paidōn*) (cf. 1227 [*paidōn . . . eis eron*] [Creusa]), *Archel.* fr. 2.19–21 Austin (*teknōn erōti*); cf. Eur. *Med.* 714–715 (Aegeus). There may be a similar usage at Aesch. *PV* 865 (*paidōn himeros*), but *paidōn* here is probably partitive with *mian*.
44. Eur. *HF* 634–636, cf., e.g., *Andr.* 418–420, *Pho.* 965–966, *Supp.* 506–508, fr. 103, 316, 346, 518, 652N.²
45. Mikalson (1986).
46. Masqueray (1906), especially 85.
47. Ar. *Thesm.* 502–519; Ar. *Av.* 1439–1445.
48. Theophr. *Char.* 20.5–6, cf. 7.10, Ar. *Nub.* 1380–1390 (for other involved fathers). For other pet names, see Aeschin. 1.126, Men. *Sam.* 240–244, Plut. *Thes.* 14.2, and cf. Ar. *Plut.* 1011, where the affectionate diminutives are probably taken, as often, from language used with children (Ferguson [1964] 111).
49. Theophr. *Char.* 2.6, cf. 5.5.
50. Arist. *Rh.* 1.1360b20; Solon 23W.
51. Arist. *Gen. An.* 3.753a8, cf. *NE* 8.1155a17.
52. Painter of Munich 2413, about 460, Munich 2413, *ARV²* 495.1, 1656, *Paralipomena* 380, Boardman (1975) pl. 350.1, 2.
53. Collected by Hirsch-Dyczek (1983); cf. Charlier and Raepsaet (1971) 603–604, Raepsaet and Decocq (1987) 3–8.
54. Oaths: Dem. 29.26, 52, 54; 54.38, 40 (where this is called too dramatic to be trustworthy), cf. Lys. 32.13, Andoc. 1.31. Children in court: Ar. *Vesp.* 568–573, 976–978, Lys. 20.34–36, Dem. 19.310, 21.99, 186–188, [Dem.] 25.84, Aeschin. 2.152, 179, Isoc. 15.321, Pl. *Ap.* 34C, Hyper. *Phil.* 9, *Euxen.* 41.
55. E.g., Lys. 4.20, Dem. 28.20.
56. Dem. 50.62. Similarly, Euxitheus of Mytilene tells an Athenian jury that it was hard for his father to leave his native city because there were strong ties that bound him there: children and property (Antiph. 5.76, cf. Dem. 23.136).

57. [Dem.] 34.37; Arist. *Rh.* 3.1417a5 (on Hdt. 2.30.4).
58. Arist. *AthPol* 56.6, cf. Xen. *Mem.* 2.2.13, Lys. 13.91, Isae. 8.32, Aeschin. 1.13 (cf. 28), Dem. 10.40, 24.105–107, Hyper. *Euxen.* 6, Harpoc. s. *kakōseōs.* Solon: Dem. 24.103, Aeschin. 1.6, 13, Plut. *Sol.* 22.1, 4, Diog. Laert. 1.55, cf. Ar. *Av.* 1353–1357. Legally, at least, this responsibility fell to sons; cf. Hdt. 2.35.4.
59. Arist. *AthPol* 55.3–4, cf. Xen. *Mem.* 2.2.13, Dem. 57.70, Din. *Aristog.* 17–18.
60. See, e.g., Xen. *Oec.* 7.12, 19, cf. [Arist.] *Oec.* 1.1343b20.
61. Stanford (1983) 39.
62. Vernier (1977) 49–51. We might recall too that in some cultures the more familiar relations are marked by formal terms of address; cf. Stanford (1983) 93.
63. For puns on the word *tokos,* "offspring" and "interest," see, e.g., Ar. *Nub.* 1156 (cf. 34), *Thesm.* 845, Pl. *Resp.* 6.506C–507A, 8.555E, Arist. *Pol.* 1.1258b6, cf. Plaut. *Men.* 59 (from a third-century Greek original). The relation of interest and affection was an issue in antiquity too; see Democr. 68 B 278D.-K., Plutarch's essay *On Affection for Offspring* (*Mor.* 493A–497E), and the comments by Lambert (1982) 11–14.
64. E. P. Thompson, *New Society* 41 (1977) 501.
65. It may be that some mothers resented the father's prerogative, especially when exercised against their firstborn; see Pl. *Tht.* 151C, cf. Ter. *Haut.* 633–643, 664–665; Schmidt (1983–1984) 136–137, K. J. Dover, *CR* 34 (1984) 342.
66. See, e.g., Peterson (1975) 205.
67. Xen. *Lac.* 1.3, cf. *Oec.* 7.6, Arist. *HA* 9.608b15; Scrimshaw (1984) 450–452, Johansson (1984).
68. Humphreys (1983) 126 n. 18.
69. Men. *Dysc.* 17–20. For a more neutral response to a daughter's birth, see Men. fr. 723E.
70. *IG* 2² 10891, 10892, both 400–300; 10660, 390–365. None is certainly the daughter of an Athenian citizen. Among post-classical writers, Plutarch says that fathers prefer daughters to sons (because the daughters need them), but mothers prefer sons (*Mor.* 143B). Cf. the discussion of alliances within the household in Chapter 6 of the present volume.
71. Vorster (1983) 249–251 (on statues of children).
72. I follow Collard's text and interpretation of these lines (1975). For "sweet endearments," note the statements in *Anecd. Bekk.* 855.29, *Anecd. Ox.* 4.273 Cramer, that girls were especially fond of diminutives.
73. Ar. *Thesm.* 289–291. For the reading *posthaliskon,* see Taillardat

(1961). For an extended series of puns involving forms of *khoiros,* "pig" and "vagina," applied by a father to young daughters, see Ar. *Ach.* 729–835; Golden (1988c).

74. For the sexual content of such kisses, cf. Ar. *Thesm.* 130–133. According to a fragment of the comic poet Diphilus, an ugly girl is one even a father won't kiss (fr. 91K.-A.).

75. For such stories in tragedy, see Foley (1985) 65–105, Lefkowitz (1986) 95–103, Loraux (1987) 31–48.

76. *Domōn agalma:* Aesch. *Ag.* 208. In Euripides, the war deprives Agamemnon and the other Greeks of the pleasures (*hēdonai*) of their children (Eur. *Tro.* 371–372, 392–393).

77. E.g., Lys. 2.11, Pl. *Menex.* 239B, Isoc. 4.56–60, Dem. 18.186, *Epit.* 8.

78. Isae. 11.17; Xen. *Oec.* 7.24, cf. *Mem.* 1.4.7; Eur. *Pho.* 355–356, fr. 1015N.²; Arist. *Gen. An.* 3.759b7; cf. *Com. Adesp.* fr. 103e col. ii.40–42E.

79. This must not be thought of as evidence for mothers' disregard of their daughters. See, e.g., the *Homeric Hymn to Demeter* (Demeter searches for Persephone; Arthur [1977]); Aesch. *Ag.* 1417–1418 (cf. 1432), Soph. *El.* 530–581 (Clytemnestra's love for Iphigenia); Ar. *Thesm.* 689–761 (a frantic mother tries to recover her abducted baby daughter); Men. *Sam.* 37–40, cf. fr. 449a, 877E. (mothers and daughters go together to festivals).

80. Cf. Arist. *EE* 7.1241b1, *NE* 9.1166a8, 1168a23.

81. By mothers: *IG* 1² 452, 524, ?691, 2² 4588, 4593, 4613, 4671, 4883, ?4891. By fathers: *IG* 1² 555, 684, ?709, ?716, 2² 4351, 4400, 4412, ?4429, cf. 4319. By mother and father: *IG* 2² 4403.

82. Men: Solon 27W. (twenty-eight to thirty-five), Pl. *Resp.* 5.460E (twenty-five), *Leg.* 4.721B (thirty), 6.772D (twenty-five to thirty-five), 6.785B (thirty to thirty-five), Arist. *Pol.* 7.1335a29 (thirty-seven or a little before, apparently an older age than usual, cf. Hsch. s. *ekshēbos*); cf. Arist. *Rh.* 2.1390b9, [Arist.] *Probl.* 20.7.923a37. Women: Xen. *Oec.* 7.5 (fourteen), Dem. 27.4, 29.43 (fifteen), cf. Arist. *AthPol* 56.7 (fourteen). Plato sets the earliest acceptable age at sixteen (*Leg.* 6.785B) or eighteen (*Leg.* 8.833D), Aristotle at about eighteen (*Pol.* 7.1335a28), apparently correcting contemporary Greek custom. As in most preindustrial populations, women's life expectancy was probably lower than men's; Golden (1981) 322–326.

83. Isae. 7.25; Nep. *Cimon* 1.2, Philo, *Spec. Leg.* 3.22, Schol. Ar. *Nub.* 1371, and, for examples, Dem. 57.20, Plut. *Them.* 32.2.

84. Bond (1981) 190 on 485–489.

85. Eur. *Tro.* 740–763; for moving descriptions of children's distress at

being parted from their mothers, see, e.g., Eur. *Tro.* 557–559, 1089–1099.

86. Sophocles' Clytemnestra is made to show some sorrow at the report of her son Orestes' death and to explain it by commenting that not even those who suffer at their hands can hate the children they bear (Soph. *El.* 770–771).
87. For other mothers living with their sons, see Hunter (1989) 47 n. 43, who lists twelve examples.
88. Lys. 7.41, Dem. 57.70, [Dem.] 53.29, cf. Lys. 24.6, Dem. 19.283, [Dem.] 25.84. A speaker in comedy notes a mother's right to benefit from those she bears: Philemon fr. 156E.
89. So the mothers mentioned at Lys. 24.6, Dem. 57.70, are certainly widows.
90. [Dem.] 25.54, Din. *Aristog.* 8, 14, 18, 20.
91. Antiph. 5.74, [Dem.] 58.60, cf. Pl. *Phdr.* 275DE.
92. E.g., Lys. 2.72–73, 13.45, Dem. *Epit.* 36. The fathers of the dead are specifically mentioned as needing the city's support at Pl. *Menex.* 248D, apparently in order to provide a rhetorical balance to their sons; in other portions of the passage, which purports to be a funeral oration composed by Aspasia, mothers and fathers are referred to together in the customary fashion (247C, 248B, 249A). Hirsch-Dyczek (1979), studying the iconography of gravestones, asserts that sixth- and fifth-century examples never stress the separation of father and child.
93. Isoc. 1.14, cf. 2.38, Alexis fr. 280E. and the proverb ascribed to Pittacus, Apost. 12.42a. Similarly, a fragment of Euripides enjoins parents to recall that they were young once themselves (951N.²). Arnott has some perceptive comments on Menander's propensity to show sons repeating their father's youthful peccadilloes ([1979] xxxix-xlii).
94. E.g., Aesch. *Supp.* 707–709, Dicaeogenes 52 F 5 Snell, Xen. *Mem.* 4.4.20, Dem. 24.60, [Dem.] 25.66, Aeschin. 1.28, Pl. *Leg.* 4.717B–718A, Antiphanes fr. 262E., Men. fr. 715E., Arist. *NE* 9.1164b5, 1165a24.
95. Many passages are collected in Stob. *Flor.* 4.25; see also Richardson (1933) 48–58, Dover (1974) 273–275.
96. Aristotle is more forthcoming elsewhere, urging that the father not monopolize respect even if he is better (*beltiōn*) than the mother; "even Zeus doesn't get all the sacrifices" (*EE* 7.1244a14, *NE* 9.1165a15).
97. Grant (1986); cf. too Aristotle's remarks at *EE* 7.1239a6, 1242a33, and Pl. *Resp.* 8.562D–563A.
98. E.g., Eur. fr. 853N.², Antiphanes fr. 261E., Men. fr. 805E., Philemon fr. 236, 237E.

99. Ar. *Nub.* 1399–1451, *Pax* 123, Pl. *Lys.* 208E, *Prot.* 325D, Arist. *NE* 7.1149b8, cf. Ar. *Eq.* 412, Xen. *An.* 5.8.18, *Cyr.* 2.2.14, Men. *Monos.* 422. Daughters are not explicitly mentioned in any of these passages (note especially Xen. *An.* 5.8.18, which speaks only of sons); in two, mothers may administer beatings (Pl. *Lys.* 208E, *Prot.* 325D). Both parents might discipline babies (Pl. *Lys.* 212E).
100. Pl. *Resp.* 8.548B; [Arist.] *Oec.* 1.1344a6. Xenophon's Ischomachus regards methods of training as something for husband and wife to determine together (Xen. *Oec.* 7.12), but there is reason to think this portrayal owes more to Xenophon's political purposes than to popular opinion at Athens; Murnaghan (1988).
101. Lekythos, Sandal Painter, about 550, Bologna PU 204, *ABV* 70.7, *Paralipomena* 28, Boardman (1974) pl. 43.
102. Hewitt (1931) 35.
103. Men. *Monos.* 765, cf. 767.
104. Eur. fr. 952N.²; Dion. Hal. *Comp.* 14 *ad fin.*
105. Eur. fr. 950N.², cf. Philemon fr. 200E.; Eur. fr. 500N.²
106. Archippus fr. 45E., Plut. *Alcib.* 1.4. A victorious choragus set up a monument to inspire his children to follow his example (*IG* 2² 3022).
107. A number of studies of conflict between parents and children are collected in Bertman (1976). Most valuable is the overview by Reinhold (1976).
108. Cf. Reinhold (1976) 21.
109. See the survey by Rudhardt (1982), especially 749–757.
110. Rumpf (1985) 57–81, 93–107.
111. Pl. *Symp.* 195BC. One or both stories are referred to at Aesch. *Eum.* 640–643, Ar. *Nub.* 904b–906, Eur. *HF* 1317–1318, Pl. *Euthyphro* 5E–6A, *Resp.* 2.377E–378B, and Isoc. 11.38 as well.
112. Dodds (1951) 46. Similarly, though it has the authority of no less a critic than Northrop Frye, the notion that "New Comedy unfolds from . . . a comic Oedipus situation" is overstated (*English Institute Essays—1948,* 50, as quoted approvingly by MacCary and Willcock [1976] 35–36). Of the three Plautine plays cited as examples of the "amatory rivalry of father and son" in a recent general introduction to New Comedy (Hunter [1985] 96), *Asinaria* involves a father who threatens to poach on his son's girlfriend, and *Mercator* a father who falls for a girl without knowing of her tie with his son and is quite contrite when he finds out. Only *Casina* really seems to fit Frye's formulation, and even there father and son are not in direct conflict but maneuver for Casina by proxy. Perhaps the truest indication of the lack of Oedipal overtones is provided by Demeas in Menander's *Samia.* Believing (wrongly) that his son has cuckolded him with his

live-in girlfriend, he forbears to blame him, assuming that Chrysis must have taken advantage of the young man when he was drunk (321–347). (It is only fair to note that Demeas's bluff and belligerent neighbor Niceratus takes a more serious view of the matter, 506–514.)

113. Some issues are treated by Roussel (1951) 215–227, Longo (1980–1981), Maffi (1983) 10–16.

114. Isae. 12.3, cf. Lys. 19.9.

115. Isoc. 15.155–156, cf. Din. *Phil.* 18.

116. I accept the estimate of Markle (1985) 277–281, that a family of four could be fed for about 150 drachmas a year in the fourth century.

117. Pl. *Leg.* 11.932B; cf. Xen. *Mem.* 1.2.33–35.

118. Councilors: Xen. *Mem.* 1.2.35, cf. *IG* l³ 14.9–11, Arist. *AthPol* 30.2. Jurors: Arist. *AthPol* 63.3, Dem. 24.150, Poll. 8.122. Administrators of the Herakleia and the Eleusinian mysteries: *IG* l³ 3, *SEG* 30.61.A.30–31 (restored). Demotionidae: *IG* 2² 1237.33–34; Hansen (1980) 167–169, Develin (1985).

119. For the importance of wealth in public life at this time, see Davies (1981) 88–131. Rhodes (1986) discusses the political options open to young men.

120. So probably [Dem.] 47.34–35, 80; cf. Pl. *Leg.* 11.931A.

121. Cf. Lacey (1968) 106–107.

122. Xen. *Lac.* 1.6–7, *Mem.* 4.4.23, Pl. *Resp.* 5.459B, Arist. *Pol.* 7.1334b29–1335a6, cf. Eur. fr. 317N.²

123. Campbell (1964) 83–88, 161–164. Some societies (mainly in Africa) rely on more elaborate and formalized age grades to control population growth and the access to power; Bernardi (1984) 73–93.

124. [Dem.] 40.4 (eighteen: regarded as exceptional), Lys. fr. 24 Thalheim. Menestheus, the son of Iphicrates, may have married in his mid-twenties or even younger: [Dem.] 49.66 with Davies (1971) 250–251, Harris (1988) 51–52 (but if in fact he was born in 386, the marriage cannot be as early as 370/69).

125. [Dem.] 25.87–88, cf. Plaut. *Most.* 755–761 (based on an early third century comedy by Philemon): an old man wants to add a *gynaeceum* onto his house for a son and his bride. Plato views this as a recipe for conflict, and legislates against it (Pl. *Leg.* 6.776AB).

126. Dem. 55.3, [Dem.] 59.22, cf. Arist. *Gen. An.* 2.740a6, *NE* 5.1134b8. Saller (1988) 403–407 provides a useful discussion of the dynamics of father-son relations among different economic strata at Rome.

127. Arist. *Pol.* 7.1335a36, cf. *HA* 5.545b27.

128. Arist. *AthPol* 56.6, cf. Ar. *Nub.* 844–846, Xen. *Mem.* 1.2.49, Aeschin. 3.251, Pl. *Leg.* 11.928E–929E.
129. Apul. *Apol.* 37.1–2, Luc. *Macr.* 24, Plut. *Mor.* 785A, Cic. *Sen.* 7.22, cf. *Vita Soph.* 13. Not all who have struggled through the last few hundred lines of this play will find their opinion of Athenian justice improved by the verdict.
130. Note here Men. fr. 806E.: "You're crazy to bring a lawsuit against parents"; cf. Pl. *Leg.* 11.928DE.
131. A recent discussion: Piccirilli (1982).
132. S. Bellow, *Mr. Sammler's Planet* (paperback edition 1971 [1969]) 92–93.
133. Saller (1987a), cf. Saller (1986).
134. Frier (1982) 245.
135. Thury (1988) 199–202 outlines the place of this practice in the structure of a tragedy produced about fifteen years before, Euripides' *Alcestis*.
136. For example, Ar. *Vesp.* 1167, 1299, 1309–1310, 1316, 1417.
137. *Neanias:* Ar. *Vesp.* 1332–1334. Cf. the use of *neanikōs* (Ar. *Vesp.* 1307), *neoplouti trygi* (1309), to describe Philocleon.
138. *Arkhaia g' hymōn:* Ar. *Vesp.* 1336. The same joke, an old man calling a younger one old-fashioned, recurs at Ar. *Nub.* 820–821.
139. An ancient commentator spells out the joke: "He's imitating young men who say, 'If my father dies I'll give you everything'" (Schol. 1353(R.), cf. 1359).
140. By "kid" I translate a diminutive (*hyidion*), presumably used to stress the absurdity of the reversal.
141. Ar. *Vesp.* 1351–1363. The last comment has been variously explained; see MacDowell (1971) 309 on 1363, Rusten (1977). Perhaps it should be taken as Philocleon's claim to have found not just renewed youth but a new life, though not quite in the form usually promised to initiates.
142. See especially Lys. 24.16 and other references in Dover (1974) 103.

Chapter 5. Brothers, Sisters, and Grandparents

1. See van Hoorn (1951) nos. 53, 100 (Athens NM 14509), 218, 253, 270, 381, 405, 463, 746, 765, 812, 838, 839, 849, 987, 1007.
2. Tombstones: *IG* 1² 977 (cf. 1023), *IG* 2² 7839a, 11169. Dedications: *IG* 1² 472, ?559, 574, 580, 679, 775, *IG* 2² 4147, Raubitschek (1949) 243 no. 212, ?251 no. 221, *SEG* 21.192.
3. See Hardcastle (1980), Humphreys (1986), and above all Cox (1988a), especially 380–386.
4. Patrilineal half-brothers were apparently less likely to get along, be-

cause they would split the patrimony (Isae. 12.4). See also Eur. fr. 338N.², Dem. 39, [Dem.] 40 and 48, and the story, told of both Pisistratus and Cato, in which sons express concerns about a father's remarriage (Plut. *Mor.* 189D, 480D, *Cato maior* 24.4–5); Humphreys (1986) 75–76, Cox (1988a) 385–386.

5. Similarly, Sositheus boasts that he showed his family feeling by giving his daughter in marriage to his brother's son ([Dem.] 43.74, cf. 44.10, Lys. 32.4–6); Thompson (1967).

6. Dem. 55.2, cf. Antiph. 6.21, Andoc. 1.148, Lys. 13.39–42, Aeschin. 2.179, Arist. *NE* 8.1159b35, Men. fr. 1139E.

7. [Dem.] 53.28; Dem. 21.78–79, [Dem.] 47.53.

8. [Dem.] 47.11, 46; Dem. 29.15, 23; Lys. 12.34.

9. [Dem.] 25.55, 79; [Dem.] 58.28, cf. Isae 2.1 (it is shameful to deprive a dead brother of descendants).

10. Apollod. 3.11.2. The story is an old one: see already Hom. *Od.* 11.298–304.

11. Peristiany (1976) 8.

12. Arist. *Pol.* 7.1328a15 = Eur. fr. 975N.², cf. *IA* 376–377; Arist. *Pol.* 5.1305b1.

13. In another passage, Aeschines urges jurors to recall that his prosecution of Timarchus protected their sons' and brothers' chastity (Aeschin. 2.180).

14. On difference in age as a point of contention, see also Arist. *EE* 7.1242a4, 36, *NE* 8.1160b25, 1161b27.

15. Plutarch alludes only gingerly to sexual competition between brothers as a source of strife; cf. Hes. *Op.* 328–330.

16. Dem. 36.11, 34, 39.27, 29; see especially Isae. 6.26, [Dem.] 43.19; Xen. *Symp.* 4.35; Harrison (1968) 122–132.

17. West (1978) 252 on 378 removes the contradiction by taking the "second son" as a reference to a grandson, but his parallels are either ambiguous (*GVI* 961.4) or inapposite.

18. For an extended discussion of such stories with a different emphasis, see Jackson (1978).

19. Foster (1960–1961), Campbell (1964) 81, Segalen (1984).

20. See Davis (1977) 176–197.

21. For an interesting account of the lack of trust involved in the partition of the inheritance in a modern Greek village, and the elaborate precautions deemed necessary to ensure fairness, see Friedl (1962) 60–64, cf. Davis (1977) 193–194.

22. See Harrison (1968) 239–244, Fox (1985) 211–214.

23. Dem. 36.9; Lys. 32.4–6; [Dem.] 44.10, 18, Aeschin. 1.102, cf. [Dem.] 57.19–21, Isoc. 18.60.

24. Arist. *Pol.* 1.1257a22. Elsewhere, he exhibits some inconsistency

about the effectiveness of holding property in common as a strategy for avoiding quarrels: *NE* 8.1162a27, *Pol.* 2.1263b24.

25. The seclusion of women from the community's public space was an ideal, best attested in tragedy (e.g., Aesch. *Cho.* 919–921, Soph. *Ant.* 578–579, Eur. *IA* 821–834, *Tro.* 647–653) but not unknown in other sources (e.g., Xen. *Oec.* 7.30, Isoc. *Ep.* 9.10, Pl. *Resp.* 9.579B, cf. Hdt. 2.35.2—a reversal). Plato's description of women as a "race accustomed to an underground and shadowy life" is especially interesting (*Leg.* 6.781C). This ideal was realized, if at all, only among the elite; poorer women often had to work. (See Arist. *Pol.* 4.1300a4, 6.1323a3, and Herfst [1922], Cohen [1989].) But we may be sure that women with jobs still had domestic responsibilities as well, so they might welcome the elite's ideal.

26. Lys. 3.6, cf. Dem. 21.78–79, 37.46.

27. The speaker of Isaeus 6 claims that Euctemon's daughters—their age is not given—are well known (presumably by sight) to most of his fellow demesmen (10); Euctemon was wealthy enough to leave an estate worth paying Isaeus to fight for, so his daughters probably were not forced to go out to work.

28. Soph. *OC* 343; Eur. *Or.* 108, cf. *Pho.* 93–94, 1276.

29. See Isager (1978), Walker (1983).

30. See Morgan (1982) (and cf. Men. *Sam.* 232). The tower room for women slaves mentioned at [Dem.] 49.56 may be a *gynaikōnitis*. A fifth-century Attic country house, the Dema house, may have a staircase leading to a second floor. The excavators suggest there may have been "women's rooms" upstairs (Jones, Sackett, and Graham [1962] 113 n. 93, cf. Walker [1983] 85).

31. The *gynaikōnitis* might be bolted (Xen. *Oec.* 9.5, to prevent slaves from breeding, Lys. 1.13, Eur. *IA* 738 [*parthenōn*], Ar. *Thesm.* 414), or made secure by removing the ladder leading to it (cf. Plut. *Arat.* 26.2–3 [Sicyon]).

32. Cf. Pl. *Tim.* 69E–70A. Vitruvius's Greek house—late Hellenistic, not classical—has a *gynaikōnitis* on the main floor (*Arch.* 6.7). There may be a *gynaikōnitis* on the main floor of a house at Olynthus; Robinson and Mylonas (1946) 188.

33. Aesch. *Prom.* 646, Eur. *IA* 738, 1175, *IT* 826, *Pho.* 89, 194, 1275.

34. Choruses: *Suda* s. *parthenōnos*. Participants (*arktoi*): partially restored in *REG* 76 (1963) 135 (Brauron, 300–200); other examples in Brelich (1969) 303.

35. There is evidence for this in a late source: Philo, *Spec. Leg.* 3.169.

36. Cf. Xen. *Oec.* 9.19, Pl. *Leg.* 5.740A, [Arist.] *Oec* 1.1344a7, and, on the close ties of mothers with their children, Chapter 4 of the present volume.

37. About 400, Amsterdam Allard Pierson Museum 8210, *ARV*² 838.27, Beck (1975) no. X.1 pl. 349; Immerwahr (1973) 145 (illustrated by him as no. 12 *bis,* pl. 32.1A).

38. About 460, Dallas Museum of Art 1968.28A, Rühfel (1984b) no. 16; cf. the red-figure hydria, Munich 476, Keuls (1983) pl. 14.17.

39. Conze (1893–1922) no. 283, Hirsch-Dyczek (1983) illus. 78.

40. It is curious that Xenophon (*Mem.* 2.2) portrays Socrates' son Lamprocles, a *neaniskos,* as still so intimately involved with his mother; they squabble, she nurses him. Has he just left the *gynaikōnitis?* Cf. Pind. *Pyth.* 8.85, Theocr. 12.33. Note that older boys might be less welcome where women worked: Pl. *Lys.* 208D.

41. About 460, Athens T.E. 1623, *Paralipomena* 391.88 *bis.*

42. Van Hoorn (1951) no. 38 pl. 295 (Athens NM 1268), no. 184 pl. 522, no. 482 pl. 338, no. 564, no. 659, no. 832 pl. 437.

43. Other brothers and sisters also were buried together, e.g., *SEG* 10.452a, about 550; Humphreys (1983) 111–115. In tragedy, Polydorus and Polyxena share one funeral pyre (Eur. *Hec.* 895–897).

44. *IG* 2² 12147, Conze (1893–1922) no. 887 pl. 172.

45. *IG* 2² 13037, Conze (1893–1922) no. 893 pl. 174; cf. nos. 888, 891, perhaps 892.

46. Conze (1893–1922) no. 1116 pl. 225.

47. *IG* 2² 11379, Conze (1893–1922) no. 697 pl. 133.

48. *IG* 2² 11121, Conze (1893–1922) no. 836.

49. Conze (1893–1922) no. 1100 pl. 226.

50. New York Metropolitan Museum 11.185, Richter (1961) no. 37 pl. 99, 107–109.

51. For a boy and a girl (not necessarily brother and sister) outside the immediate environment of the home, see the fountain scene on a hydria by the A.D. Painter, Naples Stg. 12, *ABV* 334.3, *Paralipomena* 147, Keuls (1985) pl. 210.

52. Weisner and Gallimore (1977) 169, cf. Weisner (1982) 305–315, especially 307, Munroe, Munroe, and Shimmin (1984), especially 369–370.

53. Nag, White, and Peet (1978) 294–296.

54. Another tragic sister who takes on a maternal role is Heracles' daughter (Macaria); she asks Iolaus to raise the brothers in whose interest she intends to die (Eur. *Hcld.* 574–580).

55. Some speculation on the long-term effects of sibling childcare suggests that it restricts the development of differences in both children and adults (and so presumably makes siblings more like-minded); see Weisner and Gallimore (1977) 178–179 for a skeptical summary.

56. See Lavelle (1986a). *IG* 1² 905 was apparently set up for Glyce, a metic, by her brother.

57. *IG* 2² 12151; *IG* 2² 7227.
58. *IG* 2² 11813; cf. 13095, 13102a, and the gravestone of Apollonia (Rühfel [1984a] no. 36), apparently dedicated by her brothers.
59. Eur. *Alc.* 402–403, *Andr.* 441 (cf. 504–505), *Hcld.* 239, *HF* 71–72, *Tro.* 750–751. In Euripides' *Alcestis,* a rather older boy sings a lament on behalf of his sister and himself (Eur. *Alc.* 393–416; Dyson [1988] 17–18).
60. See Lavelle (1986b).
61. For brothers as protectors of sisters' interests, see also Ar. *Plut.* 984–985, Isae. 3.36, 39, 71, [Dem.] 59.1, 6, 12.
62. See on this point Friedl (1963), on modern Greece.
63. Cf. Lys. 13.45, Isae. 10.25, Dem. 27.66, Hyper. *Epit.* 27.
64. Isae. 8.36, cf. 41–43; [Dem.] 48.54–55.
65. According to one reckoning, "in 10 out of 28 instances of adoption . . . brother-sister ties play a dominant role in the provision of heirs to the testator" (Cox [1988a] 390).
66. Plut. *Per.* 10.4–5. Walcot (1987b) 32–33 suggests that solidarity between brother and sister increased when parents had problems, and wonders "whether the fall from grace of their father Miltiades" reinforced the ties of Cimon and Elpinice.
67. Raubitschek (1949) 304 no. 284, early fifth century.
68. Dem. 31.11–12; Isae. 8.36; Andoc. 1.48, Lys. 13.39. The philosopher Pyrrho lived in his sister's home, presumably at Athens, of which he was an honorary citizen (Diog. Laert. 9.66).
69. In a speech written by the Athenian Isocrates (but involving Siphnians and delivered in an Aeginetan court), a half-sister who came to visit her dying brother is contrasted with the speaker's opponent, another half-sister who calls the dead man brother yet not only neglected him when sick but failed even to attend his funeral (Isoc. 19.26, 30). Two Athenian sisters are criticized in court on the grounds that they didn't give their brother a son by adoption (Isae. 7.31–32).
70. Humphreys (1986) 76–78, Cox (1988a) 386–389.
71. For the debate on the authorship and interpretation of this speech, see Szlezák (1981).
72. For an interesting discussion of such stories, see Visser (1986).
73. Cf. Rudhardt (1982) 733–739.
74. My ideas on dowry were first presented at the 1986 annual meeting of the American Historical Association, held at Chicago.
75. Saller (1984b) 200.
76. Dowries for wives do not directly affect the relations of brothers and sisters, and therefore I exclude them from consideration here. I have as a consequence also left out of account all dowries in which the

relationship of the donor and the woman dowered is unknown. The amounts involved in these dowries are not significantly different from those discussed here.

77. The evidence is set out in convenient form by Casson (1976), especially 53–59, Schaps (1979) 74–88, 99, and Cox (1988a) 382–384. Discrepancies between their figures and mine stem from differing interpretations of individual pieces of evidence.

78. Lys. 19.16–17, 32.6, Isae. 5.5 and 26, 8.7–8 and 35, Dem. 27.4–5 and 28.15–16, 29.48 and 31.6–9, [Dem.] 42.27. We can come up with an eighth instance if we accept the tradition that Callias had a fortune of 200 talents and assume that it was substantially from this estate that his son paid Alcibiades a dowry of 10 talents, but our source for Callias's wealth mentions it only in the context of an argument that many rich men are poorer than they are thought to be (Lys. 19.48).

79. Dem. 27.9, 37.5 (and cf. 27.17, 23, 28.13), Aeschin. 3.104, *IG* 2^2 2492, 345/4; Billeter (1898) 10–18, cf. Thompson (1978) 417.

80. These records present special problems. We cannot be sure in any case that the sum mentioned represents the entire dowry, and it is occasionally clear that it does not. M. I. Finley, in his fundamental study of these stones (1952), regards such instances as exceptional. It sometimes appears that the sum in question is more than the dowry as well. We can only assume that these two classes more or less cancel each other out.

81. [Andoc.] 4.13–14, Plut. *Alcib.* 8.6; Plut. *Mor.* 179F.

82. Davis (1977) 189–190. However, some Athenian families seem to have made a practice of marrying their kinswomen into the same deme, apparently to consolidate political ties; Cox (1988b).

83. Isae. 2.5, 5.6, perhaps Lys. 19.16–17.

84. For the solidarity of sisters in Roman comedies based on Athenian originals, see, e.g., Plaut. *Cist.* 3–5, Ter. *Andr.* 121–136, *Eun.* 144–146.

85. Further assumptions include: men's age at first birth, thirty-two; women's age at first birth, twenty; spacing between births, 2.5 years; completed family size, 6; no population growth (Golden [1985a] 10 n. 8).

86. The expectation that a father's father be aged and gray-haired makes possible the riddle playing on two meanings of *pappos,* "grandfather" and "thistledown" (Eubulus fr. 106.16–20K.-A. = Ath. 10.450B, cf. Soph. fr. 868R.).

87. This relationship and its roots are discussed by Bremmer (1983b).

88. Cf. Ter. *Hec.* 116–123.

89. *IG* 2^2 3453 (great-grandmother), 5673 (grandmother), 6214, 6288

(grandmother), 7195, 7393 (Athenians); *IG* 2² 11375, 11998 (grandmother) (not necessarily Athenian citizens). *IG* 2² 5421a may have been set up by grandsons, *hyiōnoi*, for their grandfather; *IG* 2² 530 may be a dedication by a grandfather and his grandson.

90. *IG* 2² 10650, about 410; Kübler and Peek (1934), Garland (1985) fig. 13.
91. Athens NM 777, 425–400, Rühfel (1984a) pl. 52.
92. See *Com. Adesp.* fr. 103d (a).8–11E. for a grandfather's joy at the birth of an only daughter's son; cf. Men. *Sam.* 553–554, Ter. *Ad.* 333–334, Plaut. *Aulul.* 796–798.
93. Harrison (1968) 190–193.
94. E.g., the amphora by Lydos, 560–540, Berlin 1685, *ABV* 109.24, Boardman (1974) pl. 67; the cup by the Brygos Painter, 480–470, Paris Louvre G 152, *ARV²* 369.1, Boardman (1975) pl. 245.2. See also, e.g., Eur. *Tro.* 1209–1215; Touchefeu (1983).
95. Eur. *Andr.* 1066–1069, 1171–1225, especially 1181. Cf. Hecuba's lament over her grandson Astyanax, Eur. *Tro.* 1156–1201, especially 1182–1184.
96. Isae. 1.39, 8.32.
97. See Gernet (1955) 19–28, Bremmer (1983b) 174–177. Eurysaces is entrusted to his father's father; but his mother is a slave, and her father is dead (Soph. *Ajax* 507–509).
98. On Diogeiton's activities, see Moore (1982).
99. Radcliffe-Brown (1952) 90–116. Cf., however, the critical discussion by Apple (1956).
100. Cf. Pl. *Gorg.* 527A, *Lys.* 205D, *Resp.* 1.350E, 2.378D, *Tht.* 176B; Massaro (1977) and, on old women in general, Bremmer (1987), Henderson (1987b). For children's close attention to such stories, see Pl. *Pol.* 208E.
101. *Tēthalladous: Com. Adesp.* fr. 17E., cf. Eustath. *Il.* 971.39, Poll. 3.20. *Mammothreptos:* Phryn. *Ecl.* 267 Rutherford, Poll. 3.20, Schol. Ar. *Ach.* 49, *Ran.* 1021. A boy in a Roman comedy is said to be fortunate because he has two grandmothers (Plaut. *Truc.* 808).
102. Number of widows: Golden (1981) 328–329. Mothers living with their children: see Chapter 4 of this book.

Chapter 6. Outsiders and Alliances

1. Yanagisako (1979) 161–164; Sieder and Mitterauer (1983) 336–345.
2. Harris (1982) 146–148.
3. A regular visitor: Antiph. 1.14. Apprentices: Xen. *Eq.* 2.2. Temporary residences in the fields: Osborne (1985a), especially 126–127.

4. The speaker of Lys. 3 took in his nieces (6–7), Cleonymus his nephews (Isae. 1.15); for a returning daughter, see Isae. 8.8.
5. Dem. 45.70, Isae. 5.11.
6. Isoc. 16.26, Craterus 342 F 5, 17, Schol. Ar. *Lys.* 273; Connor (1985).
7. See also Eur. fr. 359, 491N.², and note [Arist.] *Rhet. ad Alex.* 1.1421a31. Interests of the household's blood kin were protected by restrictions on an adopted son's ability to adopt in his turn; Harrison (1968) 84–87.
8. Hes. *Op.* 825, cf. Men. *Monos.* 127; Aesch. *PV* 727 (where this epithet for Salmydessus is surely influenced by the story of Phineus and Cleopatra, cf. Soph. *Ant.* 966–987); Hdt. 4.154.2, cf. Eur. *Alc.* 313–319; Eur. *Alc.* 302–309, cf. *Ion* 1025, fr. 4, 824N.²; *Com. Adesp.* fr. 110E. Note, too, Aristotle's remark that all creatures that concern themselves with children care only for those they consider their own (Arist. *Gen. An.* 3.759a36).
9. Isae. 12.5; Lys. 32.17.
10. Hdt. 8.41.1, Thuc. 1.89.3, Lys. 2.34, M-L 23.6–8, cf. Thuc. 2.6.4, 2.78.3, 4.123.4, Isoc. 6.73–74; Lys. 16.4; Lys. 12.97, cf. Dem. 19.194, Men. *Sic.* 281–282.
11. For a boy's proposal of *xenia,* and its long-term benefits, see Xen. *Hell.* 4.1.39–40; for sons and their fathers' *xenoi,* see Lys. 5.1, 18.10, [Dem.] 50.56, cf. Isoc. 1.2, 19.10.
12. Herlihy (1985) 149–155.
13. Cf. McCracken (1983) 311.
14. Eur. *IT* 708–710, *El.* 82–83.
15. Aeschin. 3.162, Harpoc. s. *Aristiōn.*
16. Herman (1987) 142–145.
17. Golden (1985b).
18. Golden (1984).
19. For the importance of the subject, cf. Laslett (1977) 43.
20. What follows is a revised version of Golden (1988b).
21. So, for example, Vogt (1974) 103–121.
22. Slater (1974).
23. For such depictions, see Rühfel (1984b) 61–76, and, on the problems posed by these conventions in general, Himmelmann (1971).
24. About 425, Athens NM 715, Conze (1893–1922) no. 1032 pl. 204, Rühfel (1984a) nos. 56, 57.
25. For a brief sketch of the duties of these slaves, see Golden (1984) 310–311. More material is collected in Mary Rosaria (1917) 16–33, Rühfel (1988). On the activities and impact of household slaves at Rome, see Bradley (1985), (1986), Joshel (1986), Saller (1987b), Dixon (1988) 120–129, 141–155.

26. Lys. 1.41; Lys. 1.9, 12.
27. Our best evidence on the age at which babies were weaned comes from outside classical Athens, in wet-nursing contracts from Hellenistic and Roman Egypt. The terms of these agreements run from six months to three years, most stipulating a duration of two years; see Bradley (1980), Pomeroy (1984) 162.
28. Lys. 1.11; Ar. *Lys.* 908.
29. Evidence that ownership of slaves was widespread: Thuc. 3.17.4, Lys. 5.5, 24.6, Dem. 45.86, Theophr. *Char.* 25.4.
30. Note the vignette concerning Chaerea and his father's slave in New Comedy: Chaerea used to take treats to him in his little room (Ter. *Eun.* 307–310).
31. That this was so at Rome is stressed by Bradley (1985) 506–512.
32. It is strange that the relations of slaves and children have not been discussed more fully in psychoanalytic treatments of Greek myth and society such as Slater (1968); cf. Humphreys (1983) 59. Freud himself was well aware of the influence of servants, nurses in particular: see, e.g., "Some Reflections on Schoolboy Psychology" (1914) in the *Standard Edition* of his works (London 1955) 13:243: "The nature and quality of the human child's relations to people of his own and the opposite sex have already been laid down in the first six years of his life. The people to whom he is in this way fixed are his parents and his brothers and sisters . . . (we should perhaps add to his parents any other people, such as nurses, who cared for him in his infancy)."
33. Hdt. 8.75; Xen. *Cyr.* 7.3.14, cf. Eur. *Med.* 821.
34. The situation of the *titthē* in Menander's *Samia* seems rather similar; she has been freed, but is still in Demeas's service (237ff.). See also, e.g., *IG* 2² 1559 A col. 3.59–66, dedications by two *titthai* freed by Aristophon of Aphidna in the later fourth century. Note, however, that these documents provide a caution against becoming oversentimental about this relationship; they seem to indicate that Aristophon (unsuccessfully) accused his ex-slaves of failing to fulfill the conditions of their emancipation.
35. Classical Athenian gravestones for *titthai*: *IG* 2² 7873, 9112, 10843, 11647, 12242, 12387, 12559, ?12632, 13065, *AthMitt* 67 (1942) 222 no. 30, *Agora* 17:156 no. 863, 186 no. 1048; see Karouzou (1957), Möbius (1966) 154–160. For *trophoi*: *IG* 2² 12563. For *paidagōgoi*: *IG* 2² 10715, 10903, ?11932, 12433. For *maiai* (nurses or midwives): *IG* 2² 6873 (probably a midwife), Peek (1957) ?41 no. 156. Of course, we do not know the status of all of these; some certainly were not slaves (e.g., *IG* 2² 7873).
36. Aesch. *Cho.* 752; Eur. *El.* 506–508.
37. Hieronymus of Rhodes fr. 19 Wehrli. Cf. the proverb referred to in a

similar context by Plutarch: "If you dwell with a lame man, you will learn to limp" (*Mor.* 4A).

38. Stobaeus, *Flor.* 4.19 provides a convenient collection of passages on the vices of slaves.
39. For the importance of association and imitation, see, e.g., Eur. *Hel.* 940–943, Xen. *Cyr,* 7.5.86, Isoc. 15.92; Beck (1964) 309.
40. Plato praises Persian education at the hands of "the most highly approved eunuchs of the court" at the expense of Athenian upbringing by "a female nurse [*trophos*] of little worth" (*Alcib. I* 121D). The point of the contrast is to emphasize the Athenians' carelessness in giving their children to slaves with no special merit.
41. Xen. *Lac.* 2.1–2, cf. Plut. *Lyc.* 16.4–6. Similarly, a passage of fourth-century comedy, Antiphanes 159E., praises the Scythians because they don't provide *titthai* or *paidagōgoi* for their children.
42. Cf. the retort of Pistoclerus to his *paidagōgos* at Plaut. *Bacch.* 162: "Am I your slave or you mine?"
43. At Men. *Sam.* 85, Chrysis worries that Plangon's baby may be put out to a wet-nurse (*titthē*) in a tenement; but there is nothing to indicate that her status is a cause of concern.
44. Syrus, chief slave of Micio in Terence's *Adelphoe,* provides a glaring example of a bad influence from New Comedy. He claims to have raised Aeschinus and Ctesipho from birth and to have taught them all he could. But what he taught, says Demea, was all bad (961–968). And there are frequent references to Syrus's leading role in the abduction of Aeschinus's girlfriend and the deception of Demea (314, 527ff., 560). There is another slave whose services are denigrated in the *Adelphoe.* When Syrus pleads for the freedom of his wife, Phrygia, Demea is at first reluctant. He is unimpressed by the grounds of Syrus's claim, that Phrygia was the first to nurse Aeschinus's newborn son (974–976). The influence of Syrus adds a nice irony to a play that deals with the responsibility of fathers for their sons.
45. Stories: Pl. *Leg,* 7.794DE, 10.887D, *Resp.* 2.377B–378A. Orders: Pl. *Leg.* 7.790A. Food: Ar. *Eq.* 716–718, Arist. *Rh.* 3.1407a6, cf. Sext. Emp. *Rhet.* 2.42, Ter. *Hec.* 767–769, Apost. 9.55 (on Cleon). Alcohol: Arist. *Somn.* 457a14, cf. Soran. *Gyn.* 2.19.88. Older nurses had a reputation for drunkenness: see, e.g., Eubulus fr. 80K.-A., Men. *Sam.* 295–303, fr. 521E.; Oeri (1948) 53–61. A father in a third-century comedy upbraids a *paidagōgos* for leading his son to drink (Baton fr. 5K.-A.). Favorinus (in Aul. Gell. *NA* 12.1) and Plutarch (*Mor.* 3CD) later urge mothers to breast-feed their children rather than entrust them to wet-nurses, slaves in particular. Such foster mothers infect children with inferior blood and spirit and may neglect them because of their lack of natural ties of affection (cf. Tac. *Dial.* 29). On such

concerns at Rome, see Bradley (1986) 215–216. No classical Greek source makes a similar appeal on behalf of human children, but Xenophon does recommend against giving puppies to a foster mother to nurse (*Cyn.* 7.3).

46. Finley (1980) 107. S. C. Humphreys (1983) goes still further: "The ethical deficiencies attributed to slaves in antiquity—deceit and laziness—were recognised to be related to their structural position, and there was therefore no reason to suppose that they could contaminate the morals of free women and children" (76 n. 6).

47. For a brief survey of the roles of nurses and *paidagōgoi* in extant tragedies, see Bassi (1942–1943) 80–87. Bassi is not concerned with the issues I discuss here.

48. In Euripides' *Hypsipyle,* the child Opheltes is left unattended by Hypsipyle, his nurse, and is killed by a snake. Though Hypsipyle is of noble birth, she is in exile and regarded as a slave (*dmōis:* fr. 34/35.5 Bond; cf. *douleian,* fr. 61.8 Bond). When Deianira gets good advice from a slave nurse her reaction is surprise, and her words imply a lucky throw of the dice rather than conscious deliberation (Soph. *Trach.* 61–63, cf. 52–53).

49. There is no entry "esclaves" or "esclavage" in the subject index to Wartelle (1978); none of the studies listed under "nourrices, confidents, et petits gens" provides a general discussion of the role of slaves or slavery in *Oresteia.* I have not found citations of any such discussion in more recent bibliographical aids.

50. Despite Fraenkel (1950) 2:3 (on *Ag.* 3), this is the consensus of recent studies: see, e.g., Taplin (1977) 276–277, Lloyd-Jones (1979) 15, Bollack and Judet de La Combe (n.d.) 1.1.8–12 (on *Ag.* 2ff.), Verdenius (1982) 430–431.

51. So, very briefly, Taplin (1977) 440.

52. See also *Ag.* 699–700, 841–842, 1374–1376, 1561–1564.

53. For the tradition and Aeschylus's relation to it, see Prag (1985), especially 68–84 (on the literary tradition). Prag discusses Aeschylus's expansion of Cassandra's role on 79–80.

54. Line 1226 was regarded as "indubitably interpolated" by Fraenkel (1950), and branded "feeble . . . and very offensive to our taste" by Denniston and Page (1957) 181 *ad loc.* Yet, as these last note, "it contains no fault of sense, syntax, metre, or style," and they retain it in their text (as Page does in the Oxford Classical Text, 1972). Perhaps its function is simply to underscore Cassandra's status as a slave.

55. There are numerous references throughout the play to Hermes (124ab, 727, 812–818) and other denizens of the underworld (15, 40, 376–377, 399, 405, 475–476, 833).

56. For a discussion of the chorus's role, see Conacher (1974), especially 330–339.
57. Golden (1982). The only other similar use known in drama outside comedy is in a third-century satyr play by Lycophron (100 F 2.7 Snell). It seems to have been too colloquial for tragedy, and may be meant here to emphasize that prince Orestes is in disguise.
58. The passage is of course particularly untypical of tragedy if the slave actually comes on stage to deliver the line, as argued by, e.g., Bain (1981) 46 n. 1. But this is uncertain; see, *contra,* Taplin (1977) 341.
59. On the nurse, see Goheen (1955) 132–137, Rose (1982), Margon (1983).
60. See Prag (1985) 75–79.
61. Stesichorus 41P., Pherecydes 3 F 134, Pind. *Pyth.* 11.26. A Laodameia is daughter of Acastus, king of Iolcus, and wife of Protesilaus; an Arsinoe is daughter of Phegeus, king of Psophis, and wife of Alcmaeon.
62. I assume that the Furies do not appear on stage at the end of *Choephori;* see A. L. Brown (1983).
63. *Politēs: Eum.* 820, 854, 927, 980, 991, 1013. *Astos: Eum.* 487, 697, 708, 807, 862, 908, 1045, cf. 997.
64. As there is, for example, in Agamemnon's use of the phrase *prodoulon embasin podos* for his sandals (*Ag.* 945).
65. Finley (1980) 108.
66. I cite the Harper paperback edition in two volumes (New York 1971), *The Hellenic World: A Sociological Analysis* and *Enter Plato: Classical Greece and the Origins of Social Theory, Part II.*
67. Unfortunately, Finley says almost nothing about Gouldner's hypothesis in his review of the book (*New York Review of Books* 7 [18 August 1966] 27–29). As far as I know, only Reinhold (1976) 29 has made use of this aspect of Gouldner's work.
68. Cf. Genovese (1974) 3–7, 114–143, who stresses that slaves integrated the masters' values into an ideology that helped them resist dehumanization.
69. See Gathorne-Hardy (1972) 71–74. Similarly, house slaves in the antebellum South were (or at least appeared to be) more assimilated than other slaves; see, e.g., Blassingame (1976), Sutherland (1981).
70. There is some evidence that Spartan women were especially valued as nurses at Athens; see Plut. *Lyc.* 16.3, cf. *Alcib.* 1.2, and, for a gravestone for a nurse from Cythera (before 350), *IG* 2² 9112. An Athenian gravestone from the second or first century B.C. commemorates a nurse from Corinth, *IG* 2² 9080. But we hear of nurses from elsewhere as well, such as Thrace.

71. On the tendency of slaves in the U.S. South to display deference (even when they did not feel it), see Stampp (1971), especially 388. The "mask of deference" adopted by black domestics in contemporary South Africa is similar; Cock (1980) 102–106.
72. McMillen (1985).
73. Cartledge (1985). On 20–23, Cartledge provides an excellent discussion of the advantages and shortcomings of the comparative method. See also Crouch (1985).
74. Franklin's comments, composed in 1751, are quoted in Finley (1980) 29–30.
75. For the opinions of slaves, see Feldstein (1971) 224–227. For de Tocqueville on slavery, see Franklin (1956) 67. For Fanny Kemble's comments, see Calhoun (1918) 285; and for many other similar sentiments, see 281–289 of the same book.
76. Quoted in Calhoun (1918) 285–286. For similar sentiments from late nineteenth century Brazil, see Conrad (1983) 221–225.
77. For parents' insistence that their children receive deference, some examples of children exercising authority, and more indications of concern, see Genovese (1974) 515–519, Blake (1978) 113, Blassingame (1979) 267.
78. See, for example, Franklin (1956) 66–70, and others cited by Bruce (1979) 243 n. 10.
79. Jefferson (1955) 162–163.
80. Bruce (1979) 57–66.
81. Pl. *Lys.* 223A, Plut. *Lyc.* 30.6, cf. Ter. *Ad.* 562–563, *Phorm.* 71–77, 286–288 (based on a play by Apollodorus of Carystus, who lived in the generation after Menander, and set in Athens).
82. Winkler (1985) 26.
83. See, e.g., Hackney (1969), A. C. Smith (1985).
84. I suspect that contemporary South Africa, where children of the white elite are often raised by and with blacks who face severe legal and social discrimination, would provide some evidence for testing this hypothesis further. Unfortunately, my efforts to find discussions of the subject in sources from or about South Africa were unsuccessful.
85. The argument that follows is not based on any one psychological theory, but borrows from a number of different approaches. I have found especially useful the concepts of cognitive dissonance (see Festinger [1957], Cohen [1967]) and reaction formation (see Sarnoff [1962]).
86. Harrison (1968) 168–171.
87. Harrison (1971) 147–150. Thür (1977) demonstrates that slaves were not in fact tortured in the private lawsuits known to us; for

instances of slave torture in other cases, see, e.g., Andoc. 1.64, Lyc. *Leocr.* 112.

88. Cf. Dover (1972) 206.
89. Dover (1972) 11.
90. Saller (1987a) 79–82.
91. See Walcot (1987b) and the critical comments of de Vries (1988).
92. E.g., Aesch. *Eum.* 835, Xen. *Mem.* 2.2.4, Isae. 6.24, [Dem.] 59.122, Theophr. *Char.* 28.4, Men. *Dysc.* 842.
93. Cf. Aesch. *Ag.* 877–879, where Clytemnestra explains away the absence of the boy Orestes, "the guarantor of my pledge and yours."
94. Dem. 39.23, [Dem.] 40.29.
95. Thompson (1972), especially 223.
96. Xen. *Hell.* 6.4.35–37, cf. Plut. *Pelop.* 35.3.
97. Fantham (1986) 277; cf. Rawson (1986) 15. A comment by Diotima hints at the strain children's deaths could put on a marriage: homosexual companionship, which gives birth to ideas, makes for greater sharing (*koinōnian*) than that which comes with children, as ideas are both more beautiful and more undying (Pl. *Symp.* 209C). Electra's comment, "Women are *philai* of their husbands, not their children," referring as it does to Clytemnestra, is heavily ironic (Eur. *El.* 265).
98. E. M. Forster, *Where Angels Fear to Tread* (1905), Penguin ed. (1959) 10.
99. Harrison (1968) 44–45.
100. Thuc. 1.127.1 and, on the definition of the Alcmaeonidae, Dickie (1979).
101. Notably by Slater (1968); usually (and unfairly) ignored by classicists, usefully reviewed by Foley (1975), who provides due praise and devastating criticism.
102. Plato recognizes the force of compulsion in resolving this dilemma, forbidding children to forgive a parent who kills a spouse (*Leg.* 9.868C).
103. Aesch. *Ag.* 1417–1418, cf. 1432, Soph. *El.* 530–581.
104. Humphreys (1986) 88. But even these hesitant conclusions may be undermined by the fact that witnesses called by one side in a lawsuit are not necessarily hostile to the other; Cox (1988b) 392 n. 18.
105. Cf. Lee (1919) 49.
106. Cf. Eur. *IA* 638–639, where Clytemnestra says that Iphigenia loves her father more than her siblings do.

Chapter 7. Change: A Postscript on the Dowries of New Comedy

1. Davies (1981) 119–120; MacDowell (1982) (answered by P. G. McC. Brown [1983]), Turner (1984) 253–254; Humphreys (1983) 94–122; Connor (1985) 88–96.
2. Golden (1986) 257–267.
3. See Rühfel (1984b) 165–168 and my discussion in Chapter 2.
4. Raepsaet and Decocq (1987) 14–15.
5. For some pertinent remarks on the history and utility of the concept of the Hellenistic epoch, see Préaux (1965).
6. Deissmann-Merten (1984) 276–281.
7. Cf. Fantham (1975) 44–46, MacDowell (1982). P. G. McC. Brown (1983) and Turner (1984) are less convinced of Menander's reliability on details of the law.
8. Soph. fr. 87R., Eur. *Andr.* 638, *Hipp.* 309, fr. 141, 168, 377N.²; cf. Turner (1984) 244.
9. See Harrison (1968) 19.
10. Paoli (1961) 61–62 has argued that when a son was adopted as heir, a daughter's dowry was set at one-half the value of the estate by law. Unfortunately, the argument rests on the force of *dikaion* in *Dysc.* 763, and the line is corrupt; no more compelling is his proposal to emend Isae. 3.51, where Endius is criticized for dowering his adoptive sister with not even a tenth (*dekaton*) of the estate, to read "not even a just portion" (*dikaion*). Custom may have enjoined generosity in such cases, but one-half still seems very generous indeed.
11. Finley (1952) 266 n. 29 (on 267); cf. Schaps (1979) 99.
12. Casson (1976) 53–59, especially 55; cf. Arnott (1979) 302–303.
13. Gomme and Sandbach (1973) 298 on *Epitr.* 134ff.
14. Eur. fr. 502, 775 N.², Pl. *Leg.* 6.774C, Arist. *NE* 8.1161a1, Anaxandrides fr. 52E., Antiphanes fr. 329E., Men. *Epitr.* 134–135, fr. 402, 403, 583, 585E.
15. Cf. *IG* 1³ 475, 476 (409–407), with *IG* 2² 1672 (329/8–?327/6); Markle (1985) 293.
16. Lys. 19.14–16, cf. Men. fr. 103E.; for the freedom to choose a son-in-law which a large dowry afforded, see Hdt. 6.122.2, Isoc. 16.31.
17. E.g., Ter. *Eun.* 318, 526 (sixteen), *Phorm.* 1017–1018 (based on a play by Apollodorus from the early third century: about fifteen), Plaut. *Cas.* 39–41, 79–86 (based on a play by Diphilus, perhaps from the late fourth century: at least sixteen).
18. *Meirakyllion:* Men. *Dysc.* 27. *Meirakiskos:* Men. *Georg.* 4. *Meirakion:* Men. *Dysc.* 219, 269, 311, 559, 729, *Georg.* 67, *Sam.* 115, 272. *Neaniskos:* Men. *Dysc.* 39, 414, *Georg.* 69, *Fab. Incert.* 54, cf. *Com. Adesp.* fr. 335aE. For a marriageable *neanias*, see Men. fr. 530b13–15E.
19. For the indeterminacy of these words, see Chapter 1.

20. Cf. the rather similar exchange in Plaut. *Pers.* 349–368 (set in Athens, though the characters are not citizens).
21. Men. fr. 60E., Posidippus fr. 11E.
22. Men. fr. 516E. may refer to a brother acting as a guarantor for his sister in some unknown money matter.
23. Men. *Asp.* 8–10; Men. *Dysc.* 226–228, 846–847.
24. Both brothers and sisters are mentioned (without explanation) as annoyances in a fragment on the joys of having no relatives (Men. fr. 244aE.).
25. For other indications of sibling solidarity, cf. Ter. *Andr.* 292–296, *Eun.* 745–747, 952–954. In Plautus's *Trinummus* (based on a late fourth or early third century comedy by Philemon), Lesbonicus laments that his sister will be married dowryless due to his own irresponsibility (585–588). This may cause resentment on her part; and if she hates him, she will be within her rights (679–685). But there is no sign of brothers' resenting having to share the estate with their sisters.
26. When Chremes details his daughter's financial demands on him, the dowry is just one item among many (Ter. *Haut.* 836–839).
27. Men. *Epitr.* 253–255; Men. *Peric.* 806–812. Similarly, Demea wears himself out making money for his sons (Ter. *Ad.* 867–870).

Bibliography

Ahlberg, G. (1971). *Prothesis and Ekphora in Greek Geometric Art* (Göteborg).

Alexiou, M. (1974). *The Ritual Lament in Greek Tradition* (Cambridge).

Apple, D. (1956). "The Social Structure of Grandparenthood." *American Anthropologist* 58:656–663.

Ariès, P. (1973). *L'Enfant et la vie familiale sous l'ancien régime*. 2d ed. (Paris).

Arnott, W. G. (1979). *Menander* (Cambridge, Mass., and London).

Arrigoni, G. (1985). "Donne e sport nel mondo greco." In *Le donne in Grecia*, edited by Arrigoni, 55–201 (Rome and Bari).

Arthur, M. (1977). "Politics and Pomegranates: An Interpretation of the Homeric Hymn to Demeter." *Arehusa* 10:7–47.

――― (1980). "The Tortoise and the Mirror: Erinna *PSI* 1090." *CW* 74:53–65.

Bain, D. (1981). *Masters, Servants, and Orders in Greek Tragedy* (Manchester).

Barker, E. (1946). *The Politics of Aristotle* (Oxford).

Barrett, S. R. (1984). *The Rebirth of Anthropological Theory* (Toronto).

Bartsocas, C. S. (1978). "Ancient Greek Feeding-Bottles." *Transactions and Studies of the College of Physicians of Philadelphia* 45:297–298.

Bassi, D. (1942–1943). "Nutrici e pedagoghi nella tragedia greca." *Dioniso* 9:80–87.

Beazley, J. D. (1918). *Attic Red-figured Vases in American Museums* (Cambridge, Mass.).

Beck, F. A. G. (1964). *Greek Education, 450–350 B.C.* (London).

———— (1975). *Album of Greek Education: The Greeks at School and at Play* (Sydney).

———— (1986). *Bibliography of Greek Education and Related Topics* (Sydney).

Beekes, R. S. P. (1986). "'You can get new children. . . .'" *Mnemosyne* 39:225–239.

Beer, C. (1987). "Comparative Votive Religion: The Evidence of Children in Cyprus, Greece, and Etruria." In *Gifts to the Gods: Proceedings of the Uppsala Symposium 1985,* edited by T. Linders and G. Nordquist, 21–29 (Uppsala).

Bellingham, B. (1988). "The History of Childhood since the 'Invention of Childhood': Some Issues in the Eighties." *JFH* 13:347–358.

Bernardi, B. (1984). *Age Class Systems: Social Institutions and Polities Based on Age.* Translated by D. I. Kertzer (Cambridge).

Bertman, S., ed. (1976). *The Conflict of Generations in Ancient Greece and Rome* (Amsterdam).

Billeter, G. (1898). *Geschichte des Zinsfusses im griechisch-römischen Altertum bis auf Justinian* (Leipzig).

Binford, L. (1972). *An Archaeological Perspective* (New York and London).

Blake, R. L. (1978). "Ties of Intimacy: Social Values and Personal Relationships of Antebellum Slaveholders." Ph.D. diss., University of Michigan.

Blassingame, J. W. (1976). "Status and Social Structure in the Slave Community." In *Perspectives and Irony in American Slavery,* edited by H. P. Owens, 137–151 (Jackson, Miss.).

———— (1979). *The Slave Community: Plantation Life in the Antebellum South* (New York and Oxford).

Boardman, J. (1974). *Athenian Black Figure Vases: A Handbook* (London).

———— (1975). *Athenian Red Figure Vases: The Archaic Period. A Handbook* (London).

———— (1977). "The Parthenon Frieze—Another View." In *Festschrift für Frank Brommer,* edited by U. Höckmann and A. Krug, 39–49 (Mainz).

Boll, F. (1913). "Die Lebensalter." *Neue Jahrbücher für das klassische Altertum* 21:89–145.

Bollack, J., and Judet de La Combe, P. (n.d.). *L'Agamemnon d'Eschyle* (Lille).

Bond, G. W. (1981). *Euripides Heracles* (Oxford).

Booth, A. D. (1985). "Douris' Cup and the Stages of Schooling in Classical Athens." *EMC* 29:274–280.

Bourriot, F. (1976). *Recherches sur la nature du genos: Étude d'histoire sociale athénienne—périodes archaïque et classique* (Lille).

Bowersock, G. W. (1969). *Greek Sophists in the Roman Empire* (Oxford).

Bowra, C. M. (1936). "Erinna's *Lament for Baucis.*" In *Greek Poetry and Life:*

Essays Presented to Gilbert Murray . . . , edited by C. Bailey et al., 325–342 (Oxford).

Bracken, M. B., Klerman, L. V., and Bracken, M. (1978). "Abortion, Adoption, or Motherhood: An Empirical Study of Decision-Making during Pregnancy." *American Journal of Obstetrics and Gynecology* 130:251–262.

Bradley, K. R. (1980). "Sexual Regulations in Wet-Nursing Contracts from Roman Egypt." *Klio* 62:321–325.

———— (1985). "Child Care at Rome: The Role of Men." *Historical Reflections / Réflexions historiques* 12:485–523.

———— (1986). "Wet-nursing at Rome: A Study in Social Relations." In *The Family in Ancient Rome: New Perspectives,* edited by B. Rawson, 201–229 (London and Sydney).

———— (1987). "Dislocation in the Roman Family." *Historical Reflections / Réflexions historiques* 14:33–62.

Brann, E. T. H. (1959). "A Figured Geometric Fragment from the Athenian Agora." *AntK* 2:35–37.

Brelich, A. (1969). *Paides e parthenoi* (Rome).

Bremmer, J. (1983a). *The Early Greek Concept of the Soul* (Princeton).

———— (1983b). "The Importance of the Maternal Uncle and Grandfather in Archaic and Classical Greece and Early Byzantium." *ZPE* 50:173–186.

———— (1987). "The Old Women of Ancient Greece." In *Sexual Asymmetry: Studies in Ancient Society,* edited by J. Blok and P. Mason, 191–215 (Amsterdam).

Brown, A. L. (1983). "The Erinyes in the *Oresteia*: Real Life, the Supernatural, and the Stage." *JHS* 103:13–34.

Brown, P. G. McC. (1983). "Menander's Dramatic Technique and the Law of Athens." *CQ* 33:412–420.

Bruce, D. D., Jr. (1979). *Violence and Culture in the Antebellum South* (Austin and London).

Brun, P. (1985). "*IG* II² 1609 et le versement en nature de l'eisphora." *REA* 87:307–318.

Bryant, A. A. (1907). "Boyhood and Youth in the Days of Aristophanes." *HSCP* 18:73–122.

Buffière, F. (1980). *Eros adolescent: La Pédérastie dans la Grèce antique* (Paris).

Burkert, W. (1966). "Kekropidensage und Arrhephoria." *Hermes* 94:1–25.

———— (1983). *Homo necans.* Translated by P. Bing (Berkeley and Los Angeles).

Calame, C. (1977). *Les Choeurs de jeunes filles en Grèce archaïque* (Rome).

Calhoun, A. W. (1918). *A Social History of the American Family,* vol. 2 (Cleveland).

Campbell, J. K. (1964). *Honour, Family, and Patronage* (Oxford).

Canby, J. V. (1986). "The Child in Hittite Iconography." In *Ancient Anatolia: Aspects of Change and Cultural Development. Essays in Honor of Machteld J. Mellink,* edited by Canby, E. Porada, B. S. Ridgway, and T. Stech, 54–69 (Madison).

Cantarella, E. (1988). *Secondo natura: La bisessualita nel mondo antico* (Rome).

Cantarella, R. (1971). "Aristofane, Erasmo e Shakespeare: Storia di un proverbio." *Rendiconti dell' Accademia nazionale dei Lincei. Classe di Scienzi morali, storiche e filologiche* 26:113–130.

Carrière, J. (1977). *Le Choeur secondaire dans le drame grec* (Paris).

Carson, A. (1986). *Eros the Bittersweet: An essay* (Princeton).

Cartledge, P. (1985). "Rebels and Sambos in Classical Greece: A Comparative View." In *Crux: Essays Presented to G. E. M. de Ste. Croix . . . ,* edited by Cartledge and F. D. Harvey, 16–46 (Exeter).

Casson, L. (1976). "The Athenian Upper Class and New Comedy." *TAPA* 106:29–59.

Cawkwell, G. L. (1973). "The Date of I.G. II² 1609 Again." *Historia* 22:759–761.

Chantraine, P. (1968–1980). *Dictionnaire étymologique de la langue grecque* (Paris).

Charlier, M.-T., and Raepsaet, G. (1971). "Étude d'un comportement social: Les Relations entre parents et enfants dans la société athénienne à l'époque classique." *AntCl* 40:589–606.

Chirassi Colombo, I. (1979). "*Paides e gynaikes*: Note per una tassonomia del comportamento rituale nella cultura attica." *QUCC* 1:26–58.

Chisholm, J. S. (1983). *Navajo Infancy* (New York).

Cock, J. (1980). *Maids and Madams: A Study in the Politics of Exploitation* (Johannesburg).

Cohen, A. R. (1967). "Attitudinal Consequences of Induced Discrepancies between Cognitions and Behavior." In *Readings in Attitude Theory and Measurement,* edited by M. Fishbein, 332–340 (New York).

Cohen, D. (1987). "Law, Society, and Homosexuality in Classical Athens." *Past and Present* 117:3–21.

——— (1989). "Seclusion, Separation, and the Status of Women in Classical Athens." *Greece and Rome* 36:3–15.

Cole, S. G. (1981). "Could Greek Women Read and Write?" In *Reflections of Women in Antiquity,* edited by H. P. Foley, 219–245 (New York).

——— (1984). "The Social Function of Rituals of Maturation: The koureion and the arkteia." *ZPE* 55:233–244.

Collard, C. (1975). *Euripides Supplices* (Groningen).

Conacher, D. J. (1974). "Interaction between Chorus and Characters in the *Oresteia*." *AJP* 95:323–343.

Connor, W. R. (1985). "The Razing of the House in Greek Society." *TAPA* 115:79–102.

Conrad, R. E. (1983). *Children of God's Fire: A Documentary History of Black Slavery in Brazil* (Princeton).

Conze, A. (1893–1922). *Die attischen Grabreliefs* (Berlin).

Cox, C. A. (1988a). "Sibling Relationships in Classical Athens: Brother-Sister Ties." *JFH* 13:377–395.

——— (1988b). "Sisters, Daughters, and the Deme of Marriage: A Note." *JHS* 108:185–188.

Crouch, B. A. (1985). "'Booty Capitalism' and Capitalism's Booty: Slaves and Slavery in Ancient Rome and the American South." *Slavery and Abolition* 6:3–24.

Crowther, N. B. (1988). "The Age-Category of Boys at Olympia." *Phoenix* 42:304–308.

Dale, A. M. (1954). *Euripides Alcestis* (Oxford).

Danforth, L. M. (1982). *The Death Rituals of Rural Greece* (Princeton).

D'Arms, J. H. (1984). "Control, Companionship, and *Clientela:* Some Social Functions of the Roman Communal Meal." *EMC* 28:327–348.

Daux, G. (1973). "Anth. Pal. VI 280." *ZPE* 12:225–234.

Davies, J. K. (1969). "The Date of *IG* II² 1609." *Historia* 18:309–333.

——— (1971). *Athenian Propertied Families, 600–300 B.C.* (Oxford).

——— (1981). *Wealth and the Power of Wealth in Classical Athens* (Salem, N.H.).

Davis, E. N. (1986). "Youth and Age in the Thera Frescoes." *AJA* 90:399–406.

Davis, J. (1977). *People of the Mediterranean* (Cambridge).

Debut, J. (1983). "De l'usage des listes de mots comme fondement de la pédagogie dans l'antiquité." *REA* 85:261–274.

Deissmann-Merten, M. (1984). "Zur Sozialgeschichte des Kindes im antiken Griechenland." In *Zur Sozialgeschichte der Kindheit,* edited by J. Martin and A. Nitschke, 267–316 (Freiburg and Munich).

Delorme, J. (1960). *Gymnasion: Études sur les monuments consacrés à l'éducation en Grèce* (Paris).

deMause, L. (1974). "The Evolution of Childhood." In *The History of Childhood,* edited by deMause, 1–73 (New York).

Denniston, J. D., and Page, D. L. (1957). *Aeschylus Agamemnon* (Oxford).

Deubner, L. (1932). *Attische Feste* (Berlin).

Develin, R. (1985). "Age Qualifications for Athenian Magistrates." *ZPE* 61:149–159.

de Vries, G. J. (1988). "Psychohistorical Vistas." *Mnemosyne* 41:373–375.

Dickie, M. W. (1979). "Pindar's Seventh Pythian and the Status of the Alcmaeonids as *Oikos* or *Genos.*" *Phoenix* 33:193–209.

Dixon, S. (1988). *The Roman Mother* (London and Sydney).

Dodds, E. R. (1951). *The Greeks and the Irrational* (Berkeley and Los Angeles).

Dörig, J. (1958). "Von griechischen Puppen." *AntK* 1:41–52.

Dover, K. J. (1972). *Aristophanic Comedy* (Berkeley and Los Angeles).

——— (1974). *Greek Popular Morality in the time of Plato and Aristotle* (Berkeley and Los Angeles).

——— (1978). *Greek Homosexuality* (Cambridge, Mass.).

——— (1980). *Plato Symposium* (Cambridge).

Doumanis, M. (1983). *Mothering in Greece: From Collectivism to Individualism* (London).

Dunkley, B. (1935–1936). "Greek Fountain Buildings before 300 B.C." *ABSA* 36:142–204.

Durling, R. J. (1986). "Arresting Puberty." *RhM* 129:364.

Dyson, M. (1988). "'Alcestis' Children and the Character of Admetus." *JHS* 108:13–23.

Ebert, J. (1965). "Παῖδες πυθικοί." *Philologus* 109:152–156.

——— (1972). *Griechische Epigramme auf Sieger an gymnischen und hippischen Agonen* (Berlin).

Elderkin, K. M. (1918). "Jointed Dolls in Antiquity." *AJA* 34:455–479.

Elkin, F., and Handel, G. (1984). *The Child and Society: The Process of Socialization.* 4th ed. (New York).

Engels, D. (1984). "The Use of Historical Demography in Ancient History." *CQ* 34:386–393.

Étienne, R. (1977). "Ancient Medical Conscience and the Life of Children." *Journal of Psychohistory* 4:131–161.

Eyben, E. (1972). "Antiquity's View of Puberty." *Latomus* 31:677–697.

Fantham, E. (1975). "Sex, Status, and Survival in Hellenistic Athens: A Study of Women in New Comedy." *Phoenix* 29:44–74.

——— (1986). "Andromache's Child in Euripides and Seneca." In *Greek Tragedy and Its Legacy: Essays Presented to D. J. Conacher,* edited by M. Cropp, E. Fantham, and S. E. Scully, 267–280 (Calgary).

Feldstein, S. (1971). *Once a Slave: The Slaves' View of Slavery* (New York).

Ferguson, C. A. (1964). "Baby Talk in Six Languages." *American Anthropologist* 66:103–114.

Festinger, L. (1957). *A Theory of Cognitive Dissonance* (Stanford).

Finley, M. I. (1952). *Studies in Land and Credit in Ancient Athens, 500–200 B.C.* (New Brunswick, N.J.).

——— (1980). *Ancient Slavery and Modern Ideology* (New York).

——— (1981). "The Elderly in Classical Antiquity." *Greece and Rome* 28:156–171.

Fitton Brown, A. D. (1984). "The Contribution of Women to Ancient Greek Agriculture." *Liverpool Classical Monthly* 9:71–74.

Flower, M. A. (1985). "*IG* II².2344 and the Size of Phratries in Classical Athens." *CQ* 35:232–235.

Foley, H. E. (1975). "Sex and State in Ancient Greece." *Diacritics* 5.4:31–36.

——— (1985). *Ritual Irony: Poetry and Sacrifice in Euripides* (Ithaca, N.Y., and London).

Foster, G. O. (1960–1961). "Interpersonal Relations in Peasant Society." *Human Organization* 19:174–184.

Fox, R. L. (1985). "Aspects of Inheritance in the Greek World." In *Crux: Essays Presented to G. E. M. de Ste. Croix . . .*, edited by P. Cartledge and F. D. Harvey, 208–232 (Exeter).

Fraenkel, E. (1950). *Aeschylus Agamemnon* (Oxford).

Francis, E. D., and Vickers, M. (1981). "Leagros Kalos." *Proceedings of the Cambridge Philological Society* 27:97–136.

Franklin, J. H. (1956). *The Militant South, 1800–1861* (Cambridge, Mass.).

French, V. (1977). "History of the Child's Influence: Ancient Mediterranean Civilizations." In *Child Effects on Adults*, edited by R. Q. Bell and L. V. Harper, 3–29 (Hillsdale, N.J.).

Friedl, E. (1962). *Vasilika: A Village in Modern Greece* (New York).

——— (1963). "Some Aspects of Dowry and Inheritance in Boeotia." In *The Egalitarian Society*, edited by J. Pitt-Rivers, 113–135 (Paris).

Frier, B. (1982). "Roman Life Expectancy: Ulpian's Evidence." *HSCP* 86:213–251.

——— (1983). "Roman Life Expectancy: The Pannonian Evidence." *Phoenix* 37:328–344.

Frisch, P. (1988). "Die Klassifikation der παῖδες bei den griechischen Agonen." *ZPE* 75:179–185.

Gallo, L. (1984). "Un problema di demografia greca: Le donne tra la nascita e la morte." *Opus* 3:37–62.

Garland, R. (1985). *The Greek Way of Death* (London).

Gathorne-Hardy, J. (1972). *The Rise and Fall of the British Nanny* (London).

Genovese, E. D. (1974). *Roll, Jordan, Roll: The World the Slaves Made* (New York).

Gernet, L. (1955). "Fosterage et légende." In *Droit et société dans la Grèce ancienne*, 19–28 (Paris).

Gigante, M. (1973). "Atakta." *Cronache Ercolanesi* 3:85–87.

Goheen, R. F. (1955). "Aspects of Dramatic Symbolism: Three Studies in the *Oresteia*." *AJP* 76:113–137.

Golden, M. (1979). "Demosthenes and the Age of Majority at Athens." *Phoenix* 33:25–38.

——— (1981). "Demography and the Exposure of Girls at Athens." *Phoenix* 35:316–331.

———— (1982). "*Pais* in Hipp. fr. 13W." *QUCC* 12:73–75.

———— (1984). "Slavery and Homosexuality at Athens." *Phoenix* 38:308–324.

———— (1985a). "'Donatus' and Athenian Phratries." *CQ* 35:9–13.

———— (1985b). "*Pais,* 'Child' and 'Slave.'" *AntCl* 54:91–104.

———— (1986). "Names and Naming at Athens: Three Studies." *EMC* 30:245–269.

———— (1988a). "Did the Ancients Care When Their Children Died?" *Greece and Rome* 35:152–163.

———— (1988b). "The Effects of Slavery on Citizen Households and Children: Aeschylus, Aristophanes, and Athens." *Historical Reflections / Réflexions historiques* 15:455–475.

———— (1988c). "Male Chauvinists and Pigs." *EMC* 32:1–12.

Goldhill, S. (1987). "The Great Dionysia and Civic Ideology." *JHS* 107:58–76.

Gomme, A. W., and Sandbach, F. H. (1973). *Menander: A Commentary* (Oxford).

Goody, E. (1984). "Parental Strategies: Calculation or Sentiment? Fostering Practices among West Africans." In *Interest and Emotion: Essays on the Study of Family and Kinship,* edited by H. Medick and D. W. Sabean, 266–277 (Cambridge).

Gouldner, A. W. (1965). *Enter Plato: Classical Greece and the Origins of Social Theory* (New York).

Grant, J. N. (1986). "The Father-Son Relationship and the Ending of Menander's *Samia.*" *Phoenix* 40:172–184.

Gray-Fow, M. J. G. (1985). "The Nomenclature and Stages of Roman Childhood." Ph.D. diss., University of Wisconsin, Madison.

Green, J. R. (1971). "Choes of the Later Fifth Century." *ABSA* 66:189–228.

Guarducci, M. (1974). "L'Offerta di Xenokrateia nel santuario di Cefiso al Falero." In ΦΟΡΟΣ: *Tribute to Benjamin Dean Meritt,* edited by D. W. Bradeen and M. F. McGregor (Locust Valley, N.Y.).

Hackney, S. (1969). "Southern Violence." In *Violence in America: Historical and Comparative Perspectives,* edited by H. D. Graham and T. R. Gurr, 387–406 (Washington, D.C.).

Hani, J. (1978). "La Fête athénienne de l'Aiora et le symbolisme de la balançoire." *REG* 91:107–122.

Hansen, M. H. (1980). "Seven Hundred *Archai* in Classical Athens." *GRBS* 21:151–173.

Hardcastle, M. (1980). "Some Non-legal Arguments in Athenian Inheritance Cases." *Prudentia* 12:11–22.

Harré, R. (1974). "The Conditions for a Social Psychology of Childhood."

In *The Integration of a Child into a Social World*, edited by M. P. M. Richards, 245–262 (Cambridge).

Harris, E. M. (1988). "The Date of Apollodorus' Speech against Timotheus and Its Implications for Athenian History and Legal Procedure." *AJP* 109:44–52.

Harris, O. (1982). "Households and Their Boundaries." *History Workshop Journal* 13:143–152.

Harrison, A. R. W. (1968). *The Law of Athens*, vol. 1, *The Family and Property* (Oxford).

——— (1971). *The Law of Athens*, vol. 2, *Procedure* (Oxford).

Henderson, J. (1975). *The Maculate Muse: Obscene Language in Attic Comedy* (New Haven and London).

——— (1987a). *Aristophanes Lysistrata* (Oxford).

——— (1987b). "Older Women in Attic Old Comedy." *TAPA* 117:105–129.

Herfst, P. (1922). *Le Travail de la femme dans la Grèce ancienne* (Utrecht).

Herlihy, D. (1985). *Medieval Households* (Cambridge, Mass., and London).

Herman, G. (1987). *Ritualised Friendship and the Greek City* (Cambridge).

Herter, H. (1927). "Das Kind im Zeitalter des Hellenismus." *Bonner Jahrbücher* 132:250–258.

——— (1961a). "Das Leben ein Kinderspiel." *Bonner Jahrbücher* 161:73–84 = *Kleine Schriften* (Munich 1975) 584–597.

——— (1961b). "Das unschuldige Kind." *Jahrbuch für Antike und Christentum* 4:146–162 = *Kleine Schriften* (Munich 1975) 598–619.

——— (1964). "Amme oder Saugflasche." *Mullus: Festschrift Theodor Klauser. Jahrbuch für Antike und Christentum Ergänzungsband* (Münster), 1:168–172 = *Kleine Schriften* (Munich 1975) 620–625.

Hertz, R. (1960). *Death and the Right Hand*. Translated by R. and C. Needham (Oxford) = *Année sociologique* 10 (1907) 48–137.

Hett, W. S. (1931). "The Games of the Greek Boy." *Greece and Rome* 1:24–29.

Hewitt, J. W. (1931). "Gratitude to Parents in Greek and Roman Literature." *AJP* 52:30–48.

Himmelmann, N. (1971). *Archäologisches zum Problem der griechischen Sklaverei* (Wiesbaden).

Hirsch-Dyczek, O. (1979). "Przedstawienia dzieci w sztuce attyckiej V i IV w. p.n.e." *Meander* 34:251–264.

——— (1983). *Les Représentations des enfants sur les stèles funéraires attiques* (Warsaw and Cracow).

Hopfner, T. (1926). "Die Kindermedien in den griechisch-ägyptischen Zauberpapyri." In *Recueil d'études, dédiées à la mémoire de N. P. Kondakov*, 65–74 (Prague).

―――― (1938). *Das Sexualleben der Griechen und Römer*, vol. 1 (Prague).

Hopkins, K. (1983). *Death and Renewal* (Cambridge).

Howell, N. (1979). *Demography of the Dobe !Kung* (New York).

Hug, A. (1956). "Παῖδες." In *Paulys Real-Encyclopädie der classischen Altertumswissenschaft* suppl. 8:374–400.

Humphreys, S. C. (1983). *The Family, Women, and Death: Comparative Studies* (London).

―――― (1986). "Kinship Patterns in the Athenian Courts." *GRBS* 27:57–91.

Hunter, R. L. (1985). *The New Comedy of Greece and Rome* (Cambridge).

Hunter, V. J. (1989). "Women's Authority in Classical Athens." *EMC* 33:39–48.

Huntingdon, R., and Metcalf, P. (1979). *Celebrations of Death: The Anthropology of Mortuary Ritual* (Cambridge).

Immerwahr, H. R. (1964). "Book Roles on Attic Vases." In *Classical Mediaeval and Renaissance Studies in Honor of B. L. Ullman*, edited by C. Henderson, Jr., 1:17–48 (Rome).

―――― (1973). "More Book Roles on Attic Vases." *AntK* 16:143–147.

Isager, S. (1978). "*Gynaikonitis*—The Women's Quarters." *Museum Tusculanum* 32–33:39–42.

―――― (1981–1982). "The Marriage Pattern in Classical Athens: Men and Women in Isaios." *Classica et Mediaevalia* 33:81–96.

Jackson, M. (1978). "Ambivalence and the Last-Born: Birth-Order Position in Convention and Myth." *Man* 13:341–361.

Jameson, M. H. (1977–1978). "Agriculture and Slavery in Classical Athens." *CJ* 73:122–145.

Jefferson, T. (1955). *Notes on the State of Virginia*. Edited by W. Peden (Chapel Hill, N.C.).

Jenkins, I. (1983). "Is There Life after Marriage? A Study of the Abduction Motif in Vase Paintings of the Athenian Wedding Ceremony." *BICS* 30:137–145.

Johansson, S. R. (1984). "Deferred Infanticide: Excess Female Mortality during Childhood." In *Infanticide: Comparative and Evolutionary Perspectives*, edited by G. Hausfater and S. B. Hrdy, 487–502 (New York).

―――― (1987a). "Centuries of Childhood / Centuries of Parenting: Philippe Ariès and the Modernization of Privileged Infancy." *JFH* 12:343–365.

―――― (1987b). "Neglect, Abuse, and Avoidable Death: Parental Investment and the Mortality of Infants and Children in the European Tradition." In *Child Abuse and Neglect: Biosocial Dimensions*, edited by R. J. Gelles and J. B. Lancaster, 57–93 (New York).

Johnston, A. W. (1987). "*IG* II² 2311 and the Number of Panathenaic Amphorae." *ABSA* 82:125–129.

Jones, J. E., Sackett, L. H., and Graham, A. J. (1962). "The Dema House in Attica." *ABSA* 57:75–114.

Jory, E. J. (1967). "Ἀ παῖς κωμῳδός and the διὰ πάντων: Some Problems of Festival Competitions." *BICS* 14:84–90.

Joshel, S. R. (1986). "Nurturing the Master's Child: Slavery and the Roman Child-Nurse." *Signs* 12:3–22.

Kadletz, E. (1980). "The Race and Procession of the Athenian *Oscophoroi*." *GRBS* 21:363–371.

Kagan, J. (1984). *The Nature of the Child* (New York).

Kahil, L. (1965). "Autour de l'Artémis attique." *AntK* 8:20–33.

——— (1977). "L'Artémis de Brauron: Rites et mystère." *AntK* 20:86–98.

——— (1983). "Mythological Repertoire of Brauron." In *Ancient Greek Art and Iconography*, edited by W. G. Moon, 231–244 (Madison).

Karouzou, S. (1946). "Choes." *AJA* 50:122–139.

——— (1957). "Epitymbia stēlē titthēs sto Ethniko Mouseio." *Hellenika* 15:311–323.

Karras, M., and Wiesehöfer, J. (1981). *Kindheit und Jugend in der Antike: Eine Bibliographie* (Bonn).

Kassel, R. (1951). *Quomodo quibus locis apud veteres scriptores Graecos infantes atque parvuli pueri inducantur describantur commemorentur*. Dissertation, University of Mainz.

Kern, J. H. C. (1957). "An Attic 'Feeding-Bottle' of the Fourth Century B.C. in Leyden." *Mnemosyne* 10:16–21.

Keuls, E. C. (1983). "Attic Vase-Painting and the Home Textile Industry." In *Ancient Greek Art and Iconography*, edited by W. G. Moon, 209–230 (Madison).

——— (1985). *The Reign of the Phallus* (New York).

Klee, T. (1918). *Zur Geschichte der gymnischen Agone an griechischen Festen* (Leipzig and Berlin).

Klein, A. E. (1932). *Child Life in Greek Art* (New York).

Koehl, R. B. (1986). "The Chieftain Cup and a Minoan Rite of Passage." *JHS* 106:99–110.

Konner, M. (1975). "Relations among Infants and Juveniles in Comparative Perspective." In *Friendship and Peer Relations*, edited by M. Lewis and L. A. Rosenblum, 99–129 (New York).

——— (1977). "Infancy among the Kalahari Desert San." In *Culture and Infancy: Variations in the Human Experience*, edited by P. H. Leiderman, S. R. Tulkin, and A. Rosenfeld, 287–328 (New York).

Kübler, K., and Peek, W. (1934). "Die Stele der Ampharete." *AthMitt* 59:25–34.

Kurtz, D. C., and Boardman, J. (1971). *Greek Burial Customs* (London).

Kyle, D. G. (1984). "Solon and Athletics." *Ancient World* 9:91–105.

——— (1987). *Athletics in Ancient Athens* (Leiden).

Laager, J. (1957). *Geburt und Kindheit des Gottes in der griechischen Mythologie* (Winterthur).

Labarbe, J. (1953). "L'Âge correspondant au sacrifice du κούρειον et les données historiques du sixième discours d'Isée." *Bulletin de l'Académie royale de Belgique: Classe des lettres* 39:358–394.

——— (1957). *La Loi navale de Thémistocle* (Paris).

Lacey, W. K. (1968). *The Family in Classical Greece* (London).

Lambert, G. (1982). *Rhetoric Rampant: The Family under Siege in the Early Western Tradition* (London, Ont.).

Lambin, G. (1975). "Les Formules de jeux d'enfants dans la Grèce antique." *REG* 88:168–177.

——— (1977). "Jeux d'enfants (Aristophane, *Oiseaux* v. 388–392)." *REG* 90:108–113.

——— (1984). "Mots familiers en ναν(ν)α- / ναν(ν)ι- / ναν(ν)ο-, νενι- / νεν-ο, νιν(ν)ι- ετ νυννι-." *RPh* 58:83–91.

——— (1986). "Trois refrains nuptiaux et le fragment 124 Mette d'Eschyle." *AntCl* 55:66–85.

Laslett, P. (1977). *Family Life and Illicit Love in Earlier Generations* (Cambridge).

Laurens, A.-F. (1984). "L'Enfant entre l'épée et le chaudron: Contribution à une lecture iconographique." *Dialogues d'histoire ancienne* 10:203–252.

Lavelle, B. M. (1986a). "The Dating and Patronage of the Archedike-Epigram." *Hermes* 114:240–244.

——— (1986b). "The nature of Hipparchos' Insult to Harmodios." *AJP* 107:318–331.

Lee, D. R. (1919). *Child-Life, Adolescence, and Marriage in Greek New Comedy and in the Comedies of Plautus* (Menasha, Wisc.).

Lefkowitz, M. R. (1986). *Women in Greek Myth* (Baltimore).

LeVine, R. A. (1977). "Child Rearing as Cultural Adaptation." In *Culture and Infancy: Variations in the Human Experience,* edited by P. H. Leiderman, S. R. Tulkin, and A. Rosenfeld, 15–27 (New York).

Lloyd-Jones, P. H. J. (1979). *Aeschylus: Oresteia. Agamemnon* (London).

——— (1983). "Artemis and Iphigeneia." *JHS* 103:87–102.

Longo, O. (1980–1981). "Rapporti di riproduzione, 'sacrifici' di adolescenti e controllo demografico nella Grecia antica." *Atti del Centro ricerche e documentazione sull'antichità classica* 11:127–163.

Loraux, N. (1981). *Les Enfants d'Athéna: Idées athéniennes sur la citoyenneté et la division des sexes* (Paris).

——— (1987). *Tragic Ways of Killing a Woman.* Translated by A. Forster (Cambridge, Mass.).

MacCary, W. T., and Willcock, M. M. (1976). *Plautus Casina* (Cambridge).

MacDonald, M. (1981). *Mystical Bedlam: Madness, Anxiety, and Healing in Seventeenth-Century England* (Cambridge).

MacDowell, D. M. (1963). *Athenian Homicide Law in the Age of the Orators* (Manchester).

——— (1971). *Aristophanes Wasps* (Oxford).

——— (1982). "Love versus the Law: An Essay on Menander's *Aspis*." *Greece and Rome* 29:42–52.

——— (1989). "The *Oikos* in Athenian Law." *CQ* 39:10–21.

Maffi, A. (1983). "Padri e figli fra diritto positivo e diritto immaginario nella Grecia classica." In *La Paura dei padri nella società antica e medievale*, edited by E. Pellizer and N. Zorzetti, 5–27 (Rome and Bari).

Manson, M. (1975). "Le Droit de jouer pour les enfants grecs et romains." In *L'Enfant. Recueils de la Société Jean Bodin* 39 (Brussels) 117–150.

——— (1978). "*Puer bimulus* (Catulle, 17, 12–13) et l'image du petit enfant chez Catulle et ses prédécesseurs." *Mélanges d'archéologie et d'histoire de l'école française de Rome* 90:247–291.

——— (1983). "The Emergence of the Small Child in Rome (Third Century B.C.–First Century A.D.)." *History of Education* 12:149–159.

Margon, J. S. (1983). "The Nurse's View of Clytemnestra's Grief for Orestes: *Choephori* 737–740." *CW* 76:296–297.

Markle, M. M. (1985). "Jury Pay and Assembly Pay at Athens." In *Crux: Essays Presented to G. E. M. de Ste. Croix . . .*, edited by P. Cartledge and F. D. Harvey, 265–297 (Exeter).

Markler, P. T. (1980). "New Information on Nutrition in Ancient Greece." *Klio* 62:317–319.

Mary Rosaria, Sister (1917). "The Nurse in Greek Life." Ph.D. diss., Catholic University of America.

Masqueray, P. (1906). "Euripide et les enfants." *REA* 8:85–92.

Massaro, M. (1977). "Aniles fabellae." *Studi italiani di filologia classica* 49:104–135.

McCracken, G. (1983). "The Exchange of Children in Tudor England: An Anthropological Phenomenon in Historical Context." *JFH* 8:303–313.

McMillen, S. (1985). "Mothers' Sacred Duty: Breast-feeding Patterns among Middle- and Upper-Class Women in the Antebellum South." *Journal of Southern History* 51:333–356.

Merkelbach, R. (1952). "Bettelgedichte." *RhM* 95:312–327.

Mette, H. J. (1982). "Von der Jugend." *Hermes* 110:258–268.

Metzger, H. (1965). *Recherches sur l'imagerie athénienne* (Paris).

Mikalson, J. D. (1986). "Zeus the Father and Heracles the Son in Tragedy." *TAPA* 116:89–98.

Miller, S. G. (1975). "The Pentathlon for Boys at Nemea." *California Studies in Classical Antiquity* 8:199–201.

Mills, S. P. (1980–1981). "The Death of Ajax." *CJ* 76:129–135.

Mitterauer, M., and Sieder, R. (1982). *The European Family*. Translated by K. Oosterveen and M. Hörzinger (Oxford).

Möbius, H. (1966). "Eigenartige attische Grabreliefs." *AthMitt* 81:136–160.

Mommsen, A. (1898). *Feste der Stadt Athen* (Leipzig).

Moon, W. G. (1983). "The Priam Painter: Some Iconographic and Stylistic Considerations." In *Ancient Greek Art and Iconography,* edited by Moon, 97–118 (Madison).

Moore, J. D. (1982). "Diogeiton's *Dioikisis*: Persuasive Language in Lysias 32." *GRBS* 23:351–355.

Morgan, G. (1982). "Euphiletos' House: Lysias 1." *TAPA* 112:115–123.

Morris, I. (1987). *Burial and Ancient Society: The Rise of the Greek City-State* (Cambridge).

Moseley, D. T., Follingstad, D. R., Harley, H., and Heckel, R. V. (1981). "Psychological Factors that Predict Reaction to Abortion." *Journal of Clinical Psychology* 37:276–279.

Muir, J. V. (1984). "A Note on Ancient Methods of Learning to Write." *CQ* 34:236–237.

Munroe, R. H., Munroe, R. L., and Shimmin, H. S. (1984). "Children's Work in Four Cultures: Determinants and Consequences." *American Anthropologist* 86:369–379.

Murnaghan, S. (1988). "How a Woman Can Be More Like a Man: The Dialogue between Ischomachus and His Wife in Xenophon's *Oeconomicus*." *Helios* 15:9–22.

Murray, O. (1983a). "The Greek Symposion in History." In *Tria corda: Scritti in onore di Arnaldo Momigliano,* edited by E. Gabba, 257–272 (Como).

———— (1983b). "The Symposion as Social Organisation." In *The Greek Renaissance of the Eighth Century B.C.: Tradition and Innovation,* edited by R. Hägg, 195–200 (Stockholm).

Mylonas, G. (1961). *Eleusis and the Eleusinian Mysteries* (Princeton).

Nag, M., White, B. N. F., and Peet, R. C. (1978). "An Anthropological Approach to the Study of the Economic Value of Children in Java and Nepal." *Current Anthropology* 19:293–306.

Nash, L. L. (1978). "Concepts of Existence: Greek Origins of Generational Thought." *Daedalus* 107 (no. 4):1–21.

Néraudau, J.-P. (1984). *Être enfant à Rome* (Paris).

———— (1987). "La Loi, la coutume et le chagrin: Réflexions sur la mort des enfants." In *La mort, les morts et l'au-delà dans le monde romain: Actes du colloque de Caen 20–22 novembre 1985,* edited by F. Hinard, 195–208 (Caen).

Oakley, J. H. (1982). "The Anakalypteria." *Archäologischer Anzeiger,* 113–118.

Oepke, A. (1934). "'Ἀμφιθαλεῖς im griechischen und hellenistischen Kult." *Archiv für Religionswissenschaft* 31:42–56.

Oeri, H. G. (1948). *Der Typ der komischen Alten in der griechischen Komödie* (Basel).

Oldenziel, R. (1987). "The Historiography of Infanticide in Antiquity: A Literature Stillborn." In *Sexual Asymmetry: Studies in Ancient Society,* edited by J. Blok and P. Mason, 87–107 (Amsterdam).

Osborne, R. (1985a). "Buildings and Residence on the Land in Classical and Hellenistic Greece: The Contribution of Epigraphy." *ABSA* 80:119–128.

———— (1985b). *Demos: The Discovery of Classical Attika* (Cambridge).

Page, D. L. (1942). *Greek Literary Papyri,* vol. 1 (London).

Paoli, U. E. (1961). "Note giuridiche sul δύσκολος di Menandro." *Museum Helveticum* 18:53–62.

Papadimitriou, J. (1963). "The Sanctuary of Artemis at Brauron." *Scientific American* 208:111–120.

Parke, H. W. (1977). *Festivals of the Athenians* (London).

Parker, R. (1983). *Miasma: Pollution and Purification in Early Greek Religion* (Oxford).

Patterson, C. (1981). *Pericles' Citizenship Law of 451–50 B.C.* (New York).

———— (1985). "'Not Worth the Rearing': The Causes of Infant Exposure in Ancient Greece." *TAPA* 115:103–123.

Peek, W. (1957). *Attische Grabinschriften,* vol. 2 (Berlin).

Peristiany, J. G., ed. (1976). *Mediterranean Family Structures* (Cambridge).

Perlman, P. (1983). "Plato *Laws* 833C–834D and the Bears of Brauron." *GRBS* 24:115–130.

Peterson, W. (1975). *Population.* 3d ed. (New York).

Piccirilli, L. (1982). "L''apokeryxis' di Temistocle." In *Studi in onore di A. Biscardi* 1:343–355 (Milan).

Pickard-Cambridge, A. W. (1968). *The Dramatic Festivals of Athens.* 2d ed. Edited by J. Gould and D. M. Lewis (Oxford).

Pinchbeck, I., and Hewitt, M. (1969). *Children in English Society,* vol. 1 (London).

Pinney, G. F. (1986). "Money-bags?" *AJA* 90:218.

Pollock, L. A. (1983). *Forgotten Children: Parent-Child Relations from 1500 to 1900* (Cambridge).

Pomeroy, S. B. (1975). *Goddesses, Whores, Wives, and Slaves: Women in Classical Antiquity* (New York).

———— (1977). "*Technikai kai mousikai*: The Education of Women in the Fourth Century and in the Hellenistic Period." *American Journal of Ancient History* 2:51–68.

—— (1978). "Supplementary Notes on Erinna." *ZPE* 32:17–22.

—— (1984). *Women in Hellenistic Egypt from Alexander to Cleopatra* (New York).

Prag, A. J. N. W. (1985). *The Oresteia: Iconographic and Narrative Tradition* (Warminster).

Préaux, C. (1965). "Réflexions sur l'entité hellénistique." *Chronique d'Égypte* 40:129–139.

Queyrel, A. (1988). "Les Muses à l'école: Images de quelques vases du peintre de Calliope." *AntK* 31:90–102.

Rabel, R. J. (1984). "The Lost Children of the *Oresteia*." *Eranos* 82:211–213.

—— (1987). "Aeschylus, *Ag.* 393–95: The Boy and the Winged Bird." *CJ* 82:289–292.

Radcliffe-Brown, A. R. (1952). *Structure and Function in Primitive Society* (London).

Raepsaet, G., and Decocq, C. (1987). "Deux regards sur l'enfance athénienne à l'époque classique." *Les Études classiques* 55:3–15.

Raubitschek, A. E. (1949). *Dedications from the Athenian Acropolis* (Cambridge, Mass.).

Rawson, B., ed. (1986). *The Family in Ancient Rome: New Perspectives* (London and Sydney).

Redfield, J. (1982). "Notes on the Greek Wedding." *Arethusa* 15:181–201.

Reinhold, M. (1976). "The Generation Gap in Antiquity." In *The Conflict of Generations in Ancient Greece and Rome,* edited by S. Bertman, 15–54 (Amsterdam).

Reinmuth, O. (1971). *The Ephebic Inscriptions of the Fourth Century B.C.* (Leiden).

Rhodes, P. J. (1981). *A Commentary on the Aristotelian "Athenaion Politeia"* (Oxford).

—— (1986). "Political Activity in Classical Athens." *JHS* 106:132–144.

Richardson, B. E. (1933). *Old Age among the Ancient Greeks* (Baltimore).

Richter, G. M. A. (1961). *The Archaic Gravestones of Attica* (London).

Ridgway, B. S. (1987). "Ancient Greek Women and Art: The Material Evidence." *AJA* 91:399–409.

Rizza, G. (1960). "Una nuova pelike a figure rosse e lo 'splanchnoptes' di Styppax." *Annuario della Scuola archeologica de Atene* 37/38:321–345.

Robbins, E. I. (1987). "Nereids with Golden Distaffs: Pindar, *Nem.* 5." *QUCC* 25:25–33.

Robert, L. (1939). "Inscriptions grecques d'Asie mineure." In *Anatolian Studies Presented to W. H. Buckler,* edited by W. M. Calder and J. Keil, 227–248 (Manchester).

Robertson, M. (1975). *The Parthenon Frieze* (New York).

Robertson, N. (1983). "The Riddle of the Arrhephoria at Athens." *HSCP* 87:241–288.

Robinson, D. M., and Mylonas, G. E. (1946). *Excavations at Olynthus*, vol. 12, *Domestic and Public Architecture* (Baltimore).

Roesch, P. (1982). *Études béotiennes* (Paris).

Rogoff, B., Sellers, M. J., Pirrotta, S., Fox, N., and White, S. H. (1975). "Age of Assignment of Roles and Responsibilities to Children: A Cross-Cultural Survey." *Human Development* 18:353–369.

Rose, A. R. (1982). "The Significance of the Nurse's Speech in Aeschylus' *Choephoroe*." *CB* 58:49–50.

Rosenblatt, P. C. (1983). *Bitter, Bitter Tears: Nineteenth-Century Diarists and Twentieth-Century Grief Theories* (Minneapolis).

Rouse, W. H. D. (1902). *Greek Votive Offerings: An Essay in the History of Greek Religion* (Cambridge).

Roussel, D. (1976). *Tribu et cité: Études sur les groupes sociaux dans les cités grecques aux époques archaïque et classique* (Paris).

Roussel, P. (1951). "Étude sur le principe de l'ancienneté dans le monde hellénique du Vᵉ siècle av. J.-C. à l'époque romaine." *Mémoires de l'Institut national de France, Académie des Inscriptions et Belles-Lettres* 43:123–227.

Rousselle, A. (1983). *Porneia: De la maîtrise du corps à la privation sensorielle, IIᵉ-IVᵉ siècles de l'ère chrétienne* (Paris).

Rudhardt, J. (1982). "De l'inceste dans la mythologie grecque." *Revue française de psychanalyse* 46:731–763.

Rühfel, H. (1984a). *Das Kind in der griechischen Kunst: Von der minoisch-mykenischen Zeit bis zum Hellenismus* (Mainz).

——— (1984b). *Kinderleben im klassischen Athen: Bilder auf klassischen Vasen* (Mainz).

——— (1988). "Ammen und Kinderfrauen im klassischen Athen." *Antike Welt* 19 (no. 4):43–57.

Rumpf, A. (1961). "Attische Feste—Attische Vasen." *Bonner Jahrbücher* 161:208–214.

Rumpf, E. (1985). *Eltern-Kind-Beziehungen in der griechischen Mythologie* (Frankfurt am Main).

Rusten, J. S. (1977). "*Wasps* 1360–1369: Philokleon's τωθασμός." *HSCP* 81:157–161.

Rutherford, I., and Irvine, J. (1988). "The Race in the Athenian Oschophoria and an Oschophoricon by Pindar." *ZPE* 72:43–51.

Sacco, G. (1979). "Sui νεανίσκοι dell'età ellenistica." *Rivista di filologia e di instruzione classica* 107:39–49.

Sagan, E. (1979). *The Lust to Annihilate: A Psychoanalytic Study of Violence in Ancient Greek Culture* (New York).

Saller, R. P. (1984a). *"Familia, Domus,* and the Roman Conception of the Family." *Phoenix* 38:336–355.

———— (1984b). "Roman Dowry and the Devolution of Property in the Principate." *CQ* 34:195–205.

———— (1986). *"Patria Potestas* and the Stereotype of the Roman Family." *Continuity and Change* 1:7–22.

———— (1987a). "Men's Age at Marriage and Its Consequences in the Roman Family." *CP* 82:21–34.

———— (1987b). "Slavery and the Roman Family." *Slavery and Abolition* 8:65–87.

———— (1988). *"Pietas,* Obligation, and Authority in the Roman Family." In *Alte Geschichte und Wissenschaftsgeschichte: Festschrift für Karl Christ zum 65. Geburtstag,* edited by P. Kneissl and V. Losemann, 393–410 (Darmstadt).

Saller, R. P., and Shaw, B. D. (1984). "Tombstones and Roman Family Relations in the Principate: Civilians, Soldiers, and Slaves." *JRS* 74:124–156.

Sanford, M. (1975). "To Be Treated as a Child of the Home: Black Carib Child Lending in a British West Indian Society." In *Socialization and Communication in Primary Groups,* edited by T. R. Williams, 159–181 (The Hague).

Sarnoff, I. (1962). *Personality Dynamics and Development* (New York).

Scanlon, T. F. (1988). *"Virgineum Gymnasium:* Spartan Females and Early Greek Athletics." In *The Archaeology of the Olympics,* edited by W. J. Raschke, 185–216 (Madison).

Schaps, D. M. (1979). *Economic Rights of Women in Ancient Greece* (Edinburgh).

Schefold, K. (1981). *Die Göttersage in der klassischen und hellenistischen Kunst* (Munich).

Scheper-Hughes, N. (1987a). "'Basic Strangeness': Maternal Estrangement and Infant Death—A Critique of Bonding Theory." In *The Role of Culture in Developmental Disorder,* edited by C. M. Super, 131–151 (San Diego).

———— (1987b). "The Cultural Politics of Child Survival." In *Child Survival: Anthropological Approaches to the Treatment and Maltreatment of Children,* edited by Scheper-Hughes, 1–29 (Dordrecht).

Schiff, H. S. (1978). *The Bereaved Parent* (Harmondsworth).

Schildkrout, E. (1978). "Age and Gender in Hausa Society: Socioeconomic Roles of Children in Urban Kano." In *Sex and Age as Principles of Social Differentiation,* edited by J. S. La Fontaine, 109–137 (London).

Schmidt, E. (1971). *Spielzeug und Spiele der Kinder im klassischen Altertum* (Meiningen).

Schmidt, M. (1983–1984). "Hephaistos lebt—Untersuchungen zur Frage der Behandlung behinderter Kinder in der Antike." *Hephaistos* 5–6:133–161.

Schmidt, R. (1977). *Die Darstellung von Kinderspielzeug und Kinderspiel in der griechischen Kunst* (Vienna).

Schmitt-Pantel, P. (1980). "Les Repas au prytanée et à la tholos dans l'Athènes classique. *Sitesis, trophé, misthos*: Réflexions sur le mode de nourriture démocratique." *Annali del seminario di studi del mondo classico* 2:55–68.

Schwartzman, H. B. (1978). *Transformations: The Anthropology of Children's Play* (New York).

Scrimshaw, S. C. M. (1984). "Infanticide in Human Populations: Societal and Individual Concerns." In *Infanticide: Comparative and Evolutionary Perspectives*, edited by G. Hausfater and S. B. Hrdy, 439–462 (New York).

Seaford, R. (1984). *Euripides Cyclops* (Oxford).

——— (1987). "The Tragic Wedding." *JHS* 107:106–130.

Segalen, M. (1984). "'Avoir sa part': Sibling Relations in Partible Inheritance Brittany." In *Interest and Emotion: Essays on the Study of Family and Kinship,* edited by H. Medick and D. W. Sabean, 129–144 (Cambridge).

——— (1986). *Historical Anthropology of the Family.* Translated by J. C. Whitehouse and S. Matthews (Cambridge).

Shaw, B. D. (1984). "Latin Funerary Epigraphy and Family Life in the Later Roman Empire." *Historia* 33:457–497.

Shorter, E. (1976). *The Making of the Modern Family* (New York).

Sieder, R., and Mitterauer, M. (1983). "The Reconstruction of the Family Life Course: Theoretical Problems and Empirical Results." In *Family Forms in Historic Europe,* edited by R. Wall (with J. Robin and P. Laslett), 309–345 (Cambridge).

Sifakis, G. M. (1979a). "Boy Actors in New Comedy." In *Arktouros: Hellenic Studies Presented to Bernard M. W. Knox . . . ,* edited by G. W. Bowersock et al., 199–208 (Berlin and New York).

——— (1979b). "Children in Greek Tragedy." *BICS* 26:67–80.

Simantiras, C. (1975). "L'Enfant dans la Grèce antique: L'Incapacité juridique en tant que protection du mineur d'âge." In *L'Enfant. Recueils de la Société Jean Bodin* 39 (Brussels) 199–209.

Simon, E. (1983). *Festivals of Attica: An Archaeological Commentary* (Madison).

Skinner, M. B. (1987). "Greek Women and the Metronymic: A Note on an Epigram by Nossis." *Ancient History Bulletin* 1:39–42.

Slater, P. (1968). *The Glory of Hera: Greek Mythology and the Greek Family* (Boston).

Slater, W. J. (1974). "Pueri, turba minuta." *BICS* 21:133–140.

Smith, A. C. (1985). "'Southern violence' Reconsidered: Arson as Protest in Black-Belt Georgia, 1865–1910." *Journal of Southern History* 51:527–564.

Smith, R. C. (1985). "The Clans of Athens and the Historiography of the Archaic Period." *EMC* 29:51–61.

Sommerstein, A. H. (1980). *Aristophanes Acharnians* (Warminster).

Sourvinou, C. (1971). "Aristophanes, *Lysistrata*, 641–647." *CQ* 21:339–342.

Sourvinou-Inwood, C. (1987). "A Series of Erotic Pursuits: Images and Meanings." *JHS* 107:131–153.

Sprague, R. K. (1984). "Plato and Children's Games." In *Greek Poetry and Philosophy: Studies in Honour of Leonard Woodbury,* edited by D. E. Gerber, 275–284 (Chico, Calif.).

Stampp, K. (1971). "Rebels and Sambos: The Search for the Negro's Personality in Slavery." *Journal of Southern History* 37:367–392.

Stanford, W. B. (1983). *Greek Tragedy and the Emotions: An Introductory Study* (London).

Stanley-Porter, D. P. (1973). "Mute Actors in the Tragedies of Euripides." *BICS* 20:68–93.

Steinhoff, P. G. (1985). "The Effects of Induced Abortion on Future Family Goals of Young Women." In *Perspectives on Abortion,* edited by P. Sachdev, 117–129 (Metuchen, N.J., and London).

Stephanopoulos, T. (1983). "Drei alt- und neugriechische Babywörter." *Glotta* 61:12–15.

Stern, E. M. (1978). "Kinder-Kännchen zum Choenfest." *Castrum peregrini* 132–133:27–37.

Stinton, T. C. W. (1976). "Iphigeneia and the Bears of Brauron." *CQ* 26:11–13.

Stone, L. (1977). *The Family, Sex, and Marriage in England, 1500–1800* (London).

Stroud, R. S. (1971). "Theozotides and the Athenian Orphans." *Hesperia* 40:280–301.

Strubbe, J. H. M. (1982). "Het jonge kind in de oudheid." *Kleio* 12:49–77.

Stuart, D. R. (1921). "On Vergil *Eclogue* iv.60–63." *CP* 16:209–230.

Sussman, G. D. (1982). *Selling Mothers' Milk: The Wet-nursing Business in France, 1715–1914* (Urbana, Ill.).

Sutherland, D. E. (1981). "A Special Kind of Problem: The Response of Household Slaves and Their Masters to Freedom." *Southern Studies* 20:151–166.

Sutton, D. F. (1981). "Satyr Play and Children in the Audience." *Prudentia* 13:71–74.

——— (1987). "The Theatrical Families of Athens." *AJP* 108:9–26.

Szemerényi, O. (1977). "Das griechische Verwandtschaftsnamensystem vor dem Hintergrund des indogermanischen Systems." *Hermes* 105:385–405.

Szlezák, T. A. (1981). "Bemerkungen zur Diskussion um *Sophokles, Antigone 904–920.*" *RhM* 124:108–142.

Taillardat, J. (1961). "Ποσθαλίων et ποσθαλίσκος (Ar. *Thesm.* 291)." *RPh* 35:249–250.

———— (1967). *Suétone.* Περὶ βλασφημιῶν. Περὶ παιδιων (*Extraits byzantins*). (Paris).

Taplin, O. (1977). *The Stagecraft of Aeschylus* (Oxford).

Thompson, W. E. (1967). "The Marriage of First Cousins in Athenian Society." *Phoenix* 21:273–282.

———— (1972). "Athenian Marriage Patterns: Remarriage." *California Studies in Classical Antiquity* 5:211–225.

———— (1978). "The Athenian Investor." *Rivista di studi classici* 26:403–423.

Thür, G. (1977). *Beweisführung vor den Schwurgerichtshöfen Athens: Die Proklesis zur Basanos* (Vienna).

Thury, E. M. (1988a). "A Study of Words Relating to Youth and Old Age in the Plays of Euripides and Its Special Implications for Euripides' *Suppliant Women.*" *Computers and the Humanities* 21:293–306.

———— (1988b). "Euripides' *Alcestis* and the Athenian Generation Gap." *Arethusa* 21:197–214.

Touchefeu, O. (1983). "Lecture des images mythologiques: Un Exemple d'images sans texte, la mort d'Astyanax." In *Image et céramique grecque,* edited by F. Lissarague and F. Thélamon, 21–29 (Rouen).

Treu, U. (1981). "Herondas 3, 24–26 und die Schulpraxis." *QUCC* 8:113–116.

Turner, E. (1984). "Menander and the New Society." In *Proceedings of the Seventh Congress of the International Federation of the Societies of Classical Studies,* edited by J. Harmatta, 243–259 (Budapest) = *Chronique d'Égypte* 54 (1979) 106–126.

Valsiner, J. (1988). "Ontogeny of Co-construction of Culture within Socially Organized Environmental Settings." In *Child Development within Culturally Structured Environments,* edited by Valsiner, 283–297 (Norwood, N.J.).

van Hoorn, G. (1909). *De vita atque cultu puerorum monumentis antiquis explanato* (Amsterdam).

———— (1951). *Choes and Anthesteria* (Leiden).

Vann, R. T. (1982). "The Youth of *Centuries of Childhood.*" *History and Theory* 21:279–297.

Van Sichelin, L. (1987). "Nouvelles orientations dans l'étude de l'arrhéphorie attique." *AntCl* 56:88–102.

van Straten, F. T. (1981). "Gifts for the Gods." In *Faith, Hope, and Worship: Aspects of Religious Mentality in the Ancient World,* edited by H. S. Versnel, 65–151 (Leiden).

——— (1987). "Greek Sacrificial Representations: Livestock Prices and Religious Mentality." In *Gifts to the Gods. Proceedings of the Uppsala Symposium 1985,* edited by T. Linders and G. Nordquist, 159–170 (Uppsala).

Vekemans, M., and Dohmen, B. (1982). "Induced Abortion in Belgium: Clinical Experience and Psychosocial Observations." *Studies in Family Planning* 13:355–364.

Verdenius, W. J. (1982). "Notes on the Prologue of Aeschylus' Agamemnon." In *Actus: Studies in Honour of H. L. W. Nelson,* edited by J. den Boeft and A. H. M. Kessels, 429–440 (Utrecht).

Vernier, B. (1977). "Émigration et dérèglement du marché matrimoniale." *Actes de la recherche en sciences sociales* 15:31–58.

Vidal-Naquet, P. (1981). "The Black Hunter and the Origin of the Athenian *Ephebeia.*" In *Myth, Religion, and Society,* edited by R. L. Gordon, 147–162 (Cambridge).

Vílchez, M. (1983). "Sobre los períodos de la vida humana en la lírica arcaica y la tragedia griega." *Emérita* 51:63–95, 215–253.

Visser, M. (1986). "Medea: Daughter, Sister, Wife, and Mother. Natal Family *versus* Conjugal Family in Greek and Roman Myths about Women." In *Greek Tragedy and Its Legacy: Essays Presented to D. J. Conacher,* edited by M. Cropp, E. Fantham, and S. E. Scully, 149–165 (Calgary).

Vogt, J. (1974). *Ancient Slavery and the Ideal of Man.* Translated by T. Wiedemann (Oxford).

Vorster, C. (1983). *Griechische Kinderstatuen* (Köln).

Wagner, J. (1976). *Seleukeia am Euphrat/Zeugma* (Wiesbaden).

Walbank, M. B. (1981). "Artemis Bear-Leader." *CQ* 31:276–281.

Walcot, P. (1987a). "Plato's Mother and Other Terrible Women." *Greece and Rome* 34:12–31.

——— (1987b). "Romantic Love and True Love: Greek Attitudes to Marriage." *Ancient Society* 18:5–33.

Walker, S. (1983). "Women and Housing in Classical Greece: The Archaeological Evidence." In *Images of Women in Antiquity,* edited by A. Cameron and A. Kuhrt, 81–91 (Detroit).

Wartelle, A. (1978). *Bibliographie historique et critique d'Eschyle et de la tragédie grecque, 1518–1974* (Paris).

Webster, T. B. L. (1972). *Potter and Patron in Classical Athens* (London).

Weisner, T. S. (1982). "Sibling Interdependence and Child Caretaking: A Cross-cultural View." In *Sibling Relationships: Their Nature and Significance across the Lifespan,* edited by M. E. Lamb and B. Sutton-Smith, 305–327 (Hillsdale, N.J.).

Weisner, T. S., and Gallimore, R. (1977). "My Brother's Keeper: Child and Sibling Caretaking." *Current Anthropology* 18:169–190.

West, M. L. (1977). "Erinna." *ZPE* 25:95–119.

——— (1978). *Hesiod Works & Days* (Oxford).

White, B. (1975). "The Economic Importance of Children in a Javanese Village." In *Population and Social Organization,* edited by M. Nag, 127–146 (The Hague).

Wiedemann, T. (1989). *Adults and Children in the Roman Empire* (London).

Wilson, S. (1984). "The Myth of Motherhood a Myth: The Historical View of European Child-Rearing." *Social History* 9:181–198.

——— (1988). "Infanticide, Child Abandonment, and Female Honour in Nineteenth-Century Corsica." *Comparative Studies in Society and History* 30:762–783.

Winkler, J. (1982). "Akko." *CP* 77:137–138.

——— (1985). "The Ephebes' Song: *Tragôidia* and *Polis*." *Representations* 11 (Summer): 26–62.

Woodford, S. (1983). "The Iconography of the Infant Herakles Strangling Snakes." In *Image et céramique grecque,* edited by F. Lissarague and F. Thélamon, 121–133 (Rouen).

Yanagisako, S. J. (1979). "Family and Household: The Analysis of Domestic Groups." *Annual Review of Anthropology* 8:161–205.

Young, D. C. (1984). *The Olympic Myth of Greek Amateur Athletics* (Chicago).

Zeller, A. C. (1987). "A Role for Women in Hominid Evolution." *Man* 22:528–557.

Zoepffel, R. (1985). "Geschlechtsreife und Legitimation zur Zeugung im alten Griechenland." In *Geschlechtsreife und Legitimation zur Zeugung,* edited by E. W. Müller, 319–401 (Freiburg and Munich).

255

Index

Index

Silenus, 9–10, 56, 147; children portrayed as, 43
Simon, 122
Simonides, 71, 171
Sisters, 135–136; and brothers, 18, 38, 72, 98, 121–136, 140, 142, 178–179. *See also* Siblings
Skin, of children, 16
Skinner, M., 189n.6
Slavery, children sold into, 193n.48, 194n.58
Slaves, 80, 81; child, 21, 146; concern about, 148–154; grouped with children, 7, 9, 35, 41, 44, 59–60, 145, 152; effects on children, 155–163, 164; relations with children, xiv, 13, 55–56, 60, 73, 92, 94, 107, 128, 141, 145–163
Smicrines, 119, 178
Smiles, of children, 1, 10
Socialization, xiv-xv, 1, 81; methods of, 4, 24, 33, 38, 46–49, 54, 55–56, 59, 64–65, 155–156
Socrates, 15, 20, 38, 40, 52, 53, 160, 161; in Plato, xiii, 2, 5, 10, 25, 55, 90, 149; in Xenophon, 61, 96, 103–104, 119
Solon, 21, 33, 57, 71, 91, 92, 136
Sons. *See* Fathers; Mothers
Sophocles, 6, 9, 85, 90, 110, 118–119, 166; *Ajax*, 18; *Ant.*, 11, 131; *El.*, 128; *Lovers of Achilles*, 7–8; *Phil.*, 46
Soranus, 17
Sositheus, 217n.5
Sostratus, 149
Sourvinou-Inwood, C., 199n.114
Sparta, 5, 81, 139, 195n.66, 227n.70; boys at, 52, 186n.64; 187n.79, 196n.68; children at, 17, 68, 149; girls at, 10–11, 72, 76, 206n.105
Speech, of children, 9, 21–22
Speeches, law-court, xvi, 160; children in, 21, 40–41, 91–92, 97, 186n.69; dowries in, 132–134; family relations in, 100, 115–117, 120, 166. *See also names of individual orators*
Stages: of childhood, xiv, 2, 14–22,

62–63, 70, 123, 146; of life, 2, 8, 10, 14–15, 39
Stephanus, 142, 190n.15
Stepmothers, 105, 141, 143
Stone, L., 82–87
Stories, for children, 10, 43, 49, 139, 149
Strato, 57
Strepsiades, 11, 41, 101
Strophius, 143, 144
Swaddling, 17–18, 20, 48
Symposia, 36–38, 61
Syrus, 167, 225n.44

Teachers, 20, 38, 123, 138
Teasing, by adults, 7
Teeth, of children, 21
teknidion, 15
teknon, 12–13, 15
Telemachus, 100
Tellus, 136
Temenus, 90
Terence, xvi, 167, 179
tēthalladous, 139
Thebes, 125
Themistocles, 147, 194n.57
Theocrines, 117
Theocritus, 171–172
Theophrastus, 91, 107
Theotime, 130
Thera, 191n.17
Therippides, 107
Theseus, 43–44, 70, 105, 138
Thompson, E. P., 93
Thrace, 227n.70
Thrasyllus, 190n.11
Thucydides, 89
Thucydides (son of Melesias), 72
Thudippus, 120
thygatēr, 33
Timocrates, 130
Tiresias, 11
Tissaphernes, 6
tokos, 93
Toys, 11, 41, 53, 54, 64, 72, 125, 126, 128
Tragedy, xvi; affection for children in,

ANCIENT SOCIETY AND HISTORY

The series Ancient Society and History offers books, relatively brief in compass, on selected topics in the history of ancient Greece and Rome, broadly conceived, with a special emphasis on comparative and other nontraditional approaches and methods. The series, which includes both works of synthesis and works of original scholarship, is aimed at the widest possible range of specialist and nonspecialist readers.

Published in the series:

Eva Cantarella, PANDORA'S DAUGHTERS: The Role and Status of Women in Greek and Roman Antiquity

Alan Watson, ROMAN SLAVE LAW

John E. Stambaugh, THE ANCIENT ROMAN CITY

Géza Alföldy, THE SOCIAL HISTORY OF ROME

Giovanni Comotti, MUSIC IN GREEK AND ROMAN CULTURE

Christian Habicht, CICERO THE POLITICIAN

Mark Golden, CHILDREN AND CHILDHOOD IN CLASSICAL ATHENS

Thomas Cole, THE ORIGINS OF RHETORIC IN ANCIENT GREECE

Maurizio Bettini, ANTHROPOLOGY AND ROMAN CULTURE: Kinship, Time, Images of the Soul

Suzanne Dixon, THE ROMAN FAMILY

Stephen L. Dyson, COMMUNITY AND SOCIETY IN ROMAN ITALY

Tim G. Parkin, DEMOGRAPHY AND ROMAN SOCIETY

Alison Burford, LAND AND LABOR IN THE GREEK WORLD

Alan Watson, INTERNATIONAL LAW IN ARCHAIC ROME: War and Religion